Summary

There is increasing pressure on the UK's marine sand and gravel resources. Planning constraints are tending to restrict the extraction from sand and gravel resources on land, while the exploitation of marine resources is encouraged, subject to environmental safeguards. In addition to the demand for aggregates from the construction industry, there is an increasing demand for marine sand and gravel for beach recharge in coastal defence schemes.

The distribution of sand and gravel resources offshore is uneven. The deposits vary in their thickness, grading and depth, and in their proximity to the shore. Some contain physical or chemical contaminants that may restrict their suitability. Many lie in places that are currently inaccessible to the aggregate industry - sterilised ground in the vicinity of seabed cables, pipelines and wrecks, areas of special conservation or fisheries significance, areas where the water is too deep for dredging operations, and the nearshore zone. Because the resources of marine sand and gravel are finite and unevenly distributed, and because they may be the subject of different and sometimes competing interests, there is a need to manage their extraction with a view to the anticipated material demands over the long-term.

This report provides quantitative estimates of the national demand for beach recharge material and of the resources suitable to meet that demand over the next 20 years. The likely requirements of the aggregate industry for the same material have also been taken into account. This information is presented regionally - for the south and east coasts, and the coasts of Wales and western England respectively. The results represent an extensive general view compiled from the best available sources of detailed data. They are of particular relevance in the determination of policy concerning coastal defence and minerals planning, and provide coastal authorities and engineers with information on the resource options for recharge materials. The results do not, however, obviate the need for detailed prospecting surveys. The quantified resource information covers areas that have been prospected by the aggregate industry, and selected additional areas that are considered to have resource potential.

The estimated demand for shingle (gravel) for beach recharge over the next 20 years will range from 23 to $47Mm^3$ (mostly for south coast beaches), and that for aggregate, about $200Mm^3$. The estimated demand for sand for recharge will range from 36 to $83Mm^3$ (mostly for east coast beaches), and that for aggregate, about $172Mm^3$. Resources of marine sand considerably exceed the total demand, and, even in areas outside those prospected by the aggregate industry, there are adequate potentially workable resources to meet the recharge demand in all three regions. Sources of shingle for beach recharge are more problematic; known gravel deposits outside areas prospected by the industry are generally thin.

The report considers the potential for the use in beach recharge of materials other than marine sand and gravel. These materials include land-won primary aggregates, land-sourced secondary aggregates and mineral wastes. The report also considers navigational dredgings. While some of these alternative materials may offer attractive local or opportunistic options, they are unlikely to satisfy the requirements of most major schemes.

The report highlights the need to locate new sources of shingle, particularly for south coast recharge schemes, and recommends the investigation of specific marine targets. These include some of the back-filled palaeovalleys that occur in the English Channel and off parts of the east coast, and areas within the nearshore zone.

The existing procedures for obtaining beach recharge material are set out in the *Beach Management Manual* and reviewed in Appendix A. Existing procedural constraints and other difficulties are examined and recommendations are made on topics including further resource studies, licensing arrangements and environmental data.

Report 154   1996

Beach recharge materials - demand and resources

B Humphreys
T Coates
M Watkiss
D Harrison

CIRIA

...UCTION INDUSTRY RESEARCH AND INFORMATION ASSOCIATION
CONSTR... Gate London SW1P 3AU
6 Storey's ...board@ciria.org.uk
E-mail switch... 8891
Tel: (0171) 222...   Fax: (0171) 222 1708

Beach recharge materials - demand and resources
Construction Industry Research and Information Association
Report 154, 1996
© CIRIA 1996

ISBN 086017 439 5
ISSN 0305 408 X

Keywords	
Beach recharge, aggregates, marine dredging	
Reader interest	**Classification**
Coastal engineers, aggregate companies, dredging companies, Government policy makers, environmental groups.	AVAILABILITY Controlled CONTENT Original analysis STATUS Committee guided USER Coastal engineers

Foreword

This report was produced as a result of CIRIA Research Project 482, *Beach Recharge Material Demand — Resources and Availability*. The work on demand and resources was carried out on behalf of CIRIA by a consortium led by the British Geological Survey and including HR Wallingford and Posford Duvivier. The work on availability of materials was carried out by Nick Bray under a separate contract. This report also constitutes NRA R&D Report 24 produced through NRA Project 489.

The project was run as part of a wider research programme on beach management and beach materials. The other main element of this programme was CIRIA Research Project 483, which has produced a *Beach Management Manual* (CIRIA Report 153).

This report was edited by Russell Arthurton of BGS and the main authors are:

Bernard Humphreys	BGS	Sections 1, 2, 4, 5, 6, 8 and 9
Tom Coates	HR Wallingford	Section 3
Michael Watkiss	Posford Duvivier	Section 3
David Harrison	BGS	Section 7

Appendix A was written by Nick Bray.

Contributions to the resource assessment were made by Antony Myers of BGS (volume calculations and digital cartography), Helen Glaves of BGS (database design) and Tim Jeffries-Harris of Posford Duvivier (Crown Estate data transfer).

CIRIA's Research Manager was Judy Payne, with support from Sian John who managed the *Beach Management Manual* project. Following CIRIA's usual practice, the work was guided by a Steering Group:

Chairman

Gordon Gray	CIRIA

Members

Peter Bide	DoE Minerals Division
Chris Birks	NRA
Iain Fairgrieve	Ham Dredging Ltd
Richard Leafe	English Nature
Daniel Leggett	NRA
Tony Murray	The Crown Estate
David Richardson	MAFF, Flood and Coastal Defence Division
Andrew Roberts	Canterbury City Council
Carolyn Warburton	DoE Minerals Division
Brian Wheeler	BMAPA

Corresponding members

Graham Boyes	MAFF, Marine Environmental Protection Division
David Court	SCOPAC
Chris Fleming	Sir William Halcrow & Partners Ltd
Robin McInnes	SCOPAC
Hugh Payne	Welsh Office
Phil Roland	Westminster Dredging Co Ltd
David Smart	Van Oord ACZ
Ian Townend	ABP Research and Consultancy Ltd
David Whitehead	British Ports Association

CIRIA is grateful to the following organisations who provided financial support for the project:

The Crown Estate	MAFF
DoE Minerals Division	SCOPAC
English Nature	Van Oord ACZ
Ham Dredging Ltd	Westminster Dredging Ltd
National Rivers Authority	

CIRIA and the authors also wish to thank everyone else who contributed to the project by providing marine resource data and by taking part in the consultation exercise carried out by Nick Bray. Special thanks are due to the Chairman of BMAPA, Brian Wheeler; and to BMAPA members for their attendance at a meeting organised to discuss the project, their subsequent support and provision of resource information to the project.

Organisations consulted by Nick Bray

ARC Marine Ltd	L G Mouchel & Partners, Bath
Babtie Dobbie	L G Mouchel & Partners, West Byfleet
A D Bates Partnership	NRA Anglian Region
Bournemouth Borough Council	NRA South West Region
The Crown Estate Commissioners	NRA Welsh Region
English Nature	New Forest District Council
HR Wallingford Ltd	Poole Harbour Commissioners
Ham Dredging Ltd	Posford Duvivier, Haywards Heath
Harwich Haven Authority	Posford Duvivier, Peterborough
Lancaster City Council	Restormel Borough Council
MAFF Fisheries, Burnham Laboratory	Shepway District Council
MAFF Flood and Coastal Defence Division	Shoreline Management Partnership
MAFF Marine Environmental Protection Division	Michael J Stone Partnership

BMAPA Members

ARC Marine
Britannia Aggregates
British Dredging
Civil and Marine
Kendall Brothers (Portsmouth)
Northwood (Fareham)
Northwest Sand and Ballast
South Coast Shipping
United Marine Dredging

Contents

List of Tables

List of Figures

Glossary

Aggregate
Sand, gravel and crushed rock suitable for use in the construction industry for mixing with a matrix to form concrete, macadam, mortar or plaster; or used alone as in railway ballast, unbound roadstone or graded fill.

Biogenic
Produced by organisms.

Carbonaceous
A rock or sediment rich in carbon, coaly.

China clay
Commercial term for kaolin, a clay mineral used in the manufacture of whiteware ceramics and in the filling and coating of paper.

Cleanliness
Used in the context of seabed materials to specify in qualitative terms the degree to which the sediment is composed only of mineral grains and lacks contaminants such as biogenic debris (e.g. seaweed, live organisms) and pollutants.

Composite grains
Grains composed of two or more other grains stuck together by mineral cements.

Conglomerate
A coarse-grained sedimentary rock composed of rounded pebbles or cobbles set in a fine matrix.

Contaminants
Material occurring within seabed sediments such as biogenic debris (e.g. seaweed, live organisms) and chemical pollutants (but excluding shell fragments) which diminish their usefulness for beach recharge schemes.

D_{50}
Particle size corresponding to 50% of the material.

Glauconite
Green-coloured grains of iron silicate composition.

Grab sample
Superficial seabed sample collected by use of a mechanical grab device.

Grading
Distribution of particle sizes, established by sieve analysis.

Gravel
Refer to Section 2.5.2 - Classification of seabed sediments.

Gravity core
A core sample collected in a tube-shaped barrel sunk by gravity into the seabed.

Indurated
Rock hardened by pressure, cementation or heat.

Indicated resource
A resource penetrated by boreholes, vibrocores, gravity cores or large grabs sufficient to prove its existence, very approximate extent and quality.

Inferred resource
A resource that is indicated by mapping surveys, such as side-scan sonar or seismic surveys offshore, but has not been sampled by boreholes or coring.

Layback
The distance between the side-scan sonar towfish or seismic receiver deployed by the ship and the navigation receiver on board the ship.

Lag deposit	Residual accumulation of coarse fragments left behind after currents have winnowed and washed away finer material.
Lithic	Referring to rock fragments forming a sediment.
Lithology	The general character of a rock or sediment expressed in terms of its mineral composition, its texture and grain size and included structures.
Palaeovalley	A preserved valley which has been excavated by processes no longer active, and which may be back-filled with sediment.
Phi intervals	The Phi scale is an expression of grain sizes on a logarithmic scale. The phi value (ϕ) is related to grain diameter (d) by the expression $\phi = -\log_2 d$. For example, $2\phi = 250\mu m$, $1\phi = 500\mu m$, $0\phi = 1mm$, $-1\phi = 2mm$, $-2\phi = 4mm$.
Quaternary	Approximately the last two million years represented by glacial, interglacial and post-glacial deposits which are generally not indurated.
Reserve	The quantity of workable mineral which is calculated to lie within given boundaries. Reserves are normally proved by drilling a closely spaced series of cores and analysing the material recovered.
Resource	A natural concentration of materials from which extraction of a commodity may be possible.
Sand	Used in this report to describe a sediment with a modal grain size of between 0.125mm and 2mm. Refer to Section 2.5.2 - Classification of seabed sediments. The lower size-limit for sand given in the Beach Management Manual is taken at 0.062mm, thus including material that would not normally be used for recharge.
Sand and gravel	A sediment comprising a mixture of coarse sand and gravel with a modal grain size between 2 and 5mm. This category has been adopted for this report only and is not a standard definition of grain size. Refer to Section 2.5.2.
Seismic survey	A geophysical technique for investigating the seabed and its underlying geology.
Shingle	A sediment with a modal grain size exceeding 5mm. Refer to Section 2.5.2. Note that this is a more precise definition than given in the Beach Management Manual which describes shingle as "coarse beach material".
Side-scan sonar	A geophysical technique for recording the texture and morphology of the seabed.
Superficial	Surface layer.
Towfish	The instrument towed behind the vessel during a seismic survey, usually carrying the combined transmitter and receiver.
Vibrocore	A core sample collected in a tube-shaped barrel sunk by vibration into the seabed.

Abbreviations and Acronyms

BGS   British Geological Survey
BMAPA   British Marine Aggregates Producers Association
CIRIA   Construction Industry Research and Information Association
DoE   Department of the Environment
ECCI   English China Clays International Limited
GPS   Global Positioning System
HO   Hydrographic Office
HR   HR Wallingford
Mt   Million tonnes
MPG   Mineral Planning Guidance
Mm^3 Million cubic metres
PD   Posford Duvivier
UTM   Universal Transverse Mercator

1 Introduction

1.1 PURPOSE AND LIMITATIONS

The main purpose of this report is to provide quantitative as well as qualitative resource information that will inform policy discussions concerning the long-term supply of beach recharge materials. This is achieved by comparing available material resources with the anticipated demand for marine materials both for beach recharge schemes and for use by the aggregate industry over the next 20 years. Although the report aims to indicate resources to meet the specific demands of beach recharge schemes, it is important to put this requirement in the context of the wider demand for marine materials from the industry. Marine-dredged sand and gravel are favoured for beach recharge schemes. Thus a review of their distribution, quality and volume is the main focus of this report. However, the use of alternatives to marine-dredged sand and gravel for beach recharge schemes is also considered.

Resource assessment is limited by data availability, and by the variable quality of data from a variety of sources. Information may be restricted in some areas either on grounds of poor survey coverage or by the confidential nature of information. With permission from the owners, many confidential data have been integrated into regional volume assessments in areas densely sampled by the marine aggregate industry and in such areas resource data are considered to be of high reliability. No account has been taken of the possible depletion of resources from areas dredged since the data were collected.

Projecting demand estimates over the next 20 years has inherent limitations, because demand is inextricably linked to Government policy and the general economic climate, both of which are subject to change. This is particularly so with the demand for construction aggregate. Nevertheless, forward planning by coastal authorities means that beach recharge schemes tend to be planned well in advance and future recharge demand can be predicted with considerable accuracy. Future demand for beach recharge is estimated on the basis of a range of physical parameters, though scheme implementation may also be subject to future policy changes.

This report will be of interest to coastal authorities and engineers as a guide to the offshore distribution of suitable deposits, and also to provide Government with a framework and tangible data which should be taken into account in policy development. The report provides resource information but is not intended to obviate the need for prospecting to evaluate further offshore resource materials and to determine reserves. It should be considered in conjunction with the CIRIA *Beach Management Manual* which summarises regulations, procedures and good management practices concerning beach recharge schemes.

1.2 UNITS

There are inherent problems with attempts to compare material demand with material resources because there are discrepancies between *in situ* volumes on the seabed, hopper volumes during transport, and the volume of material actually placed on a beach. The dredging process tends to increase the water content of sediment and therefore sediments loaded into a hopper may occupy a greater volume relative to somewhat compacted *in situ* sediments on the sea floor. Typically hopper volumes may exceed sea floor volumes by a factor of between 1.05% (soft sand) and 1.35% (sand/shingle/clay mixtures). Some sediment, particularly the fine fraction, will be lost during transport and placement on a beach.

For the purpose of this report all resource volumes are *in situ* volumes calculated in cubic metres. Where these estimates have been converted into tonnes the following density values have been used:

Shingle   2.0 tonnes/cubic metre
Sand and gravel   1.8 tonnes/cubic metre

| Sand | 1.6 tonnes/cubic metre |
| Fines | 1.5 tonnes/cubic metre |

The reader should be aware that global conversion factors can lead to inaccuracies and that site specific conversion factors should be used in detailed assessments of recharge schemes.

In this report estimates of material demand concern the amount of material actually required on the beach or in an aggregate stockpile and the estimates do not include allowances for losses of material during transport and placement.

1.3 LAYOUT OF REPORT

Section 2 summarises the location and state of existing data, and the methodology used to assimilate data from disparate sources by computer manipulation into regional volume estimates. Section 3 examines the anticipated demand for beach recharge materials projected over the next 20 years. It includes discussion of the selection of representative beach recharge sites, the design standards for beach recharge schemes, the impact of beach control structures and active beach management schemes, the numerical models used to estimate capital and maintenance recharge volumes, and considers whether demand may be affected by climatic change. The same section includes, for comparison and context, projected demand estimates for marine-sourced material for use by the construction industry, including the export demand. Sections 4 to 6 summarise the distribution, quality and quantity of marine materials off the south coast, east coast, and coasts of Wales and western England respectively in less than 60m water depth. Resource information is summarised in maps and tables and provides estimates of the potentially workable resource as well as estimates of the total material present. Section 7 provides information on the three main sources of alternative materials potentially useful for beach recharge. These are, respectively, land-won primary aggregates, land-sourced secondary aggregates and navigation dredgings. Section 8 briefly summarises the environmental considerations which may have an impact on decisions whether to exploit indicated resources. Section 9 draws conclusions on the potential of identified resources for meeting anticipated demand and makes recommendations for further study.

2 Existing data and resource assessment

2.1 THE EXISTING DATA SETS

Existing, accessible data on marine materials, concerning sand and gravel resources occurring on the continental shelf of England and Wales in water depths less than 60m (Figure 2.1) are summarised below. Seabed sediment data have been collected by several organisations for a variety of purposes, although in most cases the search for material suitable for beach recharge schemes was not the prime concern at the time of data collection. Separate large data sets have been collated by three main organisations:

- The British Geological Survey (BGS) has its own database for samples and shallow seismic records collected during its offshore geological mapping programme which ran from 1967 to 1992. This BGS database includes open file data supplied from other sources; by academic institutions, from publications and research theses, and data provided by companies involved with laying submarine pipelines or cables, constructing nearshore installations, sand and gravel extraction and the hydrocarbon industry.

- The Crown Estate database, held on their behalf by Posford Duvivier (PD), contains data generated by the marine aggregate industry and the reconnaissance surveys run by BGS as joint ventures with the Crown Estate and Department of the Environment (DoE). The prospecting reports of the aggregates industry are also held by PD.

- The Hydrographic Office (HO), part of the Ministry of Defence (MOD), holds detailed records of its own extensive side-scan sonar, bathymetric and seabed sampling surveys.

These databases classify information according to the needs of each organisation and are therefore not immediately compatible, nor do they necessarily record all the factors of relevance to beach recharge engineers. However, all three data sets were made available under specific conditions. Computer manipulation and appraisal of the data for reliability and quality has allowed an assessment of seabed resources to be made for large areas of the continental shelf of England and Wales.

Figures reduced from maps at 1:1 000 000 scale are used to display the density of available data, the quality and reliability of which is be discussed in accompanying text. Figures 2.2 and 2.3 show BGS-held data in grid square format. Figure 2.4 shows the position of seismic lines run by BGS in the study area and gives a visual impression of the density of seismic cover. Figure 2.5 shows areas surveyed to modern standards by the Hydrographic Office. Figure 2.6 shows areas where dense sediment sampling and seismic surveys were undertaken during reconnaissance prospecting by the marine aggregate industry, and the Crown Estate licensed dredging areas.

2.2 BGS OFFSHORE GEOLOGICAL DATA SET

2.2.1 Cover

Low density reconnaissance data are available across the whole continental shelf off England and Wales, although extensive parts of the narrow inshore zone of 1 to 5km width are only locally surveyed (Figures 2.2 and 2.3). Useful summaries of the distribution of seabed sediments on the UK continental shelf, based primarily upon BGS data, are given by Pantin *et al.*, (1990) and illustrated by the 1 : 1 000 000 BGS map entitled *Seabed Sediments around the United Kingdom* (Crosby *et al.*, 1987).

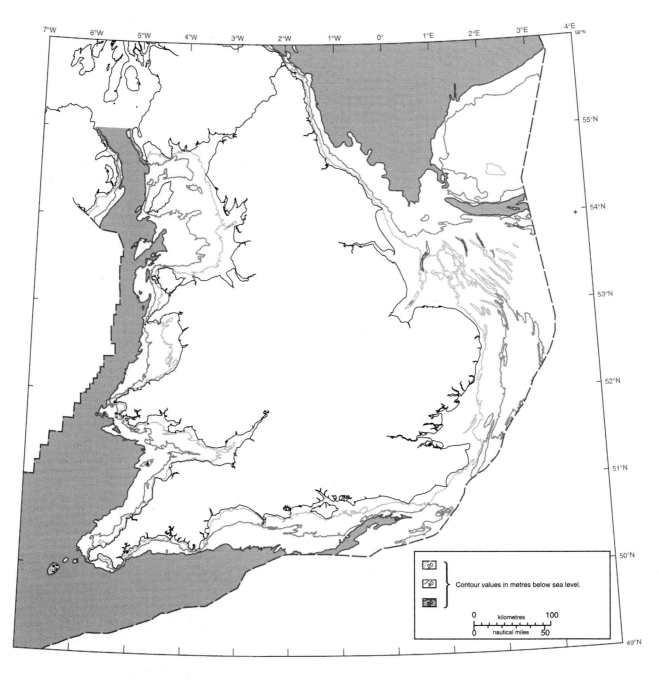

Contour values in metres below sea level.

Figure 2.1 *Bathymetry around the coast of England and Wales*

CIRIA Report 154

2.2.2 Instrumentation

BGS surveys undertaken between 1967 and 1992 employed a range of sampling and geophysical tools providing three dimensional data on the seabed sediments.

Seabed sediment samples were obtained by grab sampling, vibrocoring, gravity coring and by drilling boreholes. The normal grab sampler used by BGS, the Shipek grab, can scoop up a maximum volume of about 2kg of sediment from the sea floor when the spring-loaded grab bucket hits the seabed; the grab samples to a maximum depth of 0.15m below the seabed. Gravity corers for sediment collection are lined, hollow barrels, 1—2m long, which are dropped onto the seafloor from a height of between 10m and 15m; they can penetrate to 0.5m in sand and up to 2m in mud, and retain a core sample within the barrel when withdrawn. Vibrocorers comprising a vibrator motor housed in a pressure vessel which drives a core barrel into sediments with a vibration force of 6 tonnes can penetrate up to 6m below the seabed, recovering core 83mm wide. Vibrocores therefore provide reliable information on sediment thickness. The best data are provided by shallow boreholes, of which up to 600 have been drilled by BGS on the whole UK continental shelf. To provide an indication of data quality, the more reliable data obtained from boreholes and vibrocores are plotted separately (Figure 2.2) from the total abundance of seabed samples (Figure 2.3), which also includes large numbers of grab samples and gravity core samples from disparate sources (compare Figures 2.2 & 2.3).

BGS shallow seismic surveys giving a resolution of 15m+ below the seabed employed a sparker system, a pinger or a surface tow boomer, and a side-scan sonar system. The systems were often operated simultaneously providing comprehensive information on seabed sediments. Data from these surveys provide information on seabed topography and bedforms, and the thickness of seabed sediments (within an accuracy of $c.0.5m$). The extent of seismic survey data held by BGS is shown in Figure 2.4; commercial information is not shown. Additional data are available for the Wash, Thames Estuary, Bristol Channel and for an area offshore from Cumbria, but have not yet been included in the database. Some of the seismic lines shown in Figure 4 may be part of surveys run with a resolution too low to image the seabed sediments.

2.2.3 Navigation

BGS surveys used a range of position fixing methods:

- the Decca Main Chain navigation system, which locates positions to within 100 to 300m accuracy, was most frequently used during the sampling programme.

- before the late 1980s only limited use was made of systems giving accuracies to within 25m or closer: trisponders were used in the Bristol Channel; X-band radar was used to fix the position of boreholes in the 1970s; horizontal sextant angles were used to position samples within estuaries.

- satellite navigation systems giving accuracies to within 50m were used routinely from 1980 to position the seismic surveys, and, from 1988, for all surveys.

2.2.4 Archiving and data access

Most of the data held by BGS are not confidential, but some confidential data supplied by companies are also held. Computer-stored data can be retrieved by accessing grid rectangles defined by whole degree latitude and longitude coordinates; samples are labelled by reference to their grid square and their reference number within that square. Different sample types are distinguished on the database, e.g. vibrocores and grab samples. Each site was normally simultaneously sampled by grab sampler and gravity corer or vibrocorer. Most BGS seabed sediment size data is stored in a computerised database management system. Some data, particularly on the size of the coarser fractions, remain on paper copy. Plots of the density of seabed data are shown in Figures 2.2 & 2.3 in 5km-a-side grid squares.

Figure 2.2 *Density of BGS-held data, vibrocores and boreholes*

CIRIA Report 154

Figure 2.3 *Density of BGS-held data, all seabed samples*

Figure 2.4 *Shallow seismic lines held on BGS database*

CIRIA Report 154

2.3 HYDROGRAPHIC OFFICE MODERN SURVEY COVER

2.3.1 Cover

The extent of detailed surveys with full modern survey cover (with echo-sounded traverses at 250m intervals and full seabed coverage by side-scan sonar) is shown in Figure 2.5. This information has been digitised from the Admiralty Chart Q6090 published in March 1993 and transcribed from Mercator to National Grid projections.

HO has an on-going survey programme; the extent of cover and the areas surveyed in 1993 are shown in Figure 2.5, based on Admiralty Chart Q6090A. Some areas, already covered by modern survey, are being re-surveyed under the HO Repeat Survey Programme.

The HO surveys shown in Figure 2.5 are run to a consistent density of cover in terms of line spacing. Seabed samples were generally obtained on a rectilinear grid of closer than 2km spacing. The HO data set includes some information on the nearshore zone.

2.3.2 Instrumentation

The HO surveys provide a two-dimensional, high-density cover of the seabed deploying echo-sounders, side-scan sonars and sediment samplers. The survey lines run for the side-scan sonar are about 250m apart. Echo-sounders are run simultaneously with tidal reductions of all soundings to Lowest Astronomical Tide levels. Samples are taken by an underway sampler at 1.5—2km intervals on a rectilinear grid. The sampler penetrates to less than 0.1m into the seabed.

2.3.3 Navigation

Most modern HO surveys (post-1970) were fixed by dedicated high precision electronic systems, such as Hifix, Seafix and Loran G, giving general accuracies of $\pm$ 50m. Since 1985 GPS systems, without civilian degradation, have been used giving accuracies better than $\pm$ 10m. There is some doubt whether layback allowances have been consistently made to towfish positions which has apparently produced observed errors of up to 150m on cross-overs and on fixed sonar targets (e.g. wrecks, etc.) seen on adjacent lines.

2.3.4 Archiving and data access

The 1970-1984 survey data are archived with BGS, though not yet indexed on computer. More recently acquired HO data continues to be stored at Taunton, with an annual transfer to BGS of data more than 10 years old. 1984-1993 data are accessible to BGS at HO in Taunton on request. Surveys to the end-1993 were the most recent material available, since several months can elapse before survey data are brought ashore.

2.4 CORE DATA FROM AGGREGATES PROSPECTING SURVEYS

2.4.1 Cover

Prospecting for marine aggregates is concentrated within six main areas off England and Wales (Figure 2.6). Prospecting surveys in these areas produce better indications of the 3-D distribution of seabed samples than are provided by the more extensive BGS and HO data-sets, but the density of data varies within each prospecting area shown. The six areas shown are sufficiently generalised to avoid breaching confidentiality.

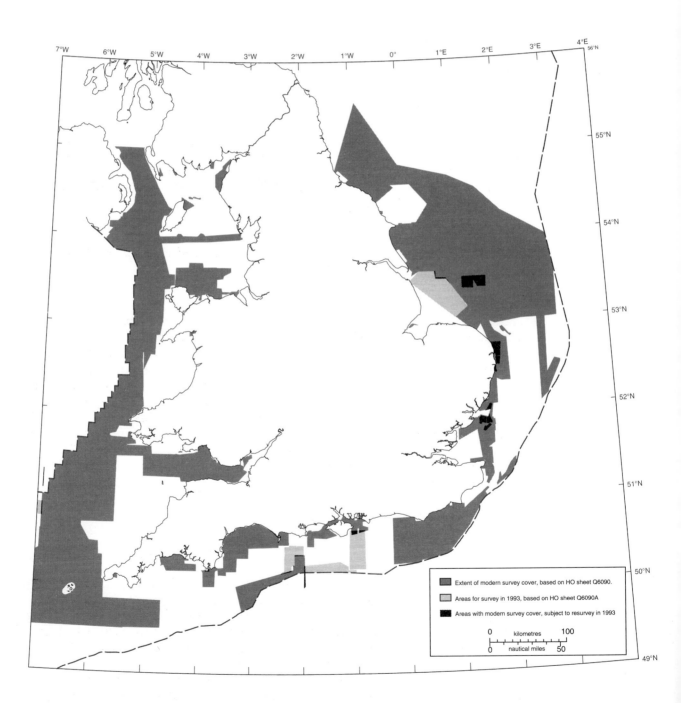

Figure 2.5 *Hydrographic Office modern survey cover*

The largest prospecting areas are located offshore from the coasts of Norfolk, a second zone offshore from Suffolk and Essex extending into the outer Thames Estuary, a third zone offshore from West Sussex extending south of the Isle of Wight, and a fourth area extending from Liverpool Bay to Anglesey. Two smaller areas have been investigated off Kent and East Sussex (Figure 2.6)

2.4.2 Available source data

Reports and samples were accessed through the archive held by PD for the Crown Estate. The data held on ARCInfo by PD refer to vibrocores. The complete company prospecting reports including shallow seismic interpretations are retained by the Crown Estate. The availability of marine aggregate industry data was subject to agreement between the Crown Estate, the aggregate industry represented by the British Marine Aggregates Producers Association (BMAPA) and the CIRIA Steering Group.

2.4.3 Navigation

Modern surveys used either Trisponder or GPS, although some of the older surveys would have used the Decca Main Chain navigation system. Sample locations are therefore fixed with high precision on modern surveys, probably to within less than 10m.

2.4.4 Data access

Use of confidential information is subject to the condition that resource data (lithology and sediment volumes) are averaged across 4km-a-side grid squares, thus avoiding release of information on individual vibrocores. Raw data used for the volumetric calculations is stored in confidence at BGS and will not be released. The use of industry data has been authorised by individual companies.

2.5 INTEGRATION AND PRESENTATION: RESOURCE ASSESSMENT

2.5.1 Introduction

In order to compare estimated resource availability with the anticipated demand for marine materials suitable for aggregate and non-aggregate purposes over the next 20 years, the volume of materials on the sea floor has been calculated for areas shown in Figures 2.7 to 2.9. A regional description of material distribution and volumes in Sections 4 to 6 provides an overview of the total offshore resource. For areas studied in detail, resource volumes within grid squares are provided and regional data are summarised in maps and tables. In order to undertake volumetric assessment of the offshore resource, a database has been created at BGS to assimilate data of variable quality from the three main sources outlined previously. Although confidentiality precludes issuing this database with the report, it is necessary to outline the methods of data assimilation and creation of the database in order to understand how the volumes were calculated.

2.5.2 Data merging

Procedure for the assimilation of data derived from different sources into digital form

Analysis of data distribution and quality has been undertaken by integrating data sets which are held by the British Geological Survey, Posford Duvivier (managing agents for the Crown Estate), and the Hydrographic Office (MOD), and for which access has been authorised. The seabed sediment data from disparate sources has been collated for insertion into a database at BGS. Crown Estate data were transferred by disc into the BGS database. The majority of the data on lithology and sediment thicknesses has been derived from the BGS and Crown Estate databases. Data from the HO have been extracted manually from available records for subsequent insertion into the BGS database. The code system used by HO to describe lithologies has been used to assess the dominant lithology within a grid square where no other data are available. HO survey sheets, and where necessary Admiralty Charts, have been used to determine the greatest and least depths below mean sea level, information on bedforms and details on contaminants within the sediments.

To protect the confidences of the owners of the data, lithology and thickness data have been manipulated into grid square format using the Intergraph software package. Data are generalised to refer to 4km-a-side grid squares where commercial considerations are paramount, and to 2km-a-side grid squares in other areas selected for study.

In this section only (Figures 2.2 and 2.3), the distribution and density of BGS data is presented in 5km-a-side grid squares.

Map projections

In order for grid squares to be used for summarising data, all data were located relative to National Grid co-ordinates and to a standard Ordnance Survey coastline of England and Wales. Data available on Mercator or Universal Transverse Mercator (UTM) projections (e.g. HO data, bathymetry data) were digitised using the Microstation system at BGS and the digital data converted to National Grid projections.

Classification of seabed sediments

In order for material resources to be meaningfully compared with the material demand, a classification of material of prime interest for beach recharge schemes has been determined. HR Wallingford have identified the nature of material anticipated to be in demand for beach recharge schemes. The material most frequently in demand around the English and Welsh coasts is 2—10mm in grain size and the smallest material that could be used is 0.110mm. Lithology is less important, and shell content is not crucial. However, general cleanliness of the resource is important, and possible contaminants such as chemical pollutants or biogenic material (seaweed and marine organisms) have been specified in the resource inventory at BGS.

There is a problem of incompatibility where grain size details and sediment nomenclature for data collated from different sources is concerned, particularly in the classification of the coarser, more economically important size fraction. Data held by the Crown Estate accords with the industry classification of marine aggregate resources: gravel is defined as sediment with a grain size greater than 5mm, sand as sediment between 5mm and 0.063mm in size, and fines less than 0.063mm in size. The different grades of sand are not differentiated.

The BGS classification used during mapping the seabed sediments prior to 1986 was a modified version of that proposed by Folk (1954) which defined gravel as greater than 2mm, sand between 0.063mm and 2mm, and mud as less than 0.063mm in size. This scheme itself is based on the grading scale of Wentworth (1922) which is a binary logarithmic scale (in that each grade limit is twice as large as the next smaller grade limit). The gravel/sand boundary is taken as 2mm, the very coarse sand/coarse sand boundary at 1mm and the medium sand/coarse sand boundary at 0.5mm. This size classification is widely accepted in the geological community, but differs from that used by beach recharge engineers and the marine aggregate extraction industry. Since 1986 some BGS samples have been re-analysed for aggregate assessment purposes and the sand/gravel boundary placed at 5mm. These data are available for the East Anglia, Flemish Bight, Ostend, and parts of the Thames Estuary and Spurn BGS area sheets published by BGS. New data have also been collected from off Beachy Head and the Humber Estuary.

The size of gravel mapped on HO survey sheets is based upon subjective criteria, and the distinction between pebbles and gravel is not clearly defined. HO visual descriptions have been reclassified to the nearest appropriate Folk category to facilitate merging with the BGS database.

Figure 2.6 *Densely sampled areas investigated for marine aggregates*

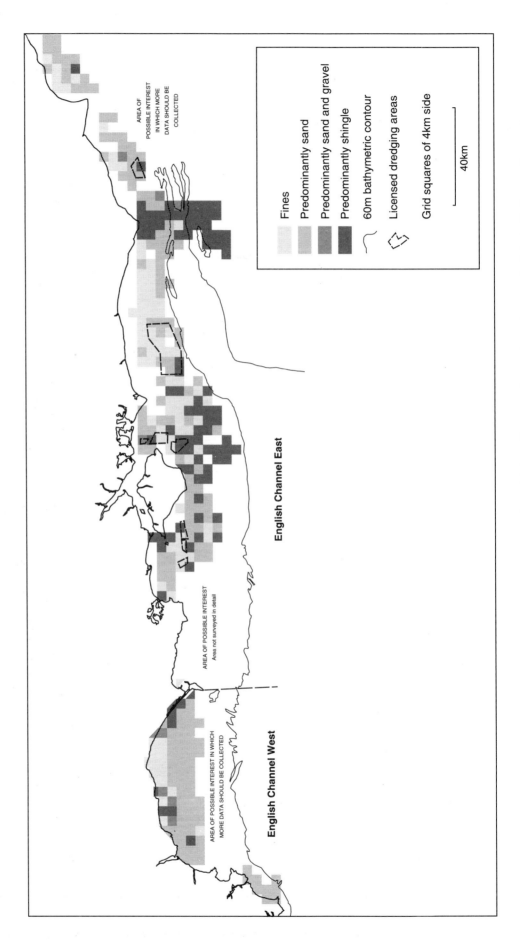

Figure 2.7 *Composite map showing all grid squares for which sediment volumes have been calculated off the south coast*

Legend:

Fines

Predominantly sand

Predominantly sand and gravel

Predominantly shingle

60m bathymetric contour

Licensed dredging areas

Grid squares of 4km side

40km

AREA OF POSSIBLE INTEREST IN WHICH MORE DATA SHOULD BE COLLECTED

English Channel East

AREA OF POSSIBLE INTEREST Area not surveyed in detail

English Channel West

AREA OF POSSIBLE INTEREST IN WHICH MORE DATA SHOULD BE COLLECTED

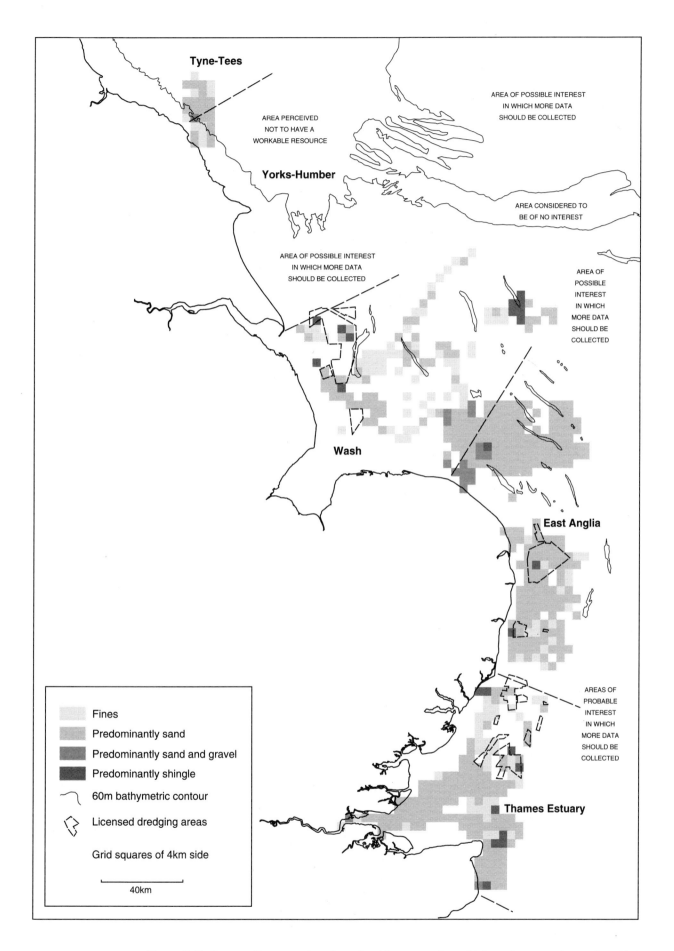

Figure 2.8 *Composite map showing all grid squares for which sediment volumes have been calculated off the east coast*

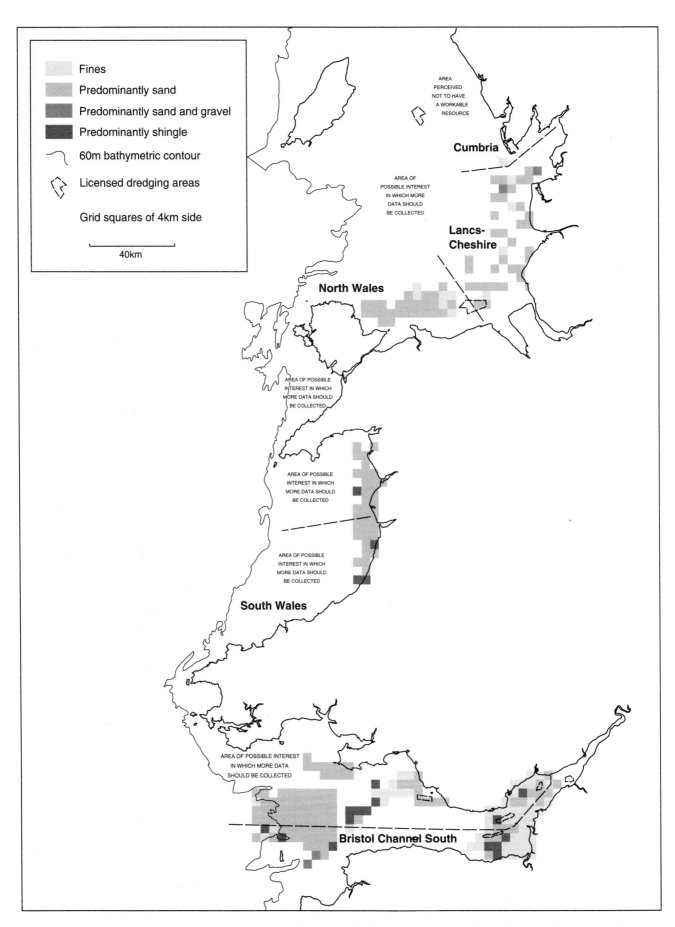

Figure 2.9 *Composite map showing all grid squares for which sediment volumes have been calculated off the coast of Wales and western England*

None of these grading systems accords with the size requirements for beach recharge material recommended by HR Wallingford. To facilitate compatibility between data sets, a sediment classification has been agreed between HR Wallingford and BGS. "Sand" is to be grouped into a single category, with a 2mm upper limit and a 0.125mm lower limit. This lower limit is adopted, because is equates with the very fine sand/fine sand Wentworth scale geological boundary and is close to the minimum size useful for beach recharge (0.110mm). A boundary at 5mm within the coarse fraction is incorporated to delimit material that would be in demand from the marine aggregate industry as well as for beach recharge. Adoption of this scheme for this report meant that the grain size of some BGS samples was reassessed.

The selected size categories and nomenclature are:

Shingle	Material > 5mm
Mixed sand and gravel	Material 2—5mm
Sand	Material 0.125mm—2mm
Fines	Material < 0.125mm (unsuitable for beach recharge)

Where feasible BGS has attempted to indicate the location of material over 50mm in size. Discussion between BGS and PD showed that data on the coarse shingle category was scarce. The coarse shingle and shingle categories have therefore been amalgamated into a single shingle category in the densely sampled areas.

Material with a modal size of 2—5mm tends to occur scattered across the region. Many sediments with abundant comminuted shell debris fall within this category. It is possible that the abundance of this category of sediment has been overestimated as a resource on the database. The reason for this is that sediment which is a mixture of coarse sand and fine shingle components can be modified by the seabed sediment sampling procedure. Grab sampling may mix shingle and sandier sediments together, giving a SG sediment in areas of high-current activity where winnowed shingle lags may rest upon sands or gravelly sands.

2.5.3 Quality control

For the detailed regional studies in Sections 4 to 6, data which has been entered into new database tables have been given an indication of reliability and perceived quality. The reliability of a grid square summary of available data is principally controlled by the number of samples taken in the grid square. Further qualification on data quality is dependent on the equipment used, the size of the sample recovered, and the subsequent analysis of the sample. In the case of BGS data, Figure 2.2 shows the most reliable seabed sediment data held (data based on vibrocores or borehole samples where adequate sample was recovered) as distinguished from the total data currently stored on the BGS database shown in Figure 2.3 which includes some very small sediment samples. Figure 2.3 includes grab samples, but the Shipek grab used by BGS in some cases only recovered small volumes (< 500g) of sediment from a coarse-grained substrate which were not adequate for full, reliable grain size analyses. For the surveys run by BGS as joint ventures with the Crown Estate and the Department of Environment, a larger Alluvial-Mining-type grab was used which had a capacity of 50kg. The HO underway core sampler was inferior to the Shipek grab now used for the most recent HO surveys.

HO sample data were determined by subjective description, and the grain size classifications derived are thus inherently less reliable than laboratory analysed samples. Both BGS and the Crown Estate hold on their databases grain size parameters determined by dry sieving techniques and this information is therefore more reliable than the sediment descriptions of HO. The Crown Estate data were extracted from marine aggregate company reports.

At BGS the grain size analysis of seabed samples was undertaken using wet sieving to separate the mud fraction (< 0.063mm) from the total sample, and dry sieving to analyse the sand and gravel fractions. Sieves at half phi (ϕ) size intervals (Wentworth scale) were used for dry sieving the sand fraction [0.063mm (4ϕ) to 2mm (-1ϕ)]. The grain size data is now stored on computer as weight percentages of half phi intervals. The weighed gravel fraction excludes composite grains. The gravel fraction was divided by hand-picking into lithic gravel and biogenic carbonate fragments (shell fragments). The carbonate content of the mud fraction was determined by the "Karbonat-Bombe" method, allowing determination of the total carbonate content of the sediment. BGS and Crown Estate data are of comparable quality, but PD have used the 5mm sand:gravel boundary favoured by the marine aggregate industry, whereas BGS have taken the same boundary at 2mm (after Wentworth, 1922). BGS holds very accurate data on the sand fractions of its samples, but data on the coarser fractions is sparse.

The grain size classes used in the report (Section 2.5.2) allow merging of the wide ranging HO data with the less extensive, but better constrained BGS and Crown Estate data. However, the HO data have provided useful information on bedforms and on sediment contamination that are not recorded on the Crown Estate data set and only locally on the BGS one.

All these factors are considered for formulating the reliability and quality index used in this report, shown on the figures summarising resource data in additional selected areas:

1   Borehole.
2   Vibrocore.
3   Amdrills, BGS grab samples with grain size analyses.
4   Grab samples which provide a subjective description of lithology, not thickness.
        Shallow seismic - provides information on thickness, but not lithology.
5   Interpreted HO side scan sonar - bedform information (subjective).

2.5.4 Parameters recorded on the database

The database created incorporating information held by BGS, and supplied by HO and PD on behalf of the Crown Estate, not only holds information on sediment type, thickness and water depths, but also details of bedforms and contaminants, including physical objects such as pipelines and wrecks. This information has been incorporated into the resource descriptions in Sections 4 to 6.

Although data from the BGS database will not be issued, on grounds of maintaining confidentiality of the data, maps illustrating particular features of the data and tables of calculated sediment volumes made possible by computer manipulation of the database have been produced. The map illustrations show grid squares shaded according to the dominant lithology and showing either the average volume of sediment within the 4km grid square or total volumes for the sub-regions studied.

The database created specifically for the report holds over 13 400 points of data which have been manipulated in 2819 2km-a-side grid squares of averaged data. A second database stores the raw data on sediment composition supplied by the Crown Estate. Again it is not possible to release these data, but they have been used for calculating the sediment volumes quoted in this report.

2.5.5 Volume assessment and data presentation

The key element in this exercise is the estimation of sediment thickness. Data are of variable quality and reliability and have been assigned a reliability index in the database (Section 2.5.3). Vibrocores and boreholes provide the most accurate information on sediment thickness in areas where the seabed sediments are very thin, less than 1m thick. Modern shallow seismic reflection profiling is able to resolve to between 1m and 2m at best. In areas where only grab sample data are available, a default value for sediment thickness of 0.1m is used, and a low reliability placed on the data in the database. However, in areas of sea floor where bedrock is extensively exposed, such as in Lyme Bay, a default sediment thickness of 0.05m is considered to be more realistic and has been adopted for the gross volume calculations.

Lithological and thickness data from all sources (principally BGS, HO and the Crown Estate) have been used for areas outside those intensely sampled by the marine aggregates industry, whereas only Crown Estate-derived data have been used in those areas where detailed prospecting by the marine aggregate industry has been undertaken. Prospecting surveys in these areas produce better indications of the 3-D distribution of seabed samples than those provided by the more extensive BGS and HO data sets, but the density of data varies within each prospecting area. Data from the prospected areas covered have been sufficiently generalised by the use of grid squares to summarise information to protect the confidences of the owners of the data. Resource estimates based on these data are compared with the anticipated demand within the region for aggregate and non-aggregate materials for the next 20 years.

In areas densely sampled by the marine aggregate industry, where volume estimates rely entirely on data supplied through the Crown Estate office, the percentage of shingle, sand and gravel, sand and fines has been estimated for each borehole core, vibrocore or amdrill core; the percentage of each size category is measured from a grading curve prepared from grain size analyses and therefore the percentage data are accurate estimates based upon analytical work. Volumes are calculated by computer manipulation of the data, multiplying the average percentage of each lithology by the mean thickness of sediment in the grid square multiplied by the area of the grid square.

All bulk volume estimates, including estimates of the volume of potentially workable material (greater than 0.5m thick, excluding the basal 0.5m of sediment cover) are initially calculated for 2km-a-side grid squares. In areas densely sampled by the marine aggregate industry commercial constraints dictate that the volume and dominant lithology data can be depicted only on 4km-a-side grid squares. The volumes recorded on 4km-a-side grid squares in Sections 4 to 6 are cumulative values derived from adding data from 2km-a-side grid squares. In many cases the 4km-a-side grid encompasses 2km grids without data. In such cases no attempt has been made to extrapolate volume estimates into 2km-a-side grid squares without data; the volumes presented are for known material only.

In selected areas of study additional to those intensely sampled by the marine aggregate industry, volume estimates utilise BGS, HO and Crown Estate low-density data sets. Point data of sediment thickness and dominant lithology are averaged for each 2km-a-side grid square. The cumulative total thickness of each lithology is divided by the total number of data points within a given grid square and multiplied by the area of the grid square.

Information is provided in tables supported by figures showing the distribution of offshore material in 4km-a-side grid squares. The use of the terms *predominantly sand, predominantly sand and gravel* and *predominantly shingle* signifies that a sediment size type is the main sediment distributed across the grid square, but the volume figures written on the grid square show the relative proportion of sand, sand and gravel and shingle respectively. The volume estimates written on each 4km-a-side grid square are for the total volume in that grid square, including the bottom 0.5m. A total volume of resource for the sub-region is presented, with additional volume estimates presented for the potentially workable resource in grid squares not dominated by fines over 0.5m thick (these values exclude the bottom 0.5m of the resource). The use of a bold line on the 4km grid to highlight a potentially workable resource greater than 0.5m in thickness provides a general idea of the distribution of offshore material, but masks the true geographic position of potential resources which may be spread very unevenly across the grid square.

All volume estimates provided in this report are for inferred resources (based on HO or seismic data only, no vibrocores) and indicated resources (borehole, vibrocore, gravity core or grab sample data available), given reliability indices 4—5 and 1—3 respectively on the database. The terms *inferred resource* and *indicated resource* follow the recommendations of Riddler (1994). No account has been taken of resources already dredged from the areas studied, although this is clearly an important consideration. The volume estimates are based on data collected between the 1970s and 1993.

Figures 2.7 to 2.9 show the areas of sea floor covered by the volumetric calculations in Sections 4 to 6.

3 Future demands for dredged sediment

3.1 INTRODUCTION

The estimated potential demand for beach recharge material and marine aggregate for England and Wales over the next 20 years is presented in this chapter. The results are sub-divided into 12 coastal regions which are based on five dredging areas (Figure 3.1 and Table 3.1). The methods are presented and comparisons are made with estimates from other sources.

Potential demands for beach recharge material are presented as ranges to reflect the uncertainties of the methods and the potential for varying demand through the use of secondary defences, beach control structures, dissimilar sediments and active beach management. It is assumed that beach recharges will be implemented and completed on all appropriate beaches within the 20-year period. The potential impact of climatic change on demand is also discussed, though such predictions of change must be considered highly speculative.

Marine sand and shingle is extracted to meet demand for primary aggregates from the construction industry. Marine materials occurring in UK territorial waters supply the UK market and are also exported to north-west Europe. Section 3.4 outlines the predicted demand for marine aggregates over the next 20 years and shows that demand is greatest from urban areas in southern England.

3.2 POTENTIAL BEACH RECHARGE DEMAND

3.2.1 Approach to beach recharge demand

Designing a successful recharged beach scheme for any location requires an understanding of all the site specific parameters which influence the local coastal environment. These include:

- wave and water level climate, including extreme events and possible future changes
- nearshore sediment budget, including all sources and sinks
- beach sediment type
- underlying geology
- nearshore bathymetry
- influence of existing coastal structures
- influence of human activities.

The designer must also define the objectives of the scheme such as the:

- acceptable level of flood risk
- acceptable level of long-term maintenance
- desirability of beach control structures or secondary defences
- type of amenity benefit required.

It is outside the scope and budget of the present project to undertake the complete design process for even one scheme. Therefore the approach adopted is to apply simplified standard numerical modelling procedures to determine the demand for a representative set of 19 beaches from around England and Wales and then to extrapolate to all of the lengths of coastline for which beach recharge schemes may be implemented. The final estimates are presented as ranges reflecting the uncertainty of the methods, the sensitivity to sediment sizes, sensitivity to wave and water level conditions, the potential for climatic change and the effect of using beach control structures or other methods of coastal defence.

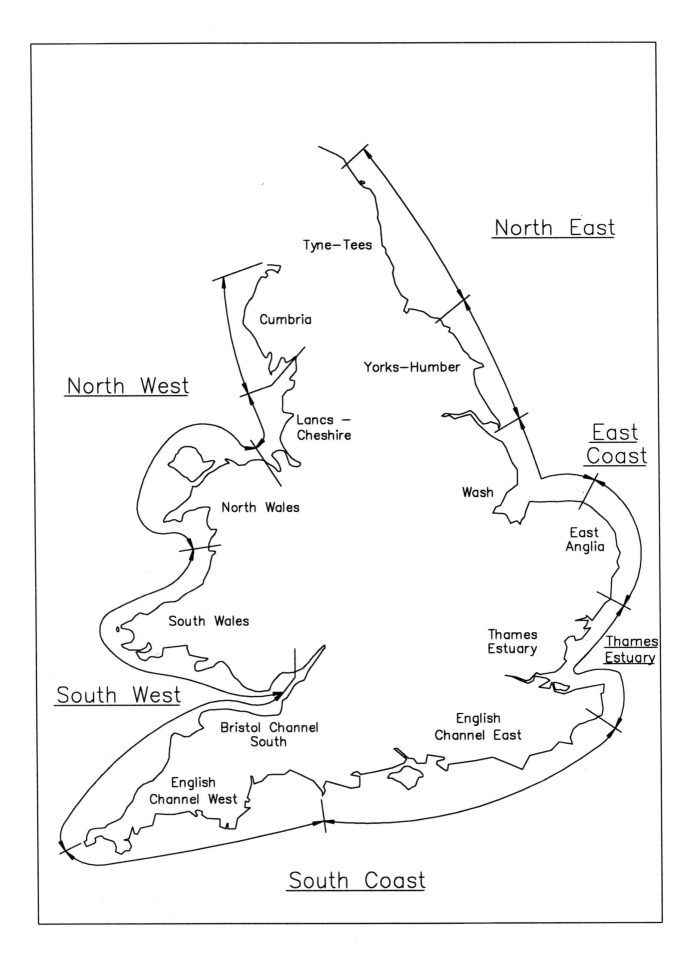

Figure 3.1 *Coastal demand regions and dredging areas*

Table 3.1 Nomenclature of regions

CIRIA	Crown Estate dredging	DoE Minerals planning	MAFF Littoral cells
Tyne-Tees	North East	Northern	Cells 1(a) to 1(e) part 1(d)
Yorks-Humber	North East	Yorks & Humber	part 1(d) Cell 2(a)
Wash	North East	East Midlands part East Anglia	Cells 2(b) to 2(d) part 3(a)
East Anglia	East Coast	East Anglia	Cell 3(b) part 3(c)
Thames Estuary	Thames Estuary	part East Anglia South East	part 3(c) Cell 3(d) Cells 4(a) to 4(b)
English Channel East	South Coast	South East part South West	Cells 4(c) to 4(d) Cells 5(a) to 5(g)
English Channel West	South Coast	South West	Cells 6(a) to 6(e)
Bristol Channel South	South West	South West	Cells 7(a) to 7(e) part 8(a)
South Wales	South West	South Wales	part 8(a) Cells 8(b) to 8(d) part 9(a)
North Wales	North West	North Wales	part 9(a) Cell 9(b) Cells 10(a) to 10(c) part 11(a)
Lancs-Cheshire	North West	North West	part 11(a) Cell 11(b) part 11(c)
Cumbria	North West	Northern	part 11(c) Cells 11(d) to 11(e)

The following sections discuss existing demand estimates from other sources, the selection of sites, the derivation of site data, the interpretation of the modelling results and the extrapolation of the estimates. The two beach response models which are used to estimate the required beach volumes for shingle and sand beaches are known respectively as SHINGLE and COSMOS. These models, plus the drift rate model DRCALC and the wave transformation model WENDIS have been developed at HR Wallingford.

3.2.2   Existing demand estimates for beach recharge material

Demand estimates have been made for some of the regions of England and Wales by the NRA. The estimates include only those beaches for which schemes have already been planned, with the exception of the Southern Region for which an attempt has been made to predict future requirements. No standard methods were used. Table 3.2 presents the available data.

Estimates for the south coast from Christchurch Bay to Ramsgate have been made by HR Wallingford (MAFF, 1993). These estimates used a similar approach to that adopted for the present project. They allow for a 300mm sea level rise but do not make allowance for beach control structures, active management or future maintenance. The estimates are presented in Table 3.3.

In addition to these two sources there is information from various sites for which beach recharge schemes have been either completed or are in the detailed design stage. This information is presented in Table 3.4.

Table 3.2 NRA demand estimates

Date	Location (and NRA region)	Sediment type	Volume (Mm³)
1992-2042	Lincolnshire (ANG)	Sand	22.0*
1995-1996	Cockersand (NW)	Sand	0.18
1995-1996	Overton (NW)	Sand	0.03
1995-1996	River Kent (NW)	Sand	0.03
1994-1996	Preston (SW)	Shingle	0.06
Post 1997	Easington (Yorkshire)	Sand	0.40
1995-	Isle of Wight (S)	Shingle	0.01
1992-2002	West Sussex (S)	Shingle	1.05
1992-2002	East Sussex (S)	Shingle	1.25
1992-2002	N. Kent (S)	Shingle	0.40
1992-2002	SE Kent (S)	Shingle & Sand	1.05

*Estimated capital and maintenance demand for Mablethorpe to Skegness scheme over 20 years in hopper m³

Table 3.3 MAFF demand estimates for shingle beaches on the south coast (from Diserens and Coates, 1993)

Location	Volume (Mm³)
Sandwick to Kinsdown	1.1
Sandgate to Pevensey	5.9
Pevensey to Langney Point	0
Seaford	0
Brighton to Littlehampton	0.75
Middleton to Portsmouth	1.54
Gosport to Hillhead	0.2
Calshot to Pankshore	0.3
Hurst to Mudeford	0.7

Some of the representative sites selected for the present study overlap with sites in Tables 3.2 to 3.4. The volume estimates derived from this study have been compared with the volumes derived from the other sources. Significant discrepancies have been investigated and modifications have been made to the proposed method for all relevant sites. These modifications are discussed later.

3.2.3 Selection and classification of representative sites

The sites chosen to represent all of the potential beach recharge locations around the UK were selected on a number of criteria. As the project scope was limited by the available budget, it was important to choose sites for which much of the of the required data was already available. HR Wallingford has a database of synthetic wave climates for many offshore locations around the UK (Figure 3.2). The first criteria was, therefore, that the beach sites had to be within the areas for which these data are relevant. The remaining criterion, in approximate order of importance, were:

- distribution around the coastlines of England and Wales
- representation of sand and shingle beaches
- recognition of an erosion or flood defence problem
- potential for implementation of a recharge scheme
- representation of different risk categories, i.e. urban or rural hinterland
- size of the recharge scheme.

Table 3.4 Beach recharge volumes for completed and planned schemes

Date	Location	Type	Capital volume (m³)	Maintenance demand (m³ pa)
1960s	Walland	Shingle	140 000	35 000
1960s	Pett	Shingle	150 000	35 000
1972	Portobello	Sand	180 000	
1975	Bournemouth	Sand	840 000	
1975	Sheerness	Shingle	180 000	3 500 (since 1986)
1975/80	Selsey	Sand	225 000	
1977/8	Cooden	Shingle	55 000	
1980	Elmer	Shingle	80 000	
1983	Bexhill	Shingle	152 000	
1985	Hayling Island	Shingle	470 000	30 000 (recycled)
1983/4	Sand Bay	Sand	300 000	
1985	Highcliffe	Shingle	44 000	
1986	Clacton/Jaywick	Sand and Shingle	100 000	
1987	Glyne Gap	Shingle	50 000	
1987	Seaford	Shingle	1 500 000	30 000 (recycled)
1988	Portobello	Sand	102 000	
1988	Shoreham	Shingle	25 000	
1989	Whitstable	Shingle	110 000	
1989	Bognor Regis	Shingle	25 000	
1990	Shoreham	Shingle	71 000	
1990	Hastings	Shingle	250 000	
1990	Bournemouth	Sand	1 000 000	
1990	Penrhyn Bay	Sand and Cobbles	75 000	
1990/1	Heacham/Hunstanton	Shingle	400 000	
1991	Aldeburgh	Shingle	40 000	
1992	Sandgate to Folkestone	Shingle	133 000	
1992	Shakespear Cliff to Folkestone	Shingle	133 000	
1992	Felixstowe	Shingle	70 000	
1992	Highcliffe	Shingle	17 000	
1992	Aberdyfi	Sand	30 000	
1992	Llandudno	Sand and Cobbles	100 000	
1993	Elmer	Shingle	150 000	
1993	Prestatyn	Sand	210 000	
1994	Sidmouth	Shingle	100 000	
1994	Dinas Dinelle	Cobbles	20 000	
1994	Reculver	Shingle	160 000	
1994-7	Mablethorpe to Skegness	Sand	10 800 000	100 000
1995	Hythe	Shingle	1 000 000	
1995	Glyne Gap	Shingle	140 000	
1995	Weymouth	Shingle	300 000	
1995	Morecambe	Sand	350 000	
1996	Happisburgh/Winterton	Sand	1 600 000	
1996	Eastbourne	Shingle	650 000	
1997	Morecambe	Sand	350 000	

Note: Volumes quoted are as placed.

The sites selected are presented in Table 3.5 and their locations are identified on the map in Figure 3.3. For the purposes of this project a simplified beach material classification has been adopted.

Material is classified by the D_{50} within the following ranges:

Sand 125μm—2mm
Shingle   >5mm

Fine material of less than 125μ is not considered to be suitable for beach recharge. Material between 2mm and 5mm is uncommon in the UK except as mixed beaches with a distinct bimodal grading distribution; the available numerical models cannot simulate complex distributions so beaches in this category have been classified as either sand or shingle depending on the dominant material of the upper beach.

Table 3.5 Sites selected for recharge demand estimates

	Site	Status	Material	Hinterland	Frontage length
1.	Hartlepool	--	Sand	Urban	0.2km
2.	Mablethorpe-Skegness	Planned	Sand	Mixed	27km
3.	Hunstanton/Heacham	Completed	Shingle	Rural	1k
4.	Cley/Salthouse	--	Shingle	Rural	2km
5.	Sheringham	Planned	Shingle	Urban	1km
6.	Aldeburgh	Completed	Shingle	Mixed	0.5km
7.	Herne Bay	--	Shingle	Mixed	2km
8.	Hythe/Sandgate	Planned	Shingle	Mixed	2km
9.	Glyne Gap	Planned	Shingle	Mixed	8km
10.	Pevensey Bay	Planned	Shingle	Mixed	1km
11.	Felpham	Planned	Shingle	Urban	1km
12.	Milford-Hurst Spit	Planned	Shingle	Rural	1km
13.	Poole Bay	--	Sand	Urban	2km
14.	Bridport	--	Shingle	Urban	0.5km
15.	Minehead	Planned	Sand	Urban	1km
16.	Aberafon	--	Sand	Urban	0.5km
17.	Aberystwyth	--	Sand	Urban	1km
18.	Kinmel Bay	--	Sand	Urban	2km
19.	Walney Island	--	Both	Rural	4km

Based on calculations undertaken prior to June 1994.

3.2.4   Selection of sites for future demand assessment

Five of the sites selected for recharge demand under present conditions were selected for demand assessment under future climatic conditions. In addition, one site (Slapton Ley) was included which is currently stable rather than at risk from erosion or flooding. Further stable or accreting sites were investigated, but none were found with suitable wave or profile information. Table 3.6 and Figure 3.4 present the selected sites and their locations.

Potential future wave conditions, based on one interpretation of climate change predictions, were applied to these sites to assess possible future demand variations. The wave conditions allow for a possible shift in the dominant wind direction at the relevant offshore wave prediction sites based on the UK Meteorological Office Global Climate Model (Jelliman *et al.*, 1991).

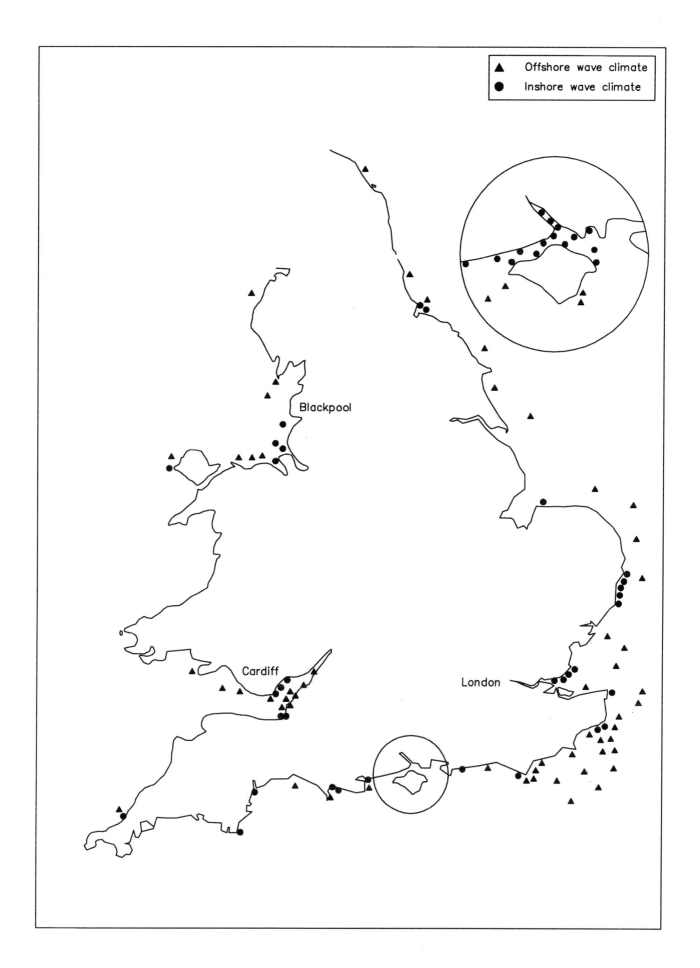

Figure 3.2 *Distribution of UK synthetic wave climate held by HR Wallingford*

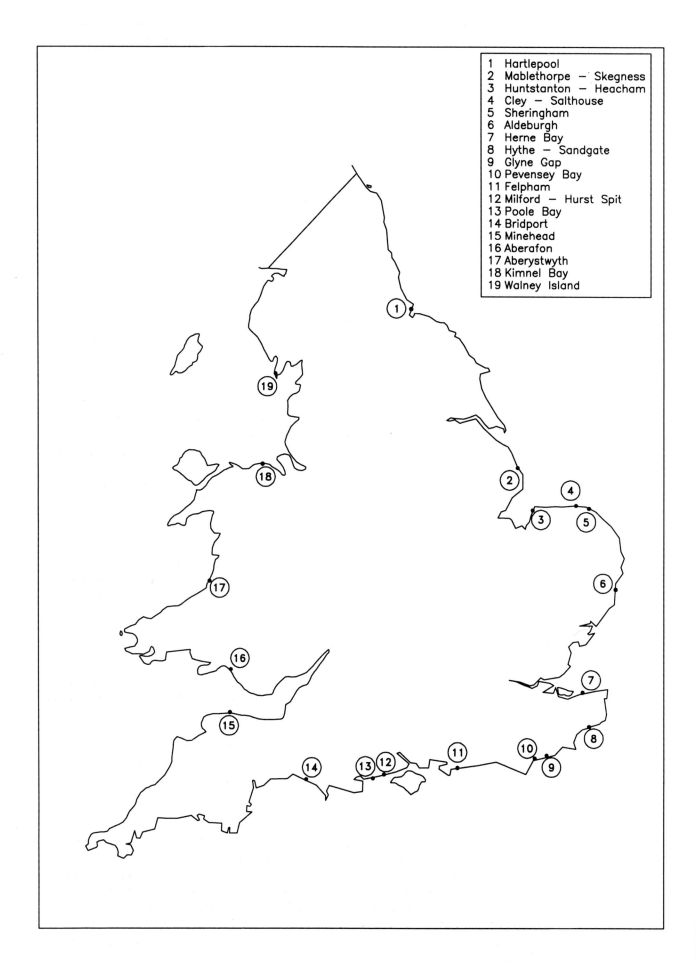

1 Hartlepool
2 Mablethorpe — Skegness
3 Huntstanton — Heacham
4 Cley — Salthouse
5 Sheringham
6 Aldeburgh
7 Herne Bay
8 Hythe — Sandgate
9 Glyne Gap
10 Pevensey Bay
11 Felpham
12 Milford — Hurst Spit
13 Poole Bay
14 Bridport
15 Minehead
16 Aberafon
17 Aberystwyth
18 Kimnel Bay
19 Walney Island

Figure 3.3 *Location of representative sites selected for recharge demand estimates*

Table 3.6 Sites selected for demand assessment due to future climate changes

	Site	Material	Present status
1.	Mablethorpe-Skegness	Sand	Eroding
2.	Cley-Salthouse	Shingle	Eroding
3.	Pevensey Bay	Shingle	Eroding
4.	Milford-Hurst Spit	Shingle	Eroding
5.	Minehead	Sand	Eroding
6.	Slapton Ley (Lyme Bay)	Shingle	Stable

3.2.5   Defence standards

Assessing risk for coastal sites is a complex process. It is generally based on predictions of the damage that may occur in the event of a given level of storm conditions. The storm conditions are classified according to the joint probability return period of the simultaneous occurrence of extreme water levels and extreme wave conditions.

The risk level is site specific, but to obtain practical standards for this project the sites have been divided into three categories: urban, rural and mixed (Table 3.5). For urban sites the worst case 200-year return period wave and water level conditions are used, while the worst case 100-year and 50-year events are used for mixed and rural sites (MAFF, 1993). The beach response required under these design conditions has been assumed to be that the initial recharged beach profile will not deform within 5m of a specified risk threshold line, which may be defined by revetments, dune lines or eroding cliffs. This basic standard may be modified according to the presence of secondary defences, such as a seawall.

3.2.6   Beach profiles

Beach profiles and additional beach management information were obtained from HR Wallingford records or from coastal authorities. Standards of information varied, but eventually a satisfactory data set was obtained. A representative profile for each site was derived and used as input to the COSMOS or SHINGLE models.

3.2.7   Derivation of wave and water level climates

All of the sites selected, except Aberystwyth in west Wales, are associated with an offshore location for which HR Wallingford holds synthetic wave data. The type of data varies, but in each case it was possible to derive a directional wave climate from which extreme wave conditions were predicted. These waves were then transformed inshore to the required beach site. The COSMOS model used for sand beach response makes the transformation without the need for further work, while for shingle beaches the WENDIS model was used; this is essentially the same as the relevant part of COSMOS so the inshore wave climates are comparable for all sites. HR Wallingford do not hold any wave data for the Aberystwyth area, so a new offshore wave climate was derived using standard hindcasting techniques.

Data is also held on the extreme water level climate (astronomical tides and storm surges) for much of the coastline. By assessing the interdependence between onshore waves and the occurrence of high water levels, a range of wave and water level conditions which have a joint probability of occurrence of either 50 years, 100 years or 200 years was determined. The interdependence depends on beach orientation and site location around the UK, and is classified into four levels varying from no interdependence to highly interdependant. From these ranges the worst case combination was identified by running sensitivity tests with the beach response models.

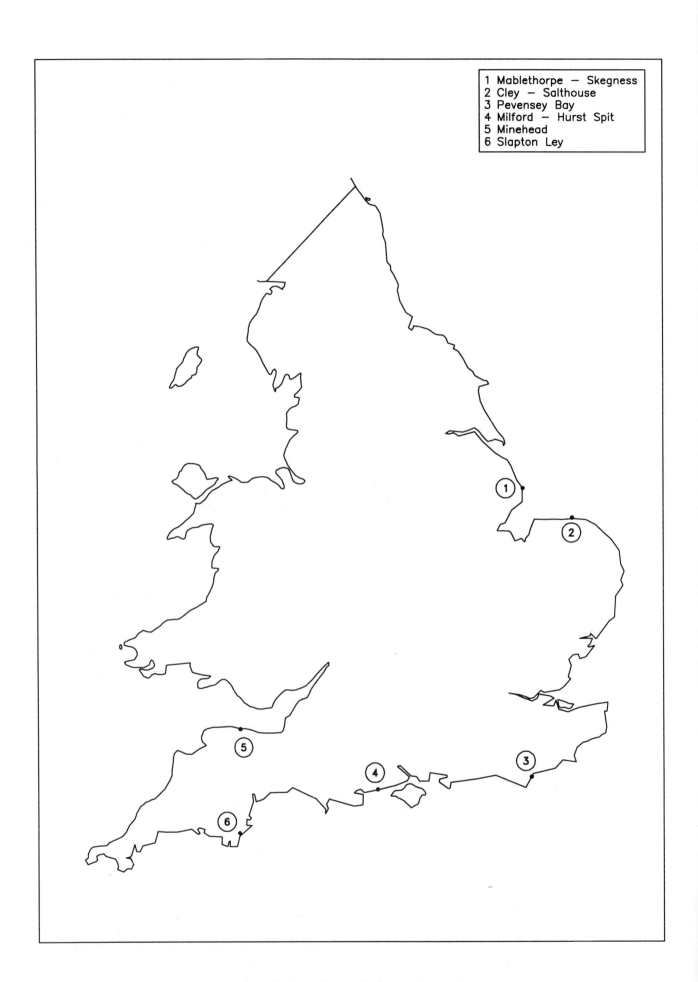

1 Mablethorpe — Skegness
2 Cley — Salthouse
3 Pevensey Bay
4 Milford — Hurst Spit
5 Minehead
6 Slapton Ley

Figure 3.4 *Location of sites selected for future demand assessment*

3.2.8   Derivation of drift rates

The beach response models SHINGLE and COSMOS were used to estimate the capital recharge volumes required for each site, but they cannot be used to determine the additional volumes that may be required for long-term maintenance. The maintenance demand depends on the rate of loss from the initial recharge. Cross-shore redistribution will account for some losses on sand beaches, but the majority of long-term losses will be caused by an imbalance in long-shore drift rates.

In order to predict losses from a recharged beach some estimates must be made of the available natural input and the potential drift rate. As a full sediment budget could not be derived for each site, the available natural drift was estimated as a proportion of the calculated potential drift rate. The potential drift rates for 0.2mm sand and 12mm shingle were calculated using the drift rate model DRCALC. Other sediment sizes and a range of wave directions were tested to determine the confidence limits. Consideration was given to the effect of structures and the input of material lost from updrift recharge sites.

3.3 RESULTS

3.3.1   Confidence limits

Estimating the demand for recharge materials over the next 20 years required that some very broad assumptions be made regarding the important parameters for the representative beaches. The estimates must therefore be expressed as a range of possible volumes, rather than as a single figure. The following points indicate the areas of uncertainty which affect the volumes.

1.   The beach response models are derived from the results of physical model studies (SHINGLE) or morphodynamic equations (COSMOS). The application of these models for this study is compromised by the lack of detailed site data.

2.   Existing beach profiles were used to determine the recharge volumes required to achieve the defence standards. They were selected to represent the "average" beach situation based on available data. These profiles may not be representative of the present beaches.

3.   The design wave conditions were derived from the transformation inshore of directional offshore climates which were, in turn, derived from land-based wind records. Both of these processes are subject to the limitations of the numerical modelling techniques and the quality and applicability of the wind records. Potential drift rates are particularly sensitive to wave energy and direction.

4.   The design water levels are derived from the probability of surge occurrence in combination with high astronomical tides. Derivation of the probability of extreme water levels is dependant on the quality and extent of measured tide data from local sources.

5.   The level of wave and water level interdependence assumed for determining joint probabilities is assessed on the basis of past experience and available site data rather than any rigorous procedures.

6.   Sediment size has an important influence on drift rates and on beach response to storm events, but the standard method applied for this project assumes a D_{50} of 0.2mm for sand and 12mm for shingle.

7.   Required defence standards vary along the coastline, depending on land use, topography, geology and the presence of existing secondary defences. As a detailed assessment of risk is not feasible, a simplified approach has been adopted. This approach allowed a standard recharge volume to be estimated for each representative site, after which minor adjustments were applied based on local knowledge.

8. The model methods provide an estimate for "as placed" material.

9. The influence of future climate change is entirely speculative, and the resulting demand estimates are only intended as a general guide to one of the possible climate change scenarios.

Tests were run to estimate the sensitivity of the results to variations in wave heights, wave periods, water levels, wave directions and sediment sizes. The results were verified against data from completed or planned schemes for which a rigorous design procedure had been applied by other consultants. The standard method used tended to underestimate volumes for sand beaches by about 20%, and an adjustment to all calculated volumes was made to compensate. Predictions for shingle beaches were found to agree with design volumes.

It should be noted that the quoted volumes have been derived only for the purposes of this study and should not be used as the basis for management decisions for the representative sites.

3.3.2 Impact of beach control structures

In addition to the accuracy limits discussed above, the volume of recharge material required can be affected by the presence of beach control structures such as groynes, detached breakwaters and sills. These structures can alter the inshore wave climate, the drift rate, the cross-shore distribution of drift and the plan shape of the beach. When correctly designed they can reduce greatly the volume of both the initial recharge and the maintenance requirements. Groynes are already in place at many of the representative sites, but in some instances they are having no beneficial impact on the beaches. The recharge estimates from this study consider the influence of correctly designed control structures on demand during the extrapolation of results from the representative sites to the full coastline.

3.3.3 Other considerations

Beach recharge schemes are not always perceived as the most appropriate solution to erosion or to flood risk for reasons which are unrelated to the hydraulic regime. These reasons are often related to material availability, construction difficulties or cost, but other factors may also be important. Schemes often require a long-term commitment to maintenance which coastal managers may be reluctant to make. Local residents are often sceptical, sometimes with good reason, about the effectiveness of a recharged beach and about the change to their familiar shoreline. An improved beach may be seen as a welcome amenity in some areas, but may also be perceived as an attraction to unwanted visitors, with associated drawbacks such as loss of privacy and traffic congestion. Similarly, local residents and their elected representatives may not be willing to accept the hydraulic effectiveness of a recharged beach as a coast defence scheme, and may prefer the apparent security offered by a sea wall. Recharged sand beaches may also create a problem with wind-blown sand.

Discussions with a sample of coastal managers from the various coastal authorities were used as a guide to the current and future acceptability of recharge schemes for the representative beaches. However, as these views may change over time, it was decided to assume that recharge schemes would take place at all sites which are appropriate from an hydraulic standpoint.

3.3.4 Extrapolation of results

The coastline of England and wales was reviewed to identify all of the frontages for which a beach recharge scheme could be considered as a means of improving coastal defences to achieve acceptable risk levels. The review was based on hydraulic conditions only, using data from HR Wallingford and the MAFF and NRA coastal surveys, from local knowledge and discussions with consultants and coastal authorities.

Figure 3.5 indicates all of the frontages identified, subdivided for sand or shingle. Each site was classified as being represented by one of the 19 selected sites. In a few cases this was not possible and the frontage was considered independently. A spreadsheet was developed which accounted for differences in tidal range, wave exposure, existing defences, required defence standards and existing beach control structures. Appendix B presents the spreadsheet with notes about the assumptions.

3.3.5 Required volumes for selected sites

Table 3.7 presents the minimum and maximum estimates for initial recharge demand and potential net drift rates for 19 sites. Two estimates are given for Walney Island, one for sand and one for shingle. The volumes and rates do not consider existing defences or beach control structures and therefore assume that the beach will be the only defence. The range of values is based on confidence limits determined from sensitivity tests. Recharge volumes are taken as $\pm30\%$, while drift rates are $\pm50\%$.

Table 3.7 Demand estimates for selected sites

Site	Location	Recharge volume (m³/m)		Nett drift rate (m³/y)	
		Minimum	Maximum	Minimum	Maximum
1	Hartlepool	175	325	25 000	75 000
2	Mablethorpe-Skegness	225	420	50 000	150 000
3	Hunstanton/Heacham	60	115	5 000	15 000
4	Cley/Salthouse	40	75	10 000	30 000
5	Sheringham	150	280	10 000	30 000
6	Aldeburgh	215	400	10 000	40 000
7	Herne Bay	75	135	5 000	15 000
8	Hythe/Sandgate	80	150	5 000	15 000
9	Glyne Gap	110	200	10 000	30 000
10	Pevensey Bay	20	35	10 000	30 000
11	Felpham	80	150	5 000	15 000
12	Milford/Hurst Spit	25	45	5 000	15 000
13	Poole Bay	90	165	20 000	60 000
14	Bridport	35	60	5 000	15 000
15	Minehead	220	405	75 000	225 000
16	Aberafon	235	435	25 000	75 000
17	Aberystwyth	225	415	5 000	15 000
18	Kimnel Bay	125	235	100 000	300 000
19	Walney Island (sand)	210	390	50 000	150 000
	(shingle)	80	150	10 000	30 000

3.3.6 Extrapolation of results

The demand volumes estimated for the 19 representative sites were extrapolated to all of the potential recharge sites identified in Figure 3.5. Volumes were estimated for each site, after which the sites were separated into 12 regions (Figure 3.1) for which demand volumes and maintenance rates of sand and shingle recharge were tabulated. Confidence levels for these extrapolated values are taken to be $\pm50\%$ for initial recharge volumes and $\pm70\%$ for maintenance volumes.

Table 3.8 presents the minimum and maximum initial recharge demand volumes assuming that all the frontages take up the option of undertaking a full recharge scheme during the next 20 years; the volumes are subdivided into sand and shingle, and include an allowance for sea level rise.

Figure 3.5 *Location of potential recharge sites around England and Wales*

CIRIA Report 154

Table 3.8 Potential initial recharge demand estimates

	Sand (Mm³)		Shingle (Mm³)	
	Max	Min	Max	Min
Tyne-Tees	7.46	4.01	0.00	0.00
Yorks-Humber	5.40	2.91	0.00	0.00
Wash	12.16	6.55	1.27	0.69
E. Anglia	0.60	0.32	4.25	2.29
Thames Estuary	3.78	2.03	10.17	5.47
English Channel E	0.85	0.46	19.20	10.34
English Channel W	1.46	0.79	0.85	0.46
Bristol Channel S	2.13	1.15	0.07	0.04
S Wales	2.68	1.44	0.00	0.00
N Wales	2.40	1.29	0.64	0.34
Lancs-Cheshire	1.69	0.91	0.00	0.00
Cumbria	2.62	1.41	0.41	0.22
TOTAL	43.23	23.28	36.86	19.85

It should be noted that the north-east region does not allow for a general recharge along the Holderness coastline. If recharge was considered for this length, then an additional volume of approximately 10Mm³ of sand could be required with a maintenance volume of about 100 000m³ per year.

Table 3.9 presents the maintenance volumes required per year following the initial recharge. The volumes assume that beach control structures or beach management schemes (recycling, regrading, selective retreat, increased risk acceptance, etc.) are implemented, and that some frontages will benefit from updrift recharge losses thereby reducing dependence on maintenance recharges. The need for active management or control structures depends to a large extent on the length of frontage and the potential drift rate. Short frontages with high drift rates will face longshore losses of a large percentage of the initial recharge, whereas long frontages will lose a much lower percentage. In the latter case, dependence on maintenance recharges may be much more cost effective than the construction of substantial beach control structures; this approach is being considered for the Mablethorpe to Skegness recharge scheme.

Table 3.9 Potential annual maintenance demand estimates

	Sand (Mm³)		Shingle (Mm³)	
	Max	Min	Max	Min
Tyne-Tees	0.68	0.23	60.00	0.00
Yorks-Humber	0.54	0.18	0.00	0.00
Wash	0.19	0.06	0.05	0.02
E. Anglia	0.64	0.21	0.09	0.03
Thames Estuary	0.09	0.03	0.09	0.03
English Channel E	0.05	0.02	0.20	0.07
English Channel W	0.02	0.01	0.14	0.05
Bristol Chan S	0.12	0.04	0.03	0.01
S Wales	0.13	0.04	0.00	0.00
N Wales	0.47	0.16	0.05	0.02
Lancs-Cheshire	0.15	0.05	0.00	0.00
Cumbria	0.38	0.13	0.02	0.01
TOTAL	3.43	1.14	0.67	0.22

The recharge demand estimates include both initial and maintenance volumes. They are extrapolated from volumes derived for 19 sites around the coast of England and Wales. Due to the simplified approach adopted for this study, the predictions and extrapolations are subject to large potential errors. The estimates are therefore presented as minimum and maximum values. The regional breakdown of demand presented in the report is summarised as follows:

Table 3.10 presents the best estimates of recharge requirements for each coastal region over the next 20 years. The figures consider the likely phasing of construction over the 20 year period.

Table 3.10 Estimated recharge demand over 20 years

	Sand (Mm³)		Shingle (Mm³)	
	Max	Min	Max	Min
Tyne-Tees	12.89	5.83	0.00	0.00
Yorks-Humber	10.27	4.53	0.00	0.00
Wash	15.35	7.61	2.07	0.95
E. Anglia	7.91	2.76	5.61	2.74
Thames Estuary	5.05	2.46	11.50	5.92
English Channel E	1.78	0.77	22.40	11.41
English Channel W	1.61	0.84	2.93	1.15
Bristol Channel S	3.33	1.55	0.67	0.24
S Wales	4.22	1.96	0.00	0.00
N Wales	9.30	3.59	1.54	0.64
Lancs-Cheshire	4.69	1.91	0.00	0.00
Cumbria	6.37	2.66	0.71	0.32
TOTAL	82.78	36.46	47.43	23.37

3.3.7 Effect of future climate change on demand

Estimates are presented for demand in the event of future climatic change. An increase in demand for sand of about 10%, mainly in the northeast and east, is forecast, while the demand for shingle may drop due to reduced drift rates. Ongoing monitoring of climate change and all recharge schemes will allow the demand forecasts to be refined in the future.

Predictions of future recharge requirements based on potential climatic changes must be considered to be highly speculative. The estimates presented in the previous section allow for a 4—6mm/year rise in sea level, but assume a constant annual wave climate. This section attempts to predict the impact of a change in the wind, and therefore wave, climate over the next 20 years. For the purposes of this report it is assumed that the only significant impact of climatic change will be a shift in wind direction, but not in storm frequency. Therefore the change in wave climate will influence the longshore drift rate and not the profile response. This assumption implies that only the maintenance recharge volumes will alter.

The best available data on future wave climates for the UK is published in Jelliman *et al.*, (1991). This work makes use of the UK Meteorological Office Global Climate Model, plus the results of international climate change research, and suggests possible wind shifts around the UK which are then transformed into drift rate changes. Briefly, the dominant wind directions with respect to coastal processes are predicted to shift to the south-east along the south coast and towards the north along the east and northwest coast. The impact of these shifts will depend on the orientations of the frontages along which beach recharge schemes may occur and on the potential influence of control structures and other management works. Percentage changes for six sites are presented in Table 3.11, while Figure 3.6 presents a summary of the possible changes to drift rates around the coastline of England and Wales. Extrapolation of these data give the regional variations in total demand presented in Table 3.12. It should be noted that if these changes occur, it will be over an undefined time period and, indeed they may not occur at all; confidence limits are therefore ±100%.

Over England and Wales as a whole, the potential increase in sand demand over 20 years due to climatic change could be of the order of 10% while the demand for shingle may actually decrease slightly.

Table 3.11 Possible change in maintenance demand for selected sites based on an assumption of future climate change

Site	Location	% change in demand
1	Mablethorpe-Skegness	+60%
2	Cley-Salthouse	-5%
3	Pevensey Bay	-80%
4	Hurst Spit	-45%
5	Minehead	-5%
6	Slapton Ley	-100%

Table 3.12 Possible regional change in maintenance demand assuming future climate change

	Sand	Shingle
	% Change	% Change
Tyne-Tees	+20	0
Yorks-Humber	+30	0
Wash	+60	0
E. Anglia	+60	+60
Thames Estuary	0	+20
English Channel E	0	-50
English Channel W	0	-70
Bristol Channel S	0	0
S Wales	0	0
N Wales	-20	0
Lancs-Cheshire	0	0
Cumbria	+20	0

Note: Some of the potential recharge beaches in the northeast are pocket beaches protected from the north, and have locally reversed drift, therefore the predicted future increases for these regions are low.

Figure 3.6 *Possible changes to drift rates due to future climatic change*

CIRIA Report 154

3.4 POTENTIAL DEMAND FOR MARINE MATERIAL BY THE AGGREGATE INDUSTRY FOR THE NEXT 20 YEARS

3.4.1 Long-term primary aggregate demand for UK

Primary aggregates can be defined as those mineral deposits which are used directly for construction purposes. Minerals used as primary aggregates are generally crushed rock, sand and gravel. In the UK sand and gravel can be both land-won and marine. Examples of secondary materials are colliery minestone, china clay sand, power station ash and blast furnace slag. Examples of recycled materials are asphalt and crushed rock from existing construction.

Minerals suitable for use as aggregates are not evenly distributed and there is also generally imbalance between the location of primary aggregates and the location of the demand from construction. This means that considerable volumes of aggregates have to be transported from source to end-use location. The provision of aggregates to meet demand is more critical in England and Wales which have about 85% of UK demand, with Scotland 10% and Northern Ireland 5%.

Guidance to mineral planning authorities in England and Wales is provided by the Minerals Division of the Department of the Environment and the Welsh Office.

The stated aim of the Mineral Planning Guidelines is to provide guidance on how an adequate and steady supply of material to the construction industry at a national, regional and local level may be maintained at the best balance of social, environmental and economic cost having considered all resources and sustainable development principles.

The Minerals Planning Guidance Note 6 (MPG 6) was first issued in 1989 but did not take account of actual production and consumption statistics beyond 1987. Prior to the Revision of MPG 6 a wide ranging consultation exercise was undertaken which included 20-year demand forecast options for England and Wales.

The Revision of MPG 6 when issued by the Department of the Environment in April 1994 related only to England and for a shortened period of 15 years to 2006. The demand forecasts for the 20-year period to 2015 are therefore estimated for the purposes of this report and are not Department of the Environment figures.

Total aggregate demand in England and Wales is forecast for this project (using data for England from MPG 6) at 4280 million tonnes in the 15-year period to 2006. Projections in MPG 6 indicate a rise in the annual rate to 450 million tonnes including Wales by 2015. This results in a demand estimate of about 7000 million tonnes for England and Wales in the 20-year period to 2015.

In the 15 years to 2006, land-won primary aggregate provision in England is envisaged to be 1200 million tonnes of sand and gravel and 1900 million tonnes of crushed rock. This is 73% of the total aggregate demand for England.

In those 15 years, 1165 million tonnes of aggregate, other than land-based production in England, will be required. This is made up of marine dredged sand and gravel (7%), imports from outside England and Wales (4%), imports from Wales (4%), and Secondary and Recycled (12%).

The planning region with the greatest demand for aggregate supply is South East England with nearly 2000 million tonnes estimated in the 20-year period to 2015. This is followed by the West Country of England with about 900 million tonnes, and East Midlands/Wash with slightly less. Lancs & Cheshire, Yorks & Humber and West Midlands all require at least 600 million tonnes for the 20-year period. Table 3.13 summarises these demand estimates.

Table 3.13 England and Wales regional total aggregate demand

Planning region	Demand forecast 15 years to 2006 (Mt)	Demand estimate 20 years to 2015 (Mt)
South East	1270	1935
West Country	610	940
East Midlands/Wash	540	840
Lancs-Cheshire	440	690
Yorks-Humber	430	615
West Midlands	490	640
Tyne-Tees/Cumbria	275	410
East Anglia	225	330
North Wales	---	200
South Wales	---	400
	4280	7000

The 15-year demand forecasts for the English regions are based on MPG6. Demand forecasts for Wales and for the English regions over the 20-year period have been estimated for this report and are not Department of the Environment figures.

3.4.2 Marine sand and gravel demand

England and Wales

The Department of the Environment and the Welsh Office accept that marine dredged material can compete with existing land-won sources, and the capacity exists to increase supply by up to 40% by 2011. They appreciate the competing demand from coastal defence authorities for soft defence beach management options. They also appreciate that present knowledge suggests a finite resource of current types of material being dredged. In addition to current dredging areas about 500 million tonnes of further such resources have been identified. The Department of the Environment and the Welsh Office have indicated that their policy remains to achieve the maximum contribution from marine aggregates consistent with the need to have regard to the protection of the marine environment, fish stocks and the coastline.

The MPG 6 Revision indicates 315 million tonnes of marine aggregate for England alone for the 15 years to 2006. For the purposes of this report the assumption can be made for England and Wales combined that in the 20-year period to 2011, the marine aggregate contribution will be 565 million tonnes. Demand in England and Wales is envisaged to rise from an average of 20 million tonnes per year in the period 1991 to 1996 to an average of 32.5 million tonnes in the period 2007 to 2011 and beyond. For the period 1996 to 2015 demand for marine aggregate in England and Wales is estimated to be approximately 565 million tonnes excluding demand for beach recharge and for export.

It must be noted however that the effect of the UK recession has caused UK aggregate landings to drop from 20 million tonnes per year in 1989/1990 to 12 million tonnes per year in 1992/1993, i.e. 60% of the original demand assumption. All the following forecast demand tonnages must be viewed in the light of this low starting level for the 20-year period. Table 3.14 presents a summary.

Table 3.14 Marine sand and gravel demand estimate from UK sea-bed 20 years to 2015

Material size range	To England and Wales from gravel areas Mt (Mm³)	To England and Wales from sand areas Mt (Mm³)	Exports to North West Europe Mt (Mm³)	Total Mt (Mm³)
Above 5mm	280 (140)	0 (0)	120 (60)	400 (200)
5mm to 2m	40 (22)	0 (0)	20 (11)	60 (33)
2m to 0.125m	125 (78)	100 (63)	50 (31)	275 (172)
Below 0.125m	20 (13)	0 (0)	10 (7)	30 (20)
TOTAL	465 (253)	100 (63)	200 (109)	765 (425)

These figures have been estimated for this report. They are not Department of the Environment figures.

Gravel areas

MPG 6 indicates that the marine gravel with sand requirements of the South East region of England amount to about 75% of the total requirement for England and Wales with the East Anglia region adding a further 2%. The average demand is expected to rise from about 15 million tonnes per year in the five years to 1997 to about 25 million tonnes per year in 2011 onwards to 2015. This report estimates that the total demand by the English Channel East, Thames Estuary and East Anglia resource sub-regions will be 435 million tonnes between 1996 and 2015, with about two thirds required by the Thames Estuary. The marine gravel with sand demand in the other planning regions (East Midlands, Yorks & Humber and Tyne & Tees) totals about 30 million tonnes in the 20-year period 1996 to 2015. Almost all of this material is gravel with sand in the proportions required for concrete. Thus the 465 million tonnes of gravel with sand can be assumed to comprise the following:

Above 5mm	280Mt	(140Mm³)
5mm to 2mm	40Mt	(22Mm³)
2mm to 0.125mm	125Mt	(78Mm³)
Below 0.125mm	20Mt	(13Mm³)

Sand areas

The most important of the remaining regions are South Wales and the West Country, with a demand of 60 million tonnes and 30 million tonnes of marine sand respectively (estimated volumes) in the 20 years to 2015. The 90 million tonnes total is from the dredging areas in the Bristol Channel/Severn Estuary. The remaining regions are Lancs & Cheshire and North Wales with a total demand of 10 million tonnes which is from the North West dredging areas in Liverpool Bay.

Most of the above 100 millions tonnes is sand for concrete and building. This total can be assumed to comprise the following:

Above 5mm	0Mt	(0Mm³)
5mm to 2mm	0Mt	(0Mm³)
2mm to 0.125mm	100Mt	(63Mm³)
Below 0.125mm	0Mt	(0Mm³)

Scotland and Northern Ireland

There are at present only small-scale marine aggregate landings in Scotland and Northern Ireland, and it is unlikely that these will increase to the extent of having a significant effect on the overall demand and supply pattern in those countries.

North West Europe

Marine gravel with sand from the UK seabed is currently supplied to four countries in North West Europe, namely Germany, Netherlands, Belgium and France. These countries generally have sufficient sources of marine sand in their own seabed.

In Germany, the current primary aggregate demand is about 300 million tonnes per year of which about 8 million tonnes is imported. About 0.25 million tonnes of gravel with sand from the UK seabed is currently landed in Germany. No forecast data is available for future aggregate demand.

In the Netherlands, the primary aggregate demand for the next 20 years is forecast at about 130 million tonnes per year, but this includes beach nourishment sand and sand for filling which will be supplied from the Netherlands seabed. Gravel and industrial sand demand is forecast to be relatively static at 23 million tonnes per year and 20 million tonnes per year respectively. Gravel imports are forecast as static at 11 million tonnes per year for at least the 20-year period to 2011. About 2.75 million tonnes per year of marine gravel with sand from the UK seabed is currently landed in the Netherlands. There is potential for marine gravel to increase its market share because of continuing difficulties with land-based supply.

In Belgium, there is no forecast data for primary aggregate demand and marine aggregate details relate only to sand for beach nourishment and filling which are supplied from the Belgian seabed. About 2.25 million tonnes per year of gravel with sand from the UK seabed are currently landed in Belgium

In France, the current primary aggregate demand is about 300 million tonnes per year of which about 3 million tonnes per year is marine aggregate. There is no forecast data for aggregate demand. About 1 million tonnes per year of gravel with sand from the UK seabed is currently landed in France.

To summarise, about 6.25 million tonnes of gravel with sand from the UK seabed are currently landed in North West Europe. In all four countries pressure on land sources favours increased demand for imported aggregates and it is anticipated that marine aggregates from the UK seabed will at least hold their current market share. Thus, if the steady growth forecast for the UK is matched in North West Europe, over the 20-year period to 2015, landings of the order of 200 million tonnes can be anticipated

As in South East England, the landings in North West Europe are almost all for concrete and can be assumed to comprise the following:

Above 5mm	120Mt	(60Mm³)
5mm to 2mm	20Mt	(11Mm³)
2mm to 0.125mm	50Mt	(31Mm³)
Below 0.125mm	10Mt	(7Mm³)

Tables 3.13 and 3.14 provide a summary of all the above demand forecasts.

3.4.3   Long-term marine aggregate industry

The present UK marine aggregate industry involves about 50 vessels operated by a dozen companies. Three of these companies operate at least eight vessels each, whereas nearly half the companies only operate one aggregate vessel each.

Organisation

The present organisation matches that of the land-based aggregate industry with the trend, certainly over the last 15 years, for concentration into fewer companies by takeover by national aggregate and readymix concrete producers. As at least 80% of marine sand and gravel is landed for concrete rather than for general building or construction purposes, the readymix concrete operators have endeavoured to control their own sources of marine supply. Hence most of the current marine aggregate companies are directly linked to readymix concrete operators.

Of the current marine landings from the UK seabed 90% are from four companies. These are (with the related aggregate or readymix company in brackets) ARC Marine (ARC), Civil and Marine (Evered Bardon), South Coast Shipping (RMC) and United Marine Dredging (Tarmac/Pioneer). Each of these companies has recently invested heavily in large riverside processing plants in strategic locations with regard to adjacent markets and road networks.

Most plants also have facilities to handle other materials such as crushed rock and some are linked to the rail network. These large strategic processing plants, offering a range of aggregate materials, have each tended to replace a number of smaller wharfs and plants where expansion was not feasible.

It is likely that concentration of aggregate processing activity into these large strategic plants will continue long term as planning permissions for further plants becomes more difficult in conurbations. This concentration on fewer plants has resulted in companies arranging to share such facilities.

Notwithstanding this concentration on large riverside processing plants in conurbations, in other areas there is always likely to be opportunity for smaller operations where particular geographic market circumstances make them economic.

Vessel capacity

The present UK marine aggregate fleet of about 50 vessels comprises a mixture of large vessels (above 3500 cargo tonnes) and medium/small vessels (below 2200 cargo tonnes). Some of the smaller vessels are static dredgers but all the others are trailers. Fourteen vessels are new, having been built in the period 1986 to 1991, but most of the others were built before 1975.

There are 12 large vessels over 4000 cargo tonnes which, with one exception, will be less than 30 years old in 2015. All these vessels generally operate in the North Sea and supply gravel with sand to South East England and North West Europe. These 12 vessels have a maximum capacity between them of about 15 million tonnes per year - 300 million tonnes in the 20 years to 2015.

There are eight large vessels over 3500 cargo tonnes which were built in the period 1971 to 1975. All were fully employed during the expansion of the late 1980s when most of the newer vessels were being built. These eight vessels have a maximum capacity between them of about 10 million tonnes per year, but some are laid up in the current recession. Major refurbishment would be necessary for any vessel to make a significant contribution in the next century.

Of the small vessels under 2000 cargo tonnes only three are new and together have a capacity of about 2 million tonnes per year - 40 million tonnes in the 20 years to 2015. The other small vessels have a combined capacity of about 10 million tonnes per year, but all are at least 20 years old and are not anticipated to contribute significantly in the next century.

To summarise, the present maximum capacity of the UK fleet is about 35 to 40 million tonnes per year. The effect of the lay-up of vessels in the current recession is to reduce this to about 30 million tonnes per year - still well in excess of the 1992/1993 aggregate extraction from the UK seabed of about 20 million tonnes per year.

Throughout the first decade of the next century, however, the maximum capacity of the present vessels still likely to be in service will probably not be much in excess of 20 million tonnes per year. Thus the maximum capacity of the present UK aggregate fleet for the 20 years to 2011 is likely to be 500 to 600 million tonnes depending on the extent of refurbishment of older vessels.

Influence of exports

At the peak of aggregate extraction from the UK seabed in 1989, nearly 24 million tonnes were landed in the UK and North West Europe. This tonnage was close to the maximum capacity of the UK fleet with many of the new vessels still under construction.

Of this total only about 2.5 million tonnes were exported, and most companies envisaged that the increased capacity generated by the new vessels coming into service would enable significant increases to be made in exports whilst continuing to supply the UK.

This increase in exports occurred to the extent that in 1992/1993 over 6 million tonnes were landed in North West Europe. In the same period, however, UK landings fell dramatically from over 21 million tonnes in 1989 to about 12 million tonnes in 1992/1993.

With the landings in both the above regions now generally static it can be seen that about one third of current aggregate extraction from the UK seabed is for export.

Of the order of £100 million was invested by the industry in those vessels ordered during the expansion period of the late 1980s with an equivalent investment in processing plants. High utilisation is necessary to justify these investments. Maintaining at least the above level of exports is crucial to the UK marine aggregate operators in keeping their vessels fully utilised and profitable in the long term.

3.4.4   Current supply pattern and trends

There are currently six main dredging regions - in clockwise order round the coast - North East, East Coast, Thames Estuary, South Coast, South West and North West. The first four are mainly gravel with sand extraction whereas the last two are mainly "sand only" extraction.

The most important gravel region is the East Coast off Great Yarmouth where, at the 1989 peak, over 9 million tonnes were dredged, most being for Thames Estuary wharves with some exports to the Netherlands, Belgium and France. Supplementing this supply in the 1989 peak was about 3 million tonnes from the Thames Estuary dredging region. This combined extraction of 12 million tonnes in 1989 had, by 1992/1993, reduced to about 10 million tonnes per year. The landings in Thames Estuary wharves had reduced drastically in this period from 10 million tonnes to 5 million tonnes per year, whereas exports increased from 2 million tonnes to over 5 million tonnes per year.

In the short and medium term, these East Coast and Thames Estuary dredging regions are likely to remain the most important extraction areas with existing production areas, on exhaustion of reserves, being later replaced by new adjacent resources already identified by recent prospecting.

The next most important gravel region is the South Coast where, at the 1989 peak, over 5 million tonnes were extracted and landed in the English Channel East wharves of Sussex and Hampshire. This extraction had fallen to just over 4 million tonnes per year in 1992/1993 with significant tonnages now being landed in the Thames Estuary wharves and for export.

In the medium term, the Hastings gravel area of the South Coast dredging region has the potential to become a major source of supply for both the English Channel East and the Thames Estuary as well as for exports. As on the East Coast/Thames Estuary dredging regions, recent prospecting has identified new resources adjacent to existing production areas in the South Coast dredging region.

The remaining gravel region is the North East where, off the Humber at the 1989 peak, about 1.5 million tonnes were extracted for landing in Yorks & Humber wharves and Tyne & Tees wharfs and for exports. Extraction has remained at that level to 1992/1993 with the reduction in landings in England being matched by increased exports.

In the medium/long-term any large-scale increase in extraction from the North East dredging region is likely to be a result of exhaustion of other gravel regions closer to the main South East England/North West Europe markets.

The most important sand region is the South West where in the Bristol Channel/Severn Estuary at the 1989 peak about 3 million tonnes were dredged and landed in South Wales and the West Country, which had reduced to just over 2 million tonnes per year in 1992/1993. The landings are directly related to the local economy and in the short/medium term are likely to rise in proportion to any local recovery.

The other sand region is the North West where from Liverpool Bay at the 1989 peak about 0.5 million tonnes were landed in Lancs & Cheshire wharves mainly on Merseyside. The effect of the recession is to reduce these levels by about half in 1992/1993. The geography of the Liverpool Bay coastline provides potential for modest penetration of the existing markets from a number of small port locations. In the medium/long-term the tonnages landed could increase if there are difficulties with land sources. Dredging peak extractions are summarised in Table 3.15 in relation to the corresponding demand regions.

Table 3.15 Regional marine sand and gravel demand from UK seabed 20 years to 2015

| Resource sub-region | Peak extraction (Mt pa) | Material size range | | | | Total (Mt) |
		Above 5mm	5mm to 2mm	2mm to 0.125m	Below 0.125m	
Tyne-Tees	---	12	2	5	1	20
Yorks-/Humber	---	6	1	2.5	0.5	10
Wash	1.5 gravel	0	0	0	0	0
East Anglia	9 gravel	6	1	2.5	0.5	10
Thames Est.	3 gravel	172	24	77	12	285
NW Europe	---	120	20	50	10	200
Eng Ch. E	5 gravel	84	12	38	6	140
Eng Ch. W	---	0	0	0	0	0
Brist Ch. S	inc below	0	0	25	0	25
South Wales	3 sand	0	0	65	0	65
North Wales	0.5 sand	0	0	1	0	1
Lancs-Chesh	inc above	0	0	9	0	9
Cumbria	---	0	0	0	0	0
TOTAL	22 gravel and sand	400	60	275	30	765

3.4.5 Summary of aggregate demand from marine sources

The demand for marine aggregate for England and Wales is likely to be about 565 million tonnes over the twenty period from 1996 to 2015, but of the current 1992/1993 level of just under 20 million tonnes per year, one third is for exports. The steady increase in demand forecast for England and Wales is also likely to occur for exports and could add a further 200 million tonnes for North West Europe.

The total of 765 million tonnes of estimated marine aggregate demand from the UK seabed for the 20 years to 2015 is summarised below.

These estimates assume that adequate quantities of marine materials will be continuously available and that costs will remain stable.

3.5 TOTAL DEMAND FOR AGGREGATES

A summary of projected demand for both beach recharge and aggregate supply is given in Table 3.16.

Table 3.16 Overall demand summary for marine material, Mm³, 1995—2015

	Shingle >5mm			Sand and gravel 2—5mm		
	Aggregate	Beach recharge	Total	Aggregate	Beach recharge	Total
Tyne-Tees	6.0	0	6.0	1.1	ND	1.1
Yorks-Humber	3.0	0	3.0	0.6	ND	0.6
Wash	0	2.07	2.07	0	ND	0
East Anglia	3.0	5.61	8.61	0.6	ND	0.6
Thames Estuary	86.0	11.50	97.5	13.3	ND	13.3
English Ch East	42.0	22.40	64.4	6.7	ND	6.7
English Ch West	0	2.92	2.92	0	ND	0
Bristol Ch South	0	0.67	0.67	0	ND	0
South Wales	0	0	0	0	ND	0
North Wales	0	1.54	1.54	0	ND	0
Lancs-Cheshire	0	0	0	0	ND	0
Cumbria	0	0.71	0.71	0	ND	0
Export	60.0	0	60.0	11.1	ND	11.1

	Sand 2—0.125mm			Fines <0.125mm		
	Aggregate	Beach recharge	Total	Aggregate	Beach recharge	Total
Tyne-Tees	3.1	12.89	15.99	0.7	US	0.7
Yorks-Humber	1.6	10.27	11.87	0.3	US	0.3
Wash	0	15.35	15.35		US	0
East Anglia	1.6	7.91	9.51	0.3	US	0.3
Thames Estuary	48.1	5.05	53.15	8.0	US	8.0
English Ch East	23.8	1.78	25.58	4.0	US	4.0
English Ch West	0	1.61	1.61	0	US	0
Bristol Ch South	15.6	3.33	18.93	0	US	0
South Wales	40.6	4.22	44.82	0	US	0
North Wales	0.6	9.30	9.9	0	US	0
Lancs-Cheshire	5.6	4.69	10.29	0	US	0
Cumbria	0	6.37	6.37	0	US	0
Export	31.3	0	31.3	6.7	US	6.7

ND   No data. Available beach recharge models cannot simulate material in the 2—5mm category. Beaches requiring this size of material are uncommon and are usually mixed beaches which have therefore been classified as either sand or shingle beaches depending on the dominant material of the upper beach.

US   Unsuitable for beach recharge

Volume estimates for aggregate demand were supplied in metric tonnes and have been converted to cubic metres using the following density values:

Shingle	2.0 tonnes/cubic metre
Sand and gravel	1.8 tonnes/cubic metre
Sand	1.6 tonnes/cubic metre
Fines	1.5 tonnes/cubic metre

Beach recharge data are best estimates of the maximum recharge requirements for each coastal sub-region, taken from Table 3.10. The values allow for the likely phasing of construction over the 20 year period and also consider the possible changes in demand in the event of future climatic change.

4 General distribution and quality of marine materials suitable for beach recharge off the south coast of England

4.1 BACKGROUND

This is the first of three sections assessing the distribution and quality of offshore material suitable for aggregate and non-aggregate purposes for comparison with the anticipated demand for these materials over the next 20 years. This Section concerns the area offshore from the South Coast, between South Foreland, Dover, in Kent and Land's End in Cornwall. The region is divided into two sub-regions, English Channel East (South Foreland to Portland) and English Channel West (Portland to Land's End) to accord with the regional areas for material demand estimates in Section 3.

An outline of the geological history and hydrography of the English Channel is provided which pertains both to the distribution and to the origin of the seabed sediments. A regional description of material distribution and volumes provides an overview of the total offshore resource. For areas studied in detail, resource volumes within grid squares are provided. The database created specifically for the project holds over 8000 points of data for the South Coast area which have been manipulated by computer into 935 2km-a-side grid squares of averaged data. Some logistical factors affecting exploitation are discussed in Section 8.

4.2 REGIONAL REVIEW

4.2.1 Sea floor topography

The topography of the present-day seabed is largely the product of a fluvial drainage regime during the Quaternary, and marine planation concomitant with periods of rising sea level, during Quaternary interglacials and since the last glaciation. The seabed takes the form of a gently inclined submarine erosion surface, locally modified by incised palaeovalleys, submerged cliff lines, enclosed deeps and the superficial sediment cover. Tidal sand ridges and sandbanks locally modify the sea floor topography by up to 20m. The occurrence of bedforms is governed by the tidal current paths in the English Channel. In general, the seabed is more irregular in the English Channel West sub-region due to the older and more resistant bedrock compared to the smoother sea floor of the English Channel East sub-region.

West of Selsey Bill a submerged cliffline follows approximately the 40m isobath, but in the east of the area a major system of palaeovalleys obscures the cliffline, although it is well developed again east of Beachy Head. The submerged cliffline at approximately 40m depth can be traced south of St Catherine's Deep across to Portland Bill. In Lyme Bay a series of cliffs marking submerged coastlines, separated by near horizontal benches, occurs below the 20m isobath. An extension of this feature may be traced intermittently along the southern coast of Devon and Cornwall between 20m and 70m depth.

West of Lyme Bay the coastal zone to 20m depth is an extension of the present cliff slope, although slopes are gentler in bays lacking a cliff surround. The sea floor then slopes steeply from the coast and the 50m bathymetric contour is mostly less than 20km offshore, although in Lyme Bay it lies some 30km south of the coast. Apart from the nearshore zone, much of the region west of Lyme Bay lies in water depths in excess of 50m.

Substantial parts of the English Channel are also in water depths of greater than 50m (Section 1). At St Catherine's Deep, 5km south of the Isle of Wight, the water depth reaches 82m within a 20km-long depression in bedrock.

4.2.2 Tidal streams

The strength of tidal and wave induced currents has an important influence on the distribution of sediment types. Winnowing of sediments to leave shingle lags and the growth of sandbanks occurs under a strong tidal current regime, whereas fine sediments tend to accumulate in sheltered bays and offshore deeps.

The behaviour of tides and currents in the English Channel is complex, but some general patterns emerge. In the Atlantic Ocean tidal streams are very weak, but as the tidal wave reaches the shallower coastal areas the magnitude of the tidal streams increases greatly. Exposure to the prevailing westerly swell decreases from west to east with the severest wave conditions being along west-facing coasts. However, the English Channel also acts in effect as a funnel and the tidal range becomes amplified as the English Channel narrows towards the east. The tidal range at mean spring tides increases from to 3.5m at the Isle of Wight to 7.0m at Dungeness.

Strong tidal currents therefore occur in the English Channel, with peak surface velocities reaching 1.75m/s in parts of the region, notably off the southern tip of the Isle of Wight and in the centre of the English Channel, SSW of the Isle of Wight. Mean spring currents in the Dover Straits may reach 1.8m/s. Apart from some inshore areas, surface velocities do not drop below 0.75m/s. In the central part of the English Channel the maximum speed of tidal currents is 0.75m/s to 1.0m/s. South of Devon and Cornwall tidal currents are of moderate strength, typically 0.75 to 1.0m/s.

Currents tend to be stronger near the headlands of Land's End, the Lizard, Start Point, Portland Bill, St Alban's Head, St Catherine's Point, Selsey Bill and Beachy Head. They are also strong in major tidal inlets such as the Solent and Southampton Water. In bays sheltered by these headlands, for example in Start Bay, Lyme Bay, Plymouth Bay, Mounts Bay, Weymouth Bay, Poole and Christchurch bays, and Rye Bay currents are weaker especially in shallow water, commonly less than 0.5m/s.

4.2.3 Solid geology

In many areas the shingle components show a relation to the lithology of the underlying bedrock. The English Channel is underlain by a variety of rock types. From the centre of Lyme Bay westwards Devonian metasediments crop out in the coastal zone with Permo-Triassic mudstones, sandstones and breccias occurring further offshore. Jurassic sandstones, limestones and mudstones extend eastwards to Durlston Head where the Isle of Wight monocline separates Cretaceous strata to the south from Tertiary sediments in the Solent extending into the Hampshire—Dieppe Basin. The Tertiary strata comprise largely unlithified sands and mudstones with some indurated limestones. Cretaceous rocks are exposed at the coast at Bognor Regis and extend to Dover, with inliers of Jurassic strata in the centre of the English Channel.

4.2.4 Quaternary geological history of the English Channel

During the Quaternary geological period the climate fluctuated between glacial and interglacial cycles. Major oscillations in sea level were associated with the growth and decline of the ice caps. These changes in sea level affected areas beyond the known limits of extent of the ice caps, such as the English Channel. During the last 250,000 years two major falls in sea level are recorded to approximately 120m below present day sea level. These periods of sea-level retreat occurred about 135,000 years before present (B.P.) during the Saalian glaciation, and about 18,000 years B.P. associated with the last (Devensian/Weichselian) glaciation. Significant sea-level falls occurred during the earlier Anglian and Cromerian glaciations, but their effect on sedimentation in the English Channel has been masked or accentuated by the two most recent periods of sea-level fall.

These changes in sea level had a profound influence on sedimentation in the English Channel. The entire sea floor became exhumed during glacial maxima and river channels drained across the emergent landscape cutting new courses, enlarging existing valleys, and depositing sediments. During the last (Devensian/Weichselian) glaciation the rivers Rhine and Meuse and rivers draining southern England flowed across the exposed English Channel floor. The complex pattern of palaeovalleys documented in the English Channel were incised by rivers during one, or perhaps more, periods of Pleistocene sea-level lowstand. It is likely that these rivers carried a substantial coarse sediment discharge, particularly when periglacial conditions affected southern Britain. Most of the sediments infilling the valleys date from the late Devensian or early Flandrian and are the product of fluvial and periglacial processes operating during these periods of lower sea level.

Where these coarse sediments have accumulated within the palaeovalleys, they may constitute a significant resource. The problem is that, even if these deposits are suitable, they may be covered by unsuitable material to a thickness that would render their extraction uneconomic. During marine transgression, notably the latest Pleistocene—early Holocene trangression, when global sea level rose by more than 100m, the palaeovalleys became tidal creeks before their eventual submergence. This phase of palaeovalley evolution is likely to have been one dominated by mud sedimentation, much the same as in the present-day ria creeks of southwest England. The thickness of mud accumulated in these relatively sheltered creeks probably varied from site to site, depending, for example, on the local tidal conditions. In some instances the palaeovalleys may have become totally filled by such fine sediments. In other cases, as the valleys became progressively submerged and subject to contemporary wave energy and associated longshore drift, substantial deposits of sand and/or shingle may have accumulated as the youngest deposits of the fill sequence.

The shingle now forming a thin veneer over parts of the sea floor comprises fluvial terrace deposits modified by the processes of marine transgression in the early Holocene. Modern addition of shingle-sized material to the sea floor is very limited, largely restricted to the release of flint nodules from the slow denudation of chalk cliffs.

Today shingle exposed at the seabed is often heavily encrusted with serpulids, bryozoa and barnacles indicating that it is not mobile there under the present tidal regime. Exceptions are gravel waves recorded, for example, in the West Solent and where wave-generated longshore drift can transport gravel in the surf zone. The distribution of shingle therefore reflects in the majority of occurrences processes no longer active at the present day.

4.2.5 Renewability of resources

It is important to note that the shingle offshore is largely a relict deposit, redistributed to some extent during the major sea level rise that took place between 8000 and 5000 years ago. The shingle deposits are not replenished after extraction, except for the shell component and some shingle clasts derived from present-day cliff erosion (e.g. flint nodules released from the Chalk) which add a small component to the current marine shingle resource. The shingle resource must therefore be considered finite and shingle removed from the South Coast area will not be replaced.

Sand deposits, depending on the local sedimentary regime, may be replenished in part. Sand is being supplied by cliff erosion from some outcrops of Lower Cretaceous bedrock, particularly on the Isle of Wight, from unlithified Tertiary deposits on the Hampshire coast, and from some Devonian and Permo-Triassic coastal outcrops in Devon and Dorset. Replenishment of dredged sand may occur in some instances where local sediment transport paths and wave currents would allow bedforms such as sandbanks to reform.

4.3 GENERAL DISTRIBUTION OF MARINE MATERIALS: RESOURCES AND VOLUME ESTIMATES

The offshore resource is considered in relation to the regional divisions proposed in Section 3. The South Coast region is divided into English Channel East and English Channel West sub-regions. The South Coast region has been widely covered by geological surveys and extensively prospected for marine aggregates. Much of the sea floor is covered by material that is potentially suitable both for beach recharge and for aggregate purposes. Muddy sediments occur only rarely in the English Channel on account of the strong tidal current activity. They tend to be confined to sheltered nearshore areas such as either side of Dungeness, and where superficial sediments may be contaminated by mud-rich bedrock such as an area southwest of Folkestone and a broad zone south of the Sussex coast. Muddy sediments occur in the inner parts of Lyme Bay where relatively weak tidal currents (less than 0.5m/s) are typical. Accumulations of fines may locally mantle coarse-grained sediments.

Palaeovalleys are a special consideration in the South Coast region, because the potential resources occurring as valley fills could greatly enhance the resource potential of the region. The broad distribution of palaeovalleys has been reported by Hamblin *et al.*, 1992. The palaeovalley fills are generally overlain by a thin veneer of seabed sediments and they may have no surface expression. The only reliable method of fixing the position of palaeovalleys is to undertake shallow reflection seismic surveys.

4.3.1 English Channel East

Deposits at the seabed are generally less than 0.5m thick over bedrock, although thicker deposits occur, either as the infills of palaeovalleys of variable thickness, or as sand and fine gravel waves generally less than 6m thick. In general, sediments up to 2m thick comprise lag deposits of shingle and sandy shingle, while sediments thicker than 2m include mobile sand bodies resting upon lag deposits. Deposits inshore may be substantially thicker (up to 25m) as both relict and active coastal spit developments (e.g. Dungeness, Hurst Castle spit, Owers Bank). These deposits of former and present coasts comprise a range of sediments from barrier spit gravels and cobbles to lagoonal muds. There are tidal sand ridges in the Dover Strait up to 10m thick (e.g. the Varne).

Current survey cover extends inshore to approximately 2km from the coast. Additionally only patchy cover exists for Poole Harbour, parts of the Solent and Southampton Water, and Owers Bank.

Shingle and coarse shingle

The seabed is formed by a thin veneer of shingle across broad swathes of the English Channel. The concentration of shingle in the surface layers is due to the winnowing of sand and finer sediment by tidal currents. The shingle may rest as a lag upon bedrock or may cap finer grained sediments. Where shingle lags are very thin there is a real possibility of contamination by underlying deposits and a significant change in the seabed character if this surface layer is removed. This lag deposit in the English Channel is generally less than 0.5m thick, of patchy distribution and interspersed with bedrock. It is almost everywhere too thin to show on seismic reflection profiles. Locally, thicker shingle deposits are present such as at Shingle Bank, offshore from Hastings, where several metres of shingle-rich sediment are preserved as a fossil beach deposit occurring at the base of a submerged cliff line. Most of Shingle Bank is licensed for aggregates production. Potential gravel resources occur offshore from Selsey Bill and on the nearshore side of Owers Bank, and in the western Solent, but dredging is constrained in these regions to avoid conseqential problems for coastal protection.

The composition of the shingle relates closely to the underlying solid geology. In general the shingle consists mostly of flint, but locally chalk, sandstone, ironstone, mudstone, phosporite, and igneous and metamorphic lithologies can be important. Shingle incorporating over 80% flint nodules extends south-east from the Isle of Wight overlying the Tertiary subcrop. South of the Isle of Wight, overlying Lower Cretaceous rocks, the shingle contains between 5% and 80% sandstone clasts, averaging 25%. Where the shingle lag is underlain by Chalk it contains up to 80% chalk clasts. Chalky shingle, dominated by large chalk clasts, occurs in areas south of the Isle of Wight and offshore Beachy Head.

Table 4.1 Summary of resources in areas densely sampled by the marine aggregate industry

		Sand		Sand and gravel		Shingle	
		Volume	Tonnage	Volume	Tonnage	Volume	Tonnage
		Mm³	Mt	Mm³	Mt	Mm³	Mt
Dungeness-Dover	A	205.8	329 3	33.0	59.4	59.8	119.6
Dungeness-Dover	B	195.5	312.8	41.8	75.2	53.5	107.0
Dungeness-Dover	C	181.1	289.8	29.0	52.2	41.7	83.4
Dungeness-Dover (includes Hastings Shingle Bank)	D	138.2	221.1	22.1	39.8	34.3	68.6
Sussex A		338.6	541.8	54.9	98.8	71.3	142.6
Sussex B		255.9	409.4	41.8	75.2	39.5	79.0
Sussex C		242.6	388.2	39.7	71.5	37.0	74.0
Sussex D		202.0	323.2	33.0	59.4	26.2	52.4
Isle of Wight A		338.5	541.6	54.2	97.6	331.9	663.8
Isle of Wight B		287.3	459.7	46.0	82.8	295.8	591.6
Isle of Wight C		192.4	307.7	30.7	55.3	254.9	509.8
Isle of Wight D		155.5	248.8	24.9	44.8	164.6	329.2

A: estimated total material identified in the areas sampled
B: as A but excluding material in grid squares where fines are the dominant lithology
C: as B but also excluding material in deposits averaging less than 0.5m thick
D: as C but excluding all material in the lowest 0.5m of the deposit

All resource estimates were calculated in cubic metres and have been converted to tonnes using the following density values:

Shingle	2.0 tonnes/cubic metre
Sand and gravel	1.8 tonnes/cubic metre
Sand	1.6 tonnes/cubic metre

In the Dover Straits chalk pebbles derived from the underlying exposed bedrock are numerous. The shingle generally has a low shell content in the eastern English Channel. The sands associated with the lag shingle deposits are generally poorly sorted of coarse grain size, with a high shell content. Shell may exceed 20% of the shingle components offshore Shoreham-Newhaven.

The size of the shingle varies considerably. Locally large clasts/cobbles over 120mm in size may occur and exceptionally boulders in excess of 500mm occur. Fine pebble gravel/shingle tends to predominate in relatively nearshore areas.

Within areas densely sampled by the marine aggregate industry the Project database indicates a potentially workable resource of 225Mm³ for the South Coast (Table 4.1). Of this, a total exceeding 190Mm³ occurs off the coast of Sussex, Hampshire and the Isle of Wight (Table 4.1; Figures 4.1 and 4.2), and 34Mm³ are estimated to occur in the vicinity of Shingle Bank off Hastings and off the Dungeness-Dover coast (Figure 4.3).

Mixed sand and gravel

Material with a modal size of 2—5 mm within gravelly sand mixtures tends to occur scattered across the study area. Many sediments with abundant comminuted shell debris fall within this category. It is possible that the abundance of this category of sediment has been overestimated as a resource on the Project database. The reason for this is that sediment which is a mixture of coarse sand and fine shingle components can be a product of the seabed sediment sampling procedure. Grab sampling may mix shingle and sandier sediments together giving a SG sediment in areas of high-current activity where winnowed shingle lags may rest upon sands or gravelly sands.

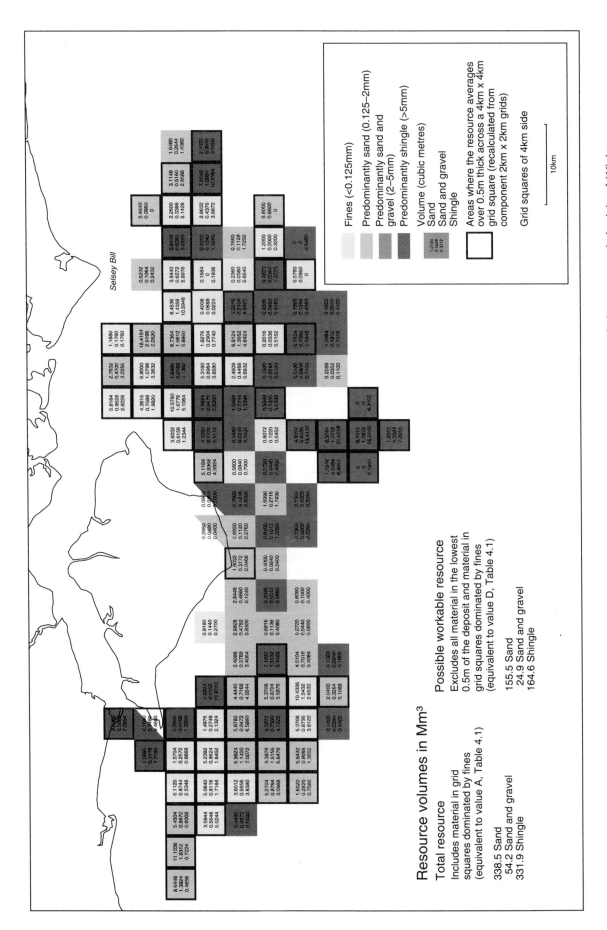

Figure 4.1 *Resource volumes in areas densely sampled by the marine aggregate industry around the Isle of Wight*

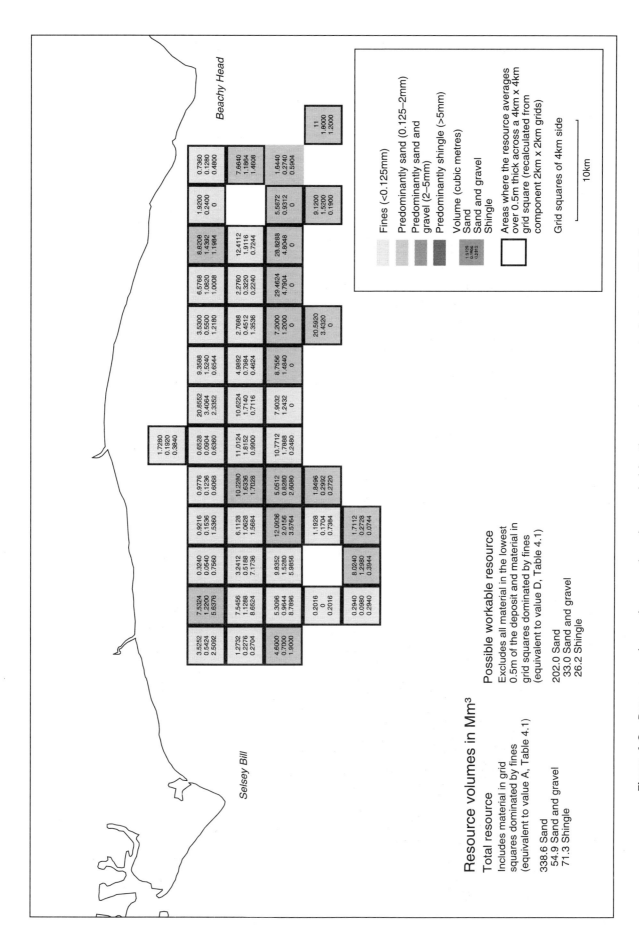

Figure 4.2 *Resource volumes in areas densely sampled by the marine aggregate industry off the Sussex coast*

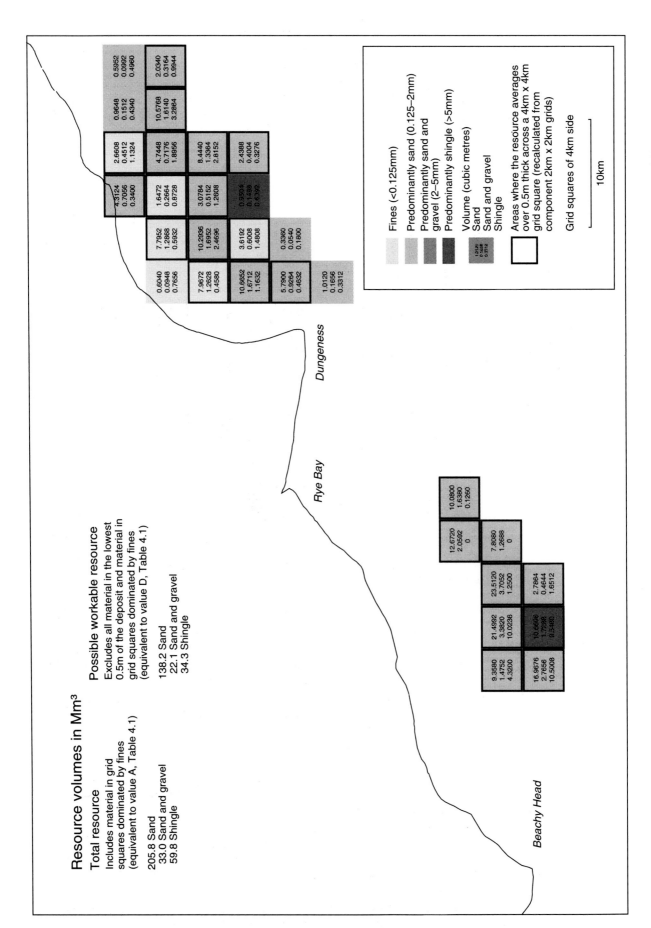

Figure 4.3 *Resource volumes in areas densely sampled by the marine aggregate industry offshore from the Sussex and Kent coasts*

Resource volumes in Mm³

Total resource

Includes material in grid
squares dominated by fines
(equivalent to value A, Table 4.1)

205.8 Sand
33.0 Sand and gravel
59.8 Shingle

Possible workable resource

Excludes all material in the lowest
0.5m of the deposit and material in
grid squares dominated by fines
(equivalent to value D, Table 4.1)

138.2 Sand
22.1 Sand and gravel
34.3 Shingle

Fines (<0.125mm)

Predominantly sand (0.125–2mm)

Predominantly sand and
gravel (2–5mm)

Predominantly shingle (>5mm)

Volume (cubic metres)
Sand
Sand and gravel
Shingle

Areas where the resource averages
over 0.5m thick across a 4km x 4km
grid square (recalculated from
component 2km x 2km grids)

Grid squares of 4km side

10km

Dungeness

Rye Bay

Beachy Head

Sand

Unlike the shingle which occurs as a thin lag over much of the English Channel floor, the distribution of sand reflects tidal current transport paths. The sand is mobile under strong tidal currents resulting in the accumulation of sand banks. Although small sandwaves, dunes and sand ribbons are found scattered on the shingle lag deposits, the most substantial resources are in areas of sand banks. Tidal sandbanks generally range between 5m and 20m in thickness and are composed typically of well sorted, medium-grained sand. The sand is quartzose with small amounts of comminuted shell debris and a little feldspar, mica and heavy minerals. Thickness of sand banks has been derived from seismic reflection profiles or HO bathymetry data.

The main accumulations of sand are:

- in the active tidal sand ridges south-west of the Dover Strait, mainly located offshore from Hastings—Dungeness (Varne, Hastings Bank and Royal Sovereign Shoals); these carry sandwaves on their surface.

- in the nearshore zone from Selsey Bill—Bognor—Worthing; however there are few data

- as an E-W accumulation of sand located 17—25km south of the coast at Brighton

- as fields of sandwaves in the eastern approaches to the Solent

- at Dolphin Bank in the south of Poole Bay where they are over 10m thick.

Within areas densely sampled by the marine aggregate industry it is estimated that up to 883Mm^3 of sand occur in the English Channel East region. In addition a further 330Mm^3 of sand are indicated to occur in areas selected for detailed study (Table 4.2).

Palaeovalley deposits

Palaeovalleys are overdeepened river channels cut during Pleistocene sea-level lowstands Some of the largest palaeovalleys, for example the Northern Palaeovalley (Hamblin et al., 1992) cut down well below 60m below sea level into the underlying bedrock. In the eastern part of the English Channel, between the Dover Strait and Selsey Bill, palaeovalleys commonly occur with a dendritic pattern. Many smaller valleys merge in a generally southerly direction and enter the Northern Palaeovalley (Hamblin et al., 1992)

The potential resource within palaeovalleys is largely speculative, but deserves special attention in this region because they may contain hitherto unexploited resources. These deposits are overlain by superficial sediments (gravel lag deposits and sand bodies). Some palaeovalleys contain up to 30m of sediment. Sediments filling palaeovalleys are rarely cored. Although flint and chalk gravels have been recorded in some palaeovalleys, on the basis of limited borehole sample data and seismic evidence a gravel fill is generally subordinate to sands, silts and clays. Of the few vibrocores penetrating these valley fills, most record well-sorted sands with comminuted shell debris of marine origin.

The amount of prospecting or other survey data available on which to base an informed judgement on the amounts of sand and/or gravel within the various palaeovalley systems is therefore generally inadequate, and makes even broad stratigraphic prediction somewhat hazardous. In view of the potential variability of the sediment fill along the length of an individual palaeovalley, the resources of sand and gravel can be determined only by carefully designed prospecting surveys, where possible identifying generic similarities between palaeovalleys forming specific linked systems.

Palaeovalleys off the Sussex coast and the eastern Solent are of most interest because of their proximity to the coast and the seismic evidence that they are largely filled with sediment. In the area between Selsey Bill and Beachy Head, vibrocores have recorded a fill of soft sediments within the upper part of the palaeovalley fills comprising clays, silts and sands with organic material and a few thin bands of shingle, believed to be estuarine deposits.

4.3.2 English Channel West

No parts of the sea floor within this sub-region are considered to have been densely sampled by the marine aggregate industry. Over much of this sub-region the cover of superficial sediment is thin (<0.3m) and bedrock is extensively exposed at seabed. Locally within bays and in the lee of headlands thicker accumulations are found. Off the south Devon and Cornwall coasts local patches of sand can occur nearshore, and thicker accumulations, up to 20m, in a series of infilled valleys. Survey cover is lacking or not accessible for most of the small and medium sized estuaries: Exe, Dart, Salcombe, Plymouth Sound, and the Fal.

Shingle and coarse shingle

There is a general paucity of shingle grade material occurring on the seabed in this area. Where it is present the shingle often includes a large shell component. The distribution of coarse sediments is also irregular, with bedrock locally widely exposed in areas scoured by strong tidal currents, such as around headlands, and in areas of high topographic relief. Supply of shingle material for recharge of shingle beaches in Lyme Bay poses some problems. The fills of palaeovalleys may offer an alternative supply, which would require further investigation and thus no estimates of the likely quantities available are included in this study.

Mixed sand and gravel

This sediment category occurs in areas of weaker tidal currents where the sand has not been winnowed. In Start Bay shell- and flint-bearing gravelly sands occur which have locally been proved to be over 6m in thickness.

Sand

Shell and flint-bearing gravelly sands occur in the vicinity of Start Bay - around 50° 10'N, 3° 00'W. They are proved to be over 6m thick at 50° 18'N, 2° 56'W, but most deposits are less than 1m. Skerries Bank occurs between 1 and 5km northeast of Start Point in the southern part of Start Bay. Coarse shelly sand forms a sediment drape over Skerries Bank, the core of which comprises silty sand (Kelland and Hails, 1972). The coarse sand drape may be up to 15m thick. Sands and muddy sands occur in a zone stretching 35km east of Torbay, locally reaching 1.5m in thickness.

Palaeovalley deposits

Apart from the nearshore zone off south Devon, palaeovalleys are generally not well developed in the English Channel West sub-region. This reflects in part the more resistant lithologies of the Palaeozoic bedrock on the sea floor south of Devon and Cornwall.

A network of buried channels occurs offshore from south Devon, with the main palaeovalley extending from Sidmouth in Lyme Bay to Start Bay (see Crosby, 1983). Little is known about the sediment fill of the main channel course, but the sediment fill exceeds 10m in thickness. In view of the occurrence of the Budleigh Salterton Beds in the cliffs onshore, the likelihood of a shingle fill within this palaeovalley is high. The main valley probably drained areas of outcrop of the Triassic pebble beds to the north during the last glaciation so it is likely that some of the products of erosion remain within the valley and form an exploitable resource.

Smaller scale palaeovalleys are found incised within Devonian slates in Start Bay. Here the bedrock surface is dissected by eight infilled valleys which appear to be former extensions of present-day valley systems. These valleys are between 100m and 450m wide, and in the case of the valley extension of the River Dart up to 30m deep. Cores (vibrocores/gravity cores) from these buried valleys prove a fill of clay, sand and shingle (Kelland and Hails, 1972). Bedrock channels and infilled depressions are also known off Falmouth Bay and St Austell Bay where they contain between 5m and 30m of sands with some gravel.

4.4 ADDITIONAL SELECTED AREAS STUDIED

4.4.1 Location

Six additional areas for detailed study were chosen which had sufficient detailed data available and are accessible to likely recharge sites. These study areas lie outside the areas intensely sampled by the aggregate industry.

4.4.2 English Channel East

South of Beachy Head

An area of sea floor extending approximately 36km due south of Beachy Head has been studied in detail (Figure 5.6). Some good quality data are available for this area, although some data points have been excluded where the water depth exceeds 60m.

Locally sandwaves, sand ribbons, rippled sand sheets and shingle lags occur. The surface sediments are underlain largely by Chalk south (to about $50° 35'N$) and west of Beachy Head, with Lower Cretaceous mudstones subcropping immediately east of Beachy Head. The bathymetry varies from around 15m just to the south of Beachy Head, but descends below 50m approximately 15km south of the headland with depressions in which the water depth exceeds 60m. The relatively deep water and stronger currents near the headland may have previously hindered exploitation of the resource in this area.

Sands and flint gravels are the dominant sediment type. The shingle contains flint pebbles up to 50cm in size, but more commonly 10—40mm in size. Both shelly sands and shell-free sands are recorded. All sediments can contain mud contaminants (in the form of mud clasts), chalk pebbles and coal fragments. Sandy sediments may contain glauconite, worm tubes, seaweed and living shells such as mussels.

The database indicates that up to $63Mm^3$ of shingle and $44Mm^3$ of sand occur in this area (Figure 4.4), although the sheets of shingle are generally too thin to be workable. However, in the same sub-region southwest of Beachy Head an infilled palaeovalley system occurs below the surface veneer of sediments which might merit further investigation.

Offshore Bexhill - Hastings

This area is underlain by Wealden mudstones and contamination by muddy material is a potential problem. Sands and mixed sands and gravels mainly occur, but a belt of dominantly muddy sediments occurs on the east side of Rye Bay separating sandy deposits from the shingle sheet close to Dungeness Point.

Data for the area closest to the shore are sparse, but BGS grab samples and HO data provide a reasonable indication of the resource in this area. Sandy deposits often contain worm tubes and can have a significant content of coal fragments. Sometimes the sediments have a black coloration on account of the mud and coal content. Phosphatic nodules are sometimes recorded.

Data are not available to allow estimates of the resources within Royal Sovereign Shoals which occur in the south-east of the area.

The database indicates that over $7Mm^3$ of sand and over $17Mm^3$ of sand and gravel occur in this area (Figure 4.5).

Table 4.2 Summary of resources in areas selected for detailed study

	Sand		Sand and gravel		Shingle	
	Volume Mm³	Tonnage Mt	Volume Mm³	Tonnage Mt	Volume Mm³	Tonnage Mt
English Channel East:						
South of Beachy Head A	43.5	69.6	2.4	4.3	63.1	126.2
South of Beachy Head B	43.5	69.6	2.4	4.3	62.7	125.4
South of Beachy Head C	27.0	43.2	0	0	4.4	8.8
South of Beachy Head D	21.0	33.6	0	0	0.4	0.8
Bexhill-Hastings A	7.4	11.8	17.3	31.1	0.5	1.2
Bexhill-Hastings B	7.2	11.5	17.3	31.1	0.5	1.2
Bexhill-Hastings C	3.0	4.8	16.0	28.8	0	0
Bexhill-Hastings D	1.0	1.6	12.0	21.6	0	0
Solent, eastern approaches A	5.3	8.5	2.1	3.8	0.4	0.8
Solent, eastern approaches B	5.0	8.0	1.8	3.2	0.4	0.8
Solent, eastern approaches C	0	0	0	0	0	0
Solent, eastern approaches D	0	0	0	0	0	0
Poole-Christchurch A	274.0	438.4	0.13	0.2	0.63	1.3
Poole-Christchurch B	274.0	438.4	0.13	0.2	0.63	1.3
Poole-Christchurch C	273.8	438.1	0.13	0.2	0.10	0.2
Poole-Christchurch D	243.9	390.2	0.08	0.1	0.06	0.12
English Channel West:						
Lyme Bay A	41.2	65.9	7.2	13.0	10.2	20.4
Lyme Bay B	40.2	64.3	6.9	12.4	9.3	18.6
Lyme Bay C	7.70	12.3	2.77	5.0	0.05	0.1
Lyme Bay D	1.64	2.6	0.86	1.5	0.02	0.04
Start Bay A	61.0	97.6	0	0	0	0
Start Bay B	61.0	97.6	0	0	0	0
Start Bay C	59.2	94.7	0	0	0	0
Start Bay D	41.2	65.9	0	0	0	0

A: estimated total material identified in the areas sampled
B: as A but excluding material in grid squares where fines are the dominant lithology
C: as B but also excluding material in deposits averaging less than 0.5m thick
D: as C but excluding all material in the lowest 0.5m of the deposit

All resource estimates were calculated in cubic metres and have been converted to tonnes using the following density values:

Shingle	2.0 tonnes/cubic metre
Sand and gravel	1.8 tonnes/cubic metre
Sand	1.6 tonnes/cubic metre

Eastern approaches to the Solent

Part of this area is already licenced for sediment extraction. However, further resources occur in the immediate vicinity of the extraction licence (Figure 4.6) and sand to shingle grade sediments may also occur within the Solent palaeovalley (Hamblin *et al.*, 1992). Volumes of seabed sediments are small, but a significant resource may occur buried in the Solent palaeovalley.

The sea floor topography is undulating in this area, with water depths varying from three to almost 30 metres. Isolated, irregular sandwaves are common, and these sandwaves and sand ribbons locally produce a thicker resource. However, few reliable thickness data are available. Several shipwrecks occur in this area which, together with sewage outfalls near the Hampshire coast, could hamper dredging. The sediments commonly include mud contaminants and may include seaweed.

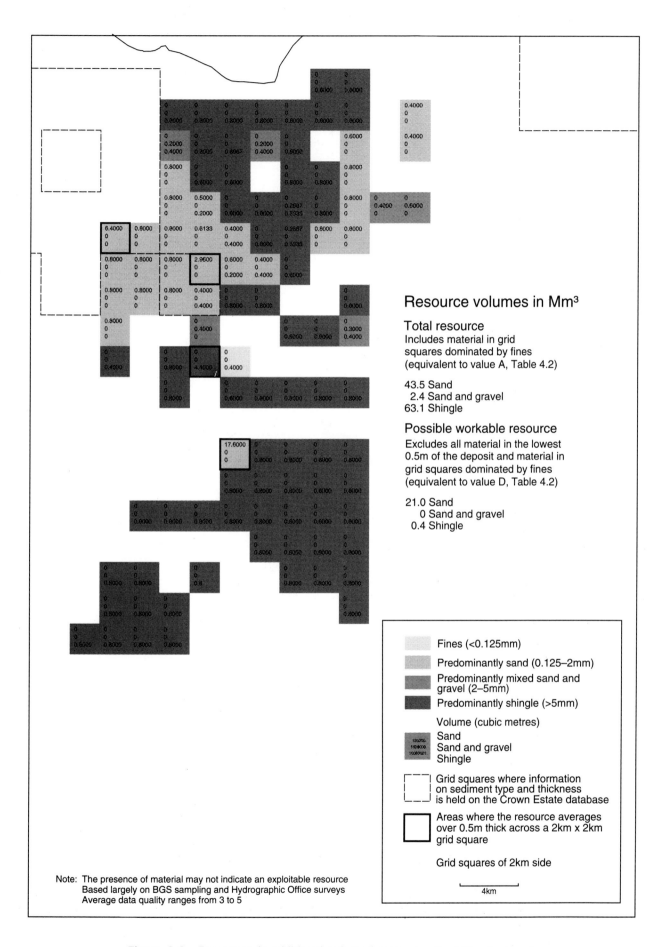

Figure 4.4 *Resources in additional selected areas: south of Beachy Head*

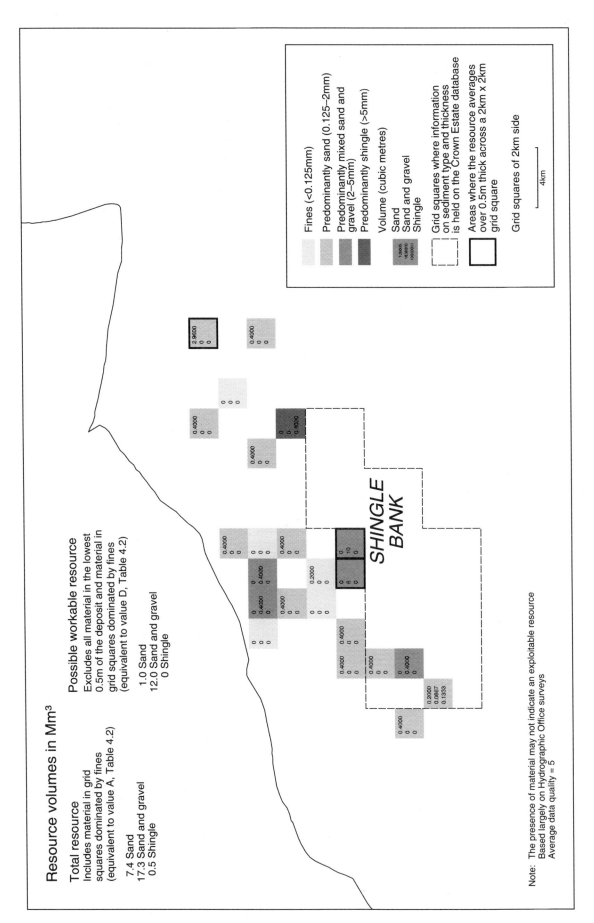

Figure 4.5 *Resources in additional selected areas: Bexhill to Hastings, inshore from Shingle Bank*

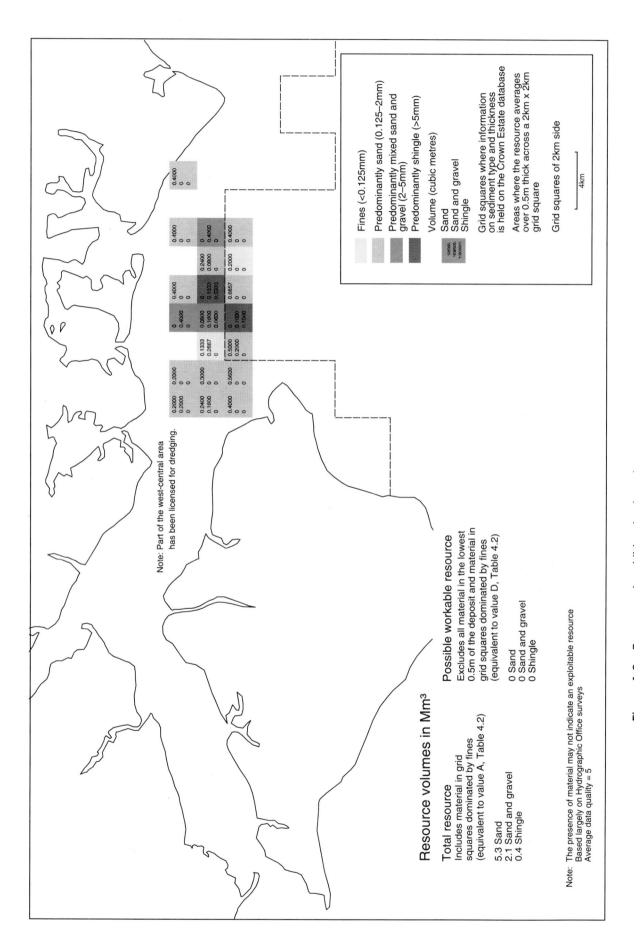

Figure 4.6 *Resources in additional selected areas: eastern approaches to the Solent*

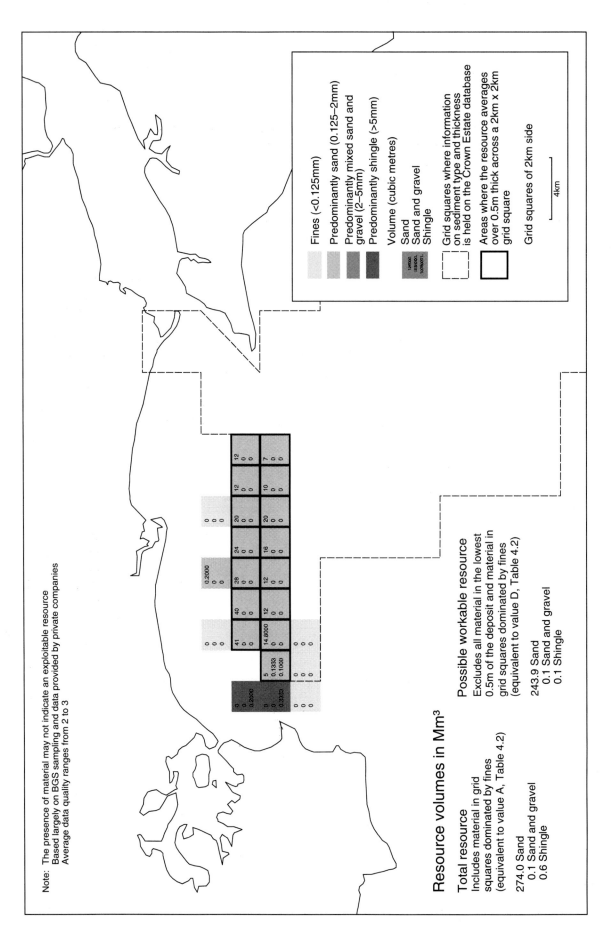

Figure 4.7 *Resources in additional selected areas: Poole Bay—Christchurch Bay*

Poole-Christchurch Bay

A large sandbank, Dolphin Sand, stretches across the southern boundary of Poole-Christchurch Bay. Sand moves westward along Dolphin Sand as a narrow, continuous train of sandwaves of about 2m in height. The sand originates from cliff erosion at Barton, and is transported in a clockwise direction via Hurst Spit, Dolphin Sand and then onshore to beaches in Poole Bay. Within Poole Bay the sea floor sediment cover is very thin.

The sand resource of Dolphin Bank is quite large (Figure 4.7). Data available to this study indicate approximately 244Mm^3 of sand within or near to Dolphin Sand.

4.4.3 English Channel West

Lyme Bay

There are extensive HO data in Lyme Bay which provide a good indication of the distribution of sediment types across the bay, and the patchy, discontinuous nature of the sediment cover. These data are supported by scattered BGS grab samples, and some vibrocore data for the west part of Lyme Bay held on the Crown Estate database. Over much of Lyme Bay thickness data are sparse, and in the absence of positive thickness data a default value of 0.05m has been used to account for the overall thin nature of the sediments in this area. Sandwaves up to 3m high do occur locally, and their approximate position is indicated by the grid squares with larger volumes shown on Figure 4.8. Sand ribbons also commonly occur. Accumulations of shell material, scattered shipwrecks, and live faunas are commonly encountered.

Despite the large size of Lyme Bay, the apparent sea floor sediment resource is moderate, comprising 10Mm^3 of shingle, 7Mm^3 of sand and gravel and 41Mm^3 of sand. The shingle, however, occurs as a thin impersistent sheet, virtually none of which is likely to be workable (Table 4.2, Figure 4.8). Localised fields of sandwaves may provide a sufficiently large accumulation of sediment that is economically viable for dredging.

Start Bay

The largest sand resource within Start Bay exists in Skerries Bank off Start Point. This bank has grown as a result of tidal flow separation, with the ebb tide dominant on the western half of the bank within Start Bay, and the flood tide dominant on the eastern half of the bank off Start Point. Coarse shelly sand forms a sediment drape over Skerries Bank, the core of which comprises silty sand (Kelland and Hails, 1972). The coarse sand drape may be up to 15m thick. The Project database does not include data for the main body of Skerries Bank. However, the sand deposts are well developed in the rest of Start Bay. Available data indicate that over 41Mm^3 of sand occur in the centre and northern parts of Start Bay (Table 4.2, Figure 4.9). Although this is a considerable resource, its close proximity to the coast and location in an environmentally sensitive are are likely to constrain any extraction.

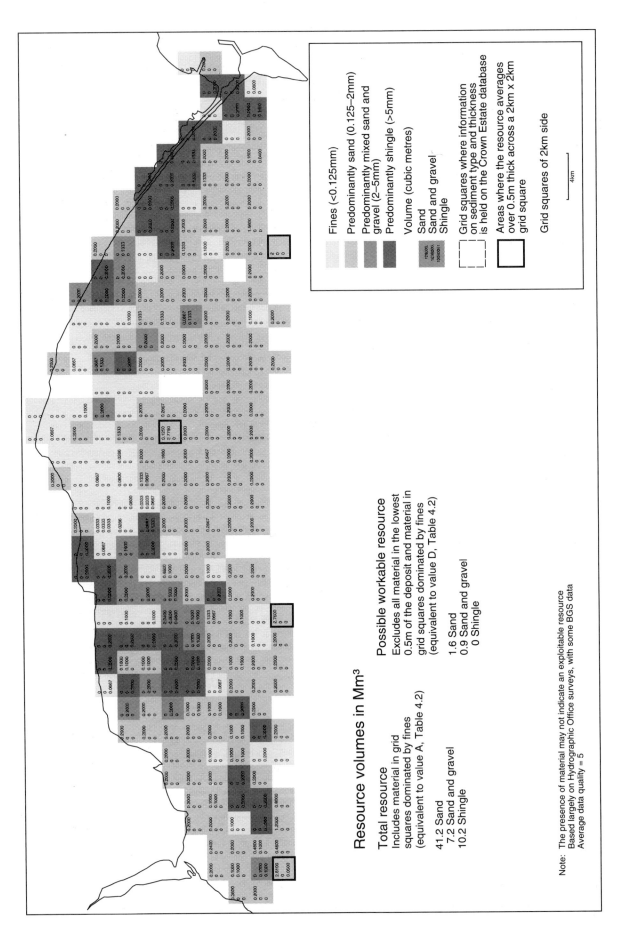

Figure 4.8 *Resources in additional selected areas: Lyme Bay*

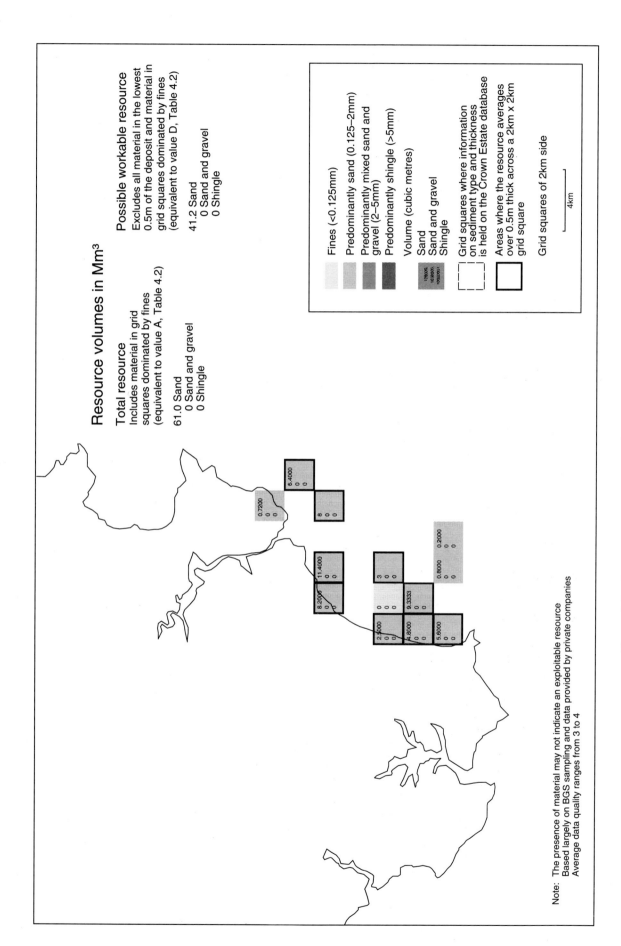

Figure 4.9 *Resources in additional selected areas: Start Bay*

5 General distribution and quality of marine materials suitable for beach recharge off the east coast of England

5.1 BACKGROUND

This is the second of three sections assessing the distribution and quality of offshore material suitable for aggregate and non-aggregate purposes for comparison with the anticipated demand for these materials over the next 20 years. This Section concerns the area offshore from the East Coast, between South Foreland, Dover, in Kent and the Scottish border at Berwick-upon-Tweed. The area is divided into five sub-regions, Thames Estuary, East Anglia, The Wash, Yorks-Humber, and Tyne-Tees to accord with the regional areas for material demand estimates in Section 3.

An outline of the geological history and hydrography of the southern North Sea is provided which pertains both to the distribution and to the origin of the seabed sediments. A regional description of material distribution and volumes provides an overview of the total offshore resource. For areas studied in detail resource volumes within grid squares are provided. The database created specifically for this project holds over 4000 points of data (excluding Crown Estate data) for the East Coast area, which have been manipulated into 1322 2km-a-side grid squares of averaged data. Some logistical factors affecting exploitation are discussed in Section 8.

5.2 REGIONAL REVIEW

5.2.1 Sea floor topography

The topography of the present-day seabed is largely the product of a fluvial drainage regime during the Quaternary, and marine planation concomitant with periods of rising sea level both during Quaternary interglacials and since the last glaciation. The seabed takes the form of a gently inclined submarine erosion surface, locally modified by incised palaeovalleys, submerged cliff lines, enclosed deeps and the superficial sediment cover. Tidal sand ridges and sandbanks locally modify the sea floor topography by up to 20m. The occurrence of bedforms is governed by the tidal current paths in the southern North Sea.

The southern North Sea is a relatively shallow part of the UK continental shelf with water depths almost everywhere less than 50m. In general, the water depth increases gradually from west to east, with the deepest waters occurring in the deep water channel lying along the Median Line between UK waters and those of the Low Countries.

North of Flamborough Head the sea floor slopes relatively steeply from the coast and the 50m isobath is between 10km and 30km offshore. South of Flamborough Head the shelf is entirely shallower than 50m except for several elongate valleys or "pits" which may be over 50km long, up to 4km wide and extend over 70m below the adjacent seabed. The largest of these is the Silver Pit which is oriented north-south and lies approximately 35km off the Humber Estuary. South of Spurn Head there are extensive nearshore zones less than 10m deep.

The Dogger Bank is an extensive area of relatively shallow (25—40m) water depths which lies at a minimum distance of 90km off the Yorkshire coast.

The most conspicuous features in the East Anglia sub-region are the coast-parallel sandbanks of the area to the north-east of Norfolk, Brown Ridge in the east of the area and Aldeburgh Napes, a nearshore sandbank in the south-west of the sub-region. These sandbanks may be over 20km long and are typically between 2km and 3km wide and 15m to 30m high above the surrounding seabed. They have accumulated under the influence of tidal currents which are strong in the southern North Sea, with surface velocities reaching over 1.5m/s in local areas off north-east Norfolk.

The floor of the Thames Estuary is covered by a splay of tidal sandbanks separated by channels seldom deeper than 20m at low water.

5.2.2 Tidal streams

The strength of tidal and wave-induced currents has an important influence on the distribution of sediment types. Winnowing of sediments to leave shingle lags and the growth of sandbanks occurs under a strong tidal current regime, whereas fine sediments tend to accumulate in sheltered bays and offshore deeps.

The behaviour of tides and currents in the southern North Sea is complex, but some general patterns emerge. Tidal ranges along the east coast of the UK are larger than those elsewhere in the North Sea. The mean spring tidal range increases from 5.0m at Flamborough Head to 6.0m in the Humber to 6.5m in the Wash.

North of the Farne Islands nearshore tidal currents during mean spring tides reach a maximum of 0.5m/s, increasing to 0.7m/s in Tees Bay. Tidal streams in some large embayments are barely perceptible, for example in Filey Bay. On the north-east coast the wave regime is severe from the north and east, but it moderates south of Flamborough Head due to the shoaling waters and protection afforded by offshore banks. Wave action in the nearshore zone south of Spurn Head is not generally severe due to the moderating effects of shoaling waters. Tidal currents do not usually exceed 1.0m/s except near the coastal headlands and in the tidal channels in the Wash and Humber. Peak velocities up to 1.5m/s are reached exceptionally both in the Wash and the Humber tidal channels. The Dogger Bank is an area of low to medium strength tidal currents (less than 0.5m/s in the east, less than 1.0m/s in the west) but is exposed to wave attack, particularly from the north. The wave regime in the Thames Estuary is relatively mild but tidal currents are moderately strong, at around 1.0m/s at peak flow. Tidal range at mean spring tide increases from 2.0m at Lowestoft to 4.0m in the outer Thames Estuary to over 5m in the inner estuary.

Despite the relatively high tidal current velocities there is little present day transport of shingle on the seabed, although wave induced currents in the nearshore zone result in movement alongshore of both sand and shingle in a north to south direction. In the Norfolk Banks and Thames Estuary strong tidal currents have swept the mobile sediments into large sandbanks with most of the intervening sea floor covered by winnowed shingle-rich sediments.

5.2.3 Geological setting

North of Flamborough Head resistant Jurassic sandstones and limestones, Permian dolomitised limestones and mudrocks, and Carboniferous sandstones occur in a rocky coastline with many sea cliffs, and form a resistant sea floor offshore from the coast. Interbedded Jurassic sandstones, limestones and mudstones crop out at seabed in the offshore area north of Filey Brigg to the Tees Estuary. North of Hartlepool Upper Magnesian Limestone comprising dolomitised limestones and intercalated evaporite deposits form the floor of the seabed in the nearshore zone. North of the Tyne Carboniferous strata crop out at seabed in a belt that extends approximately parallel with the coast. From Whitley Bay to just south of the Farne Islands the Carboniferous strata comprise Coal Measures sandstones and mudstones with coal seams. From the Farne Islands northwards the Carboniferous strata comprise rhythmic sequences which include limestones, as well as shales, sandstones and coals of various thicknesses. Basic igneous sills have, in places, intruded into the sedimentary sequences.

South of the Chalk cliffs at Flamborough Head, the Yorkshire coastline is formed of lower cliffs cut into late Pleistocene glacial deposits. The coastline of the Wash sub-region is low lying and sandy, with offshore areas floored by Quaternary deposits. Much of the offshore area extending from northeast Norfolk to Flamborough Head is underlain by fine-grained limestones of the Chalk Group. The Chalk may include layers of siliceous nodules or tabular sheets of silica (flints) and cemented hard chalk or hardgrounds. Near Flamborough, however, the Chalk is almost flint-free. Tertiary rocks, mainly mudstones and sandstones, underlie the sea floor east of the Norfolk coast. Lower Cretaceous and Jurassic heterogeneous sediments underlie the Wash, and form the sea floor north of Flamborough Head.

Much of the coast of the East Anglia sub-region comprises cliffs formed of Pleistocene marine, fluvial and glacial deposits, separated by low-lying areas with marshes. Much of the Thames Estuary is underlain by Tertiary London Clay Formation, a monotonous sequence of mudstones with occasional beds of phosphatic and carbonate nodules, and volcanic ash bands. Other Tertiary formations are thinner with heterolithic sedimentary rocks (often unlithified glauconitic sandstones, mudstones and flint conglomerates) occurring offshore from Clacton and Harwich. Plio-Pleistocene Crag deposits, bioclastic limestones and shelly sandstones, occur off the Suffolk coast.

The sea cliffs of North Foreland and South Foreland are composed of chalk.

5.2.4 Quaternary geological history of the southern North Sea

Much of the floor of the North Sea was shaped during the last glaciation, and over wide areas at present Pleistocene deposits immmediately underlie the thin veneer of seabed sediments. Although the Pleistocene deposits comprise till across many areas, this reflects the deposits of the last (Devensian) glaciation rather than the total Pleistocene succession, which includes thick deltaic and estuarine deposits as well as fluvioglacial sands, glacimarine muds and tills.

During the Quaternary geological period the climate fluctuated between glacial and interglacial cycles. Major oscillations in sea level (Section 4.2.4) were associated with the growth and decline of the ice caps, and this is reflected in the interdigitation of interglacial and glacial deposits in the southern North Sea Basin. The last major ice sheet (Devensian) reached no further south than the north Norfolk coast, but the earlier Anglian ice sheet deposited sediments (till and fluvioglacial sands) in the area offshore from Suffolk. The Pleistocene sedimentary succession in the southern North Sea is discussed and explained in Cameron *et al.* (1992).

Extensive deposits of till (Bolders Bank Formation) occur in an area lying north of a line running approximately east-north-east from Hunstanton in Norfolk to Flamborough Head in Yorkshire, extending to beyond 3°E. The till offshore from Lincolnshire is less than 5m thick, but thickens towards the coast up to 20m in places. Chalk is the most conspicuous pebble component of this till. North of Flamborough Head the sea floor of the nearshore zone is covered by a discontinuous sheet of glacial till of the Late Devensian Wee Bankie Formation. Further offshore the Bolders Bank Formation is again encountered. The till of the Wee Bankie Formation contains a variety of rock clasts; Carboniferous Limestone, Permo-Triassic dolomites and mudstones, and chalk are most commonly found as clasts. Glaciomarine muds (St Abbs Formation) occur on the seabed south from Amble towards the Tees Estuary.

Offshore from Suffolk, Early Pleistocene deposits comprise shelly sands with silt partings (Red Crag Formation) and clays and sands (Westkapelle Ground Formation). Middle Pleistocene fluviatile and estuarine sands, muds and pebbly sediments occur offshore from Lowestoft.

During much of the Pleistocene the course of the River Thames lay north of its present position. The river formed a series of terraces, covered by alluvial sediments, which are extensively preserved in southern and eastern Essex. The proto-River Thames followed several different courses and is likely to have debouched sediment into what is now the offshore area of Suffolk.

The present distribution of the shingle now forming a thin veneer over parts of the sea floor reflects the marine reworking of Pleistocene fluvial and glacial deposits during the early stages of the Holocene transgression across the area. Modern addition of shingle size material to the sea floor is very limited, largely restricted to release of flint nodules from the slow denudation of chalk cliffs.

Today shingle exposed at the seabed is often heavily encrusted with serpulids, bryozoa and barnacles indicating that it is not mobile there under the present tidal regime. The distribution of shingle therefore reflects in the majority of occurrences processes no longer active at the present day.

5.2.5 Renewability of resources

It is important to note that the shingle offshore is largely a relict deposit, redistributed to some extent during the major sea-level rise that took place between 8000 and 5000 years ago. As the shingle includes a dominant "relict" component, this resource must be considered finite. Cliffs of Pleistocene glacial till deposits on the Holderness coast retreating on average by 1.2m/year (Pringle 1985), release considerable amounts of coarser clasts to the coastal sediment budget. Sand and coarser material form c.30% of the till in the cliffs at Holderness which McCave (1987) estimated are losing 1.4 million tonnes of sediment per year to coastal erosion. Generally, though, if shingle is extracted from the East Coast area it will not be replaced.

At present rivers around the southern North Sea input very little sand; the main input is from coastal erosion. The rapidly eroding glacigenic sediments of the Holderness coast may supply 0.63Mm³ of sand per year (O'Connor, 1987), some of which is deposited on the spit at Spurn Head, some is washed into the Humber Estuary and some is transported further along the coast south of the Humber. Another important source of sediment comes from the north Norfolk coast between Weybourne and Happisburgh, where cliffs of glacigenic sediments are receding at approximately 0.9m/year (Clayton, 1989). Sediment derived from this erosion is transported to the west and south-east along the beaches by longshore drift, with the dominant transport to the southeast. Sand may ultimately be tranported offshore along a complex transport path involving nearshore parabolic banks to the offshore Norfolk Banks. The complex bank systems off the Suffolk coast may also receive contributions from coastal erosion. Replenishment of dredged sand may therefore occur in some instances where local sediment transport paths and wave currents would allow bedforms such as sandbanks to reform.

5.3 GENERAL DISTRIBUTION OF MARINE MATERIALS: RESOURCES AND VOLUME ESTIMATES

The offshore resource is considered in relation the regional divisions proposed in Section 3. The East Coast region is divided into five sub-regions - Thames Estuary, East Anglia, The Wash, Yorks-Humber and Tyne-Tees.

The East Coast area has been widely covered by geological surveys and extensively prospected for marine aggregates. Much of the sea floor is covered by material that is potentially suitable both for beach recharge and for aggregate purposes. Sandy sediments dominate over much of the region. The sand fraction covering the sea floor is mostly medium-grained. Fine-grained sand occurs in the mouths of estuaries such as the Wash, Humber and outer Thames. Much of the sand is mobile under present-day hydrodynamic conditions, and therefore its distribution relates to modern sand-transport processes. Shingle is widespread in the East Coast region but is not being transported any significant distance at present. An exception is the area between South Falls and Sandiette Banks where gravel waves have been described. The areas from which the aggregate is currently being extracted are the outer Thames Estuary, off East Anglia, and off the Humber Estuary. Production from the outer Thames has begun to decline as its reserves diminish, and the dredging industry is looking increasingly to the East Anglian area to maintain the supply of marine aggregates to south-east England.

Muddy sediments have a restricted distribution, mostly confined to intertidal areas within estuaries and tidal inlets. Most of the fine-grained sediment released by coastal erosion remains in the nearshore zone and much of it is deposited in estuaries. Mud also occurs in the large offshore depressions of the Outer Silver Pit and Markham's Hole.

Palaeovalleys are an additional consideration in the East Coast region, because the potential resources occurring as valley fills might enhance the resource potential of the region. However, although valleys formed during the decay phase of the last (Devensian) ice sheet occur frequently in the region north of the Norfolk coast (Cameron *et al.*, 1992), the infill deposits (Botney Cut Formation) comprise predominantly glaciomarine muds in the valley fills that have been cored to date. This suggests that palaeovalleys are not a high priority for exploration for future sources of sand and shingle deposits in this region.

5.3.1 Thames Estuary

This sub-region extends from Aldeburgh Napes in the north to South Foreland, Dover, in Kent and includes the whole of the outer Thames Estuary. Traditionally this area has supplied most of the marine sand and gravel produced in the UK and, although reserves are now depleted, it continues to supply substantial amounts of aggregates to London and the South East region. Several extensive dredging grounds occur between Maplin Sands and Outer Gabbard. Almost all of the offshore parts of the Thames Estuary have been prospected for marine sand and gravel with the exception of small areas adjacent to the Median Line (where the seabed is mainly sandy). The extensive, shallow water nearshore areas extending for some 10—15km from the coast have generally not been surveyed, although site investigation surveys in the Maplin Sands area have investigated resource potential. Few areas of shingle deposits remain which have not been prospected in detail, but these include north-west of the Galloper (around 51° 48'N, 1° 54'E), south of the Kentish Knock licence (around 51° 39'N, 1° 42'E), immediately inshore of Sunk Sand (around 51° 45'N, 1° 26'E) and north-west of North Hinder (around 51° 40'N, 2° 10'E).

There is generally very little mud within the sediments of this sub-region with the exception of some nearshore areas and areas which are underlain by buried channels filled with mud and silts. Very little sediment comes into this sub-region from the Thames or from other river sources and most of the sediments were probably present in the area before the present Thames Estuary area was flooded by the sea approximately 8000 years ago. Much of the mud or silty sediment is supplied to the area through the Dover Straits.

Shingle and coarse shingle

Although there are large shingle-rich deposits particularly on the north side of the estuary, these deposits usually form a thin veneer over bedrock. Some thicker deposits, however, do occur and these generally coincide with the areas which are currently licensed for dredging. Some shingle deposits extend into shallower waters in the nearshore zone, inshore of Shipwash and Gunfleet Sand, and off Herne Bay and the Isle of Sheppey.

Shingle in the Thames Estuary is dominantly composed of flint and forms thin deposits (generally less than 1.0m thick) over large areas. Rounded pebbles of chalk may occur in shingle overlying Chalk bedrock. More commonly, cobbles of indurated, calcareous mudstone and phosphorite pebbles are recorded, derived from the London Clay which underlies much of the London Basin. The shell content of the shingle is highly variable but locally may contain over 20% shell debris.

Shingle reserves in this sub-region are becoming depleted, and for the past 10—15 years there has been a steady decline in marine aggregates dredging. The following resource volume estimates should be treated with caution, mindful that dredging may have occurred after some of the survey data were collected.

Within areas densely sampled by the marine aggregate industry, the database indicates a total resource of 133.6Mm^3 for the Thames Estuary (Figure 5.1), 86.2Mm^3 of which is potentially workable. In addition, a further 10.1Mm^3 are located in the additional areas of detailed study (Table 5.2, Figure 5.5).

Table 5.1 *Summary of resources in areas densely sampled by the marine aggregate industry*

	Sand		Sand and gravel		Shingle	
	Volume Mm³	Tonnage Mt	Volume Mm³	Tonnage Mt	Volume Mm³	Tonnage Mt
Thames Estuary A	2426.3	3882.1	389.7	701.5	133.6	267.2
Thames Estuary B	2348.4	3757.4	377.0	678.6	117.7	235.4
Thames Estuary C	2327.5	3724.0	373.6	672.5	90.9	181.8
Thames Estuary D	2052.7	3284.3	329.5	593.1	86.2	172.4
East Anglia A	956.3	1530.1	153.3	275.9	202.5	405.0
East Anglia B	869.1	1390.6	139.5	251.1	190.2	380.4
East Anglia C	845.1	1352.2	135.6	244.1	180.2	360.4
East Anglia D	660.6	1057.0	106.0	190.8	143.7	287.4
Wash A	674.3	1078.9	128.3	230.9	157.0	314.0
Wash B	574.5	919.2	92.2	166.0	120.9	241.8
Wash C	545.4	872.6	87.6	157.7	82.2	164.4
Wash D	434.0	694.4	69.7	125.5	75.5	151.0

A: estimated total material identified in the areas sampled
B: as A but excluding material in grid squares where fines are the dominant lithology
C: as B but also excluding material in deposits averaging less than 0.5m thick
D: as C but excluding all material in the lowest 0.5m of the deposit

All resource estimates were calculated in cubic metres and have been converted to tonnes using the following density values:

Shingle	2.0 tonnes/cubic metre
Sand and gravel	1.8 tonnes/cubic metre
Sand	1.6 tonnes/cubic metre

Mixed sand and gravel

The amount of mixed sand and gravel with this sub-region is relatively large. Within areas densely sampled by the marine aggregate industry the database indicates a total resource of 389.7Mm³ for the Thames Estuary (Figure 5.1), 373.6Mm³ of which occur in areas where the resource on average exceeds 0.5m in thickness. In addition, a further 49.1Mm³ are located in the additional areas of detailed study (Section 4, Table 5.2, Figure 5.5).

Sand

The sands forming sandbanks in this sub-region are quartzose, with mostly less than 10% shell debris, and are of fine grain size in the estuary and medium-grained farther offshore. In the inter-bank areas the sands tend to be coarser, with the finest sands on the bank crests. The distribution of sand reflects tidal current transport paths. The sand is mobile under strong tidal currents resulting in the accumulation of sandbanks. Although small sandwaves, dunes and sand ribbons are found scattered on the shingle lag deposits, the most substantial resources are in areas of sandbanks. Tidal sandbanks generally range between 5m and 20m in thickness and are composed typically of well sorted, medium-grained sand. The sand is quartzose with small amounts of comminuted shell debris and a little feldspar, mica and heavy minerals. The thickness of sandbanks has been derived from seismic reflection profiles or HO bathymetry data.

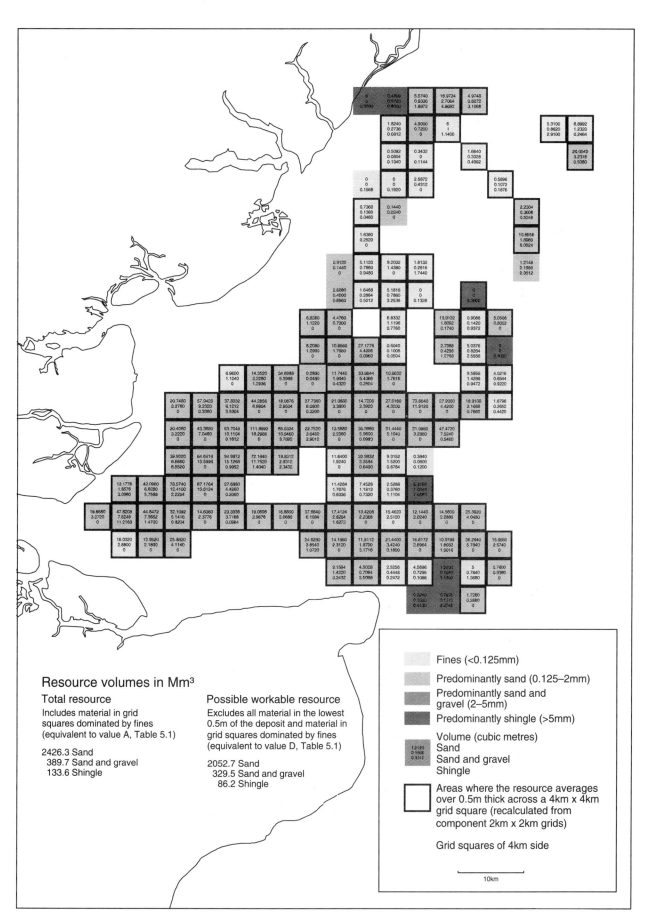

Figure 5.1 *Resources in areas densely sampled by the marine aggregate industry: Thames Estuary*

The main accumulations of sand in this sub-region are:

1. At the mouth of the Thames Estuary where sandbanks are forming due to longshore and landward transport of sediment into the estuary mouth. These banks tend to be coast-parallel and the largest bank, Long Sand, is over 45km in length. Many of the banks dry at low water and are separated by channels seldom deeper than 15m. These banks which include Long Sand, Sunk Sand and Gunfleet Sand are generally broad, with their crests very close to sea level; some are exposed at low water.

2. Further offshore NNE-SSW trending ridges occur that are not strictly coast-parallel. These banks include North and South Falls, Inner and Outer Gabbard, and the Galloper. These narrow, linear banks rise up to 35m above the surrounding sea floor and for ridges up to 65km long. Sediments of the Outer Gabbard are rich in calcium carbonate which may comprise over 50% of the sand. Much of the shell-rich material has come from reworking of carbonate-rich Tertiary formations on the sea floor.

3. Goodwin Sands off Kent. The Goodwin Sands are a large source of sand. Despite removal of 2.5Mm^3 of sand for use in the landfill for the Folkestone Terminal of the Channel Tunnel (Jones, 1989), a large resource remains.

Most of the Thames Estuary sandbanks have sandwaves on their surface.

Within areas densely sampled by the marine aggregate industry it is estimated that up to 2426.3Mm^3 of sand occur in the Thames Estuary sub-region, of which 2052.7Mm^3 are potentially workable. In addition a further 1472.9Mm^3 of sand, of which 1321.2Mm^3 are potentially workable, are indicated to occur in areas selected for detailed study (Table 5.2, Figures 5.4 and 5.5).

5.3.2 East Anglia

The sea floor of this sub-region is covered largely by sands and sandy shingle. Muds occur inshore of the 20m isobath off Aldeburgh, although muds and muddy sands lie at, or close to, seabed over large parts of the sub-region. Over most of the sub-region seabed sediments occur as a veneer less than 1m thick, mostly between 0.25m and 0.60m thick and locally less than 0.1m thick. Almost all of this region has been prospected for sand and gravel, except for the nearshore zone and for the large areas of sandy seabed east of the Norfolk Banks (east of 2° 10'E to the Median Line). Prospecting surveys and reconnaissance resource surveys (Harrison, 1988) have outlined substantial areas where the sediment cover is between 1m and 3m in thickness. Sand thickness in the tidal sand ridges may locally exceed 20m.

The major licensed dredging areas cover the largest and thickest shingle resources in the sub-region. The Great Yarmouth to Southwold area includes some of the most important marine aggregate dredging grounds in the UK. The Cross Sands licensed dredging area off Great Yarmouth is large and highly productive and this area, together with the dredging licenses off Southwold, comprise the East Coast dredging area which supplies the greatest tonnage of marine sand and gravel in the UK. There remain, however, large parts of the seabed in this area which are not licensed for dredging. Many pipelines and cable routes cross this area and several specific areas are designated as dumping grounds or MOD sites. Significant resources are sterilised by these constraints.

Shingle and coarse shingle

The concentration of shingle in the surface layers is due to the winnowing of sand and finer sediment by tidal currents. The shingle may rest as a lag upon bedrock or may cap finer grained sediments. Where shingle lags are very thin, there is a real possibility of contamination by underlying deposits.

Several large areas of shingle-rich sediment are developed off Great Yarmouth and Southwold, mainly inshore of the 35m isobath, although several smaller areas occur in deeper water. The shingle resources typically include admixed sand; a mixture of 30%-40% shingle and 60%-70% sand is often encountered. A shingle lag often occurs between the large sandbanks in this sub-region.

A potential shingle resource occurs near to the Norfolk coast at Barley Picle. Areas offshore from Cromer and Weybourne are covered by a shingle lag deposit, directly overlying till or bedrock/Chalk, but no thick deposits have been located. However, data are very limited in this nearshore area. A substantial part of the gravel area off Southwold extends from the currently licensed area into the shallower waters of the nearshore zone, mostly less than 15 m, shallowing inshore towards Dunwich Bank.

The shingle is composed largely of flint, but other rock types are important and shell debris may locally contribute 30% or more of the shingle. However, over most of the sub-region flint forms over 90% of the shingle. Most of the flint gravel is pebble size (less than 64mm) and particle shape varies from well-rounded to angular. Other rock types found in the shingle include quartzite, sandstone, ironstone and phosphorite. Quartzite pebbles are relatively common in the seabed sediments off Great Yarmouth where they may form up to 25% of the shingle. Offshore from Southwold the shingle contains large amounts of phosphatic pebbles (phosphorite) derived from underlying bedrock (London Clay and Coralline Crag).

Areas where additional shingle resources may be located, but reconnaissance data are limited, are between banks around Haisborough Sand and Winterton Ridge, north-east of Cromer, and between Dunwich Bank and the Southwold production licence.

Within areas densely sampled by the marine aggregate industry the database indicates a resource of 202.5Mm^3 for East Anglia, of which 143.7Mm^3 are potentially workable (Figure 5.2).

Mixed sand and gravel

The amount of mixed sand and gravel with this sub-region is relatively large. Within areas densely sampled by the marine aggregate industry the database indicates a resource of 153.3Mm^3 total for the Thames Estuary (Table 5.1), 106.0Mm^3 of which are potentially workable. In addition, a further 75.9Mm^3 are located in the additional areas of detailed study (Table 5.2).

Sand

Most of the sand-sized sediment is medium-grained (0.2—1.0mm), although fine sands occur in some nearshore areas. The sands are quartzose and contain variable amounts of shell debris, usually less than 10%. The sands reach a maximum thickness of 40m in the tidal sand ridges off the Norfolk coast.

The main accumulations of sand are:

1. The group of sandbanks collectively known as the Norfolk Banks. These are large sandbanks (tidal sand ridges) such as Haisborough Sand, Newarp Bank, Smiths Knoll etc. These tidal sand ridges are oriented north-west/south-east, parallel to the peak tidal flow and rise abound 15m in height above the surrounding seabed. The sandbanks rest on a relatively flat surface at 20m to 30m depth. They consist of accumulations of sand on an erosional surface of Pleistocene deposits that in the interbank areas is either composed or covered by a thin lag of shingle. The largest of the Norfolk Banks, Well Bank, is over 50km long, 1.7km wide and rises to 38m above the adjacent sea floor. The nearshore banks have a parabolic form, are connected by low cols and have sandwaves on their flanks. The outer banks generally have a linear form and smooth profile. The banks consist of fine- to medium-grained sands which show a high degree of sorting. Shell content of available samples is low, often less than 5%. However, very little is known about the internal composition of the Norfolk Banks. The environment of the sand banks may support fauna of

burrowing organisms such as sand eels and echinoids.

2.   Tidal sandbanks and fields of sandwaves lying east of the coast of Suffolk and south Norfolk.

Within areas densely sampled by the marine aggregate industry it is estimated that up to 956.3Mm³ of sand occur in (2) above (Figure 5.2). In addition a further very large resource occurs in the Norfolk Banks; 5241.2Mm³ of sand are indicated to occur in an area selected for detailed study (Figure 5.7, Table 5.2).

5.3.3 The Wash

The seabed sediments over most of the area occur as a veneer less than 1m thick, mostly between 0.1m and 0.5m thickness, directly overlying stiff glacial clays. Sandbanks and other sand accumulations can be much thicker, locally up to 20m.

A BGS reconnaissance survey (Harrison, 1992), funded by DoE and the Crown Estate, has summarised sand and gravel resources in this sub-region. The sub-region contains large resources of marine sand and gravel which occur in shallow water. Almost all of the area has been prospected for sand and gravel, except for the nearshore zone. The main shingle areas west of Sole Pit have been prospected in detail. Prospecting has confirmed commercial resources in areas west and south-west of the Silver Pit, south-east of Inner Dowsing, around Triton Knoll, Outer Dowsing, Haddock Bank and east of Dudgeon Shoal. Most of these areas are covered by production licenses but there remain large areas of seabed which are not licensed for aggregate dredging. The major licensed dredging areas in this sub-region collectively form the Humber Licence. Silts and muds generally occur only in estuaries, although muddy deposits are found where a mudstone substrate is being eroded in some seabed depressions.

Many pipelines and cable routes cross this area and several specific areas are designated as dumping grounds or MOD sites. Significant resources are sterilised by these constraints.

Shingle and coarse shingle

Shingle deposits are generally restricted to an irregular, broad zone which occurs inshore of a line drawn between Flamborough Head and Haddock Bank. Patchy areas of shingle also occur further offshore, around Well Bank Flat and around the Indefatigable Banks, and between Markham's Hole and the Outer Silver Pit. The seabed deposits are particularly rich in shingle inshore of the Silver Pit where strong tidal currents effectively winnow sand and silt from the superficial sediments but do not move the shingle.

The composition of the shingle is highly variable, although hard sandstone and igneous or metamorphic rock types predominate. Shell is locally a major component, particularly in sandy shingle in the east of the area. The shingle off the Humber Estuary is varied in composition: Carboniferous sandstone and limestone are particularly common, but chalk, Jurassic mudstone, flint and igneous and metamorphic rock types are also widespread. Clasts of Devonian sandstone and quartzite have also been noted. The size of the shingle varies considerably. Locally they can contain large cobbles or boulder-sized fragments up to several tens of centimetres in size.

Relatively thick shingle-bearing deposits which are not constrained by cables, pipelines or dumping grounds occur immediately to the south-west and north-west of the Protector Overfalls licence and an area north of Outer Dowsing, around 53° 36′N, 1° 02′E.

Possible shingle deposits occur east of 1° 30′ (Sole Pit), areas to the north-east of Well Hole (between 1° 50′E and 2° 10′E and around 53° 48′N), the area between the Indefatigable Banks and Markham's Hole, and areas between Markham's Hole and Outer Silver Pit. Although the shingle is typically less than 0.15m thick overlying till, thicker deposits (up to 0.5m) have been identified in a small area north-west of the Indefatigable Banks around 53° 37′N, 2° 20′E and in several smaller areas between Markham's Hole, the Outer Silver Pit and Botney Cut. These deposits generally contain between 20% and 40% shingle, and between 60% and 80% sand.

Within areas densely sampled by the marine aggregate industry the database indicates a resource of 157.0Mm^3 in the Wash sub-region, 75.5Mm^3 of which are potentially workable (Figure 5.3).

Mixed sand and gravel

The amount of mixed sand and gravel with this sub-region is moderately large. Within areas densely sampled by the marine aggregate industry the database indicates a resource of 128.3Mm^3 total for the Wash sub-region (Figure 5.3), 69.7Mm^3 of which are potentially workable.

Sand

Most of the sandy sediment in this sub-region is medium-grained (0.2—1.0mm) and quartzose, with less than 10% comminuted shell debris. Patches of coarse- and very coarse-grained sand occur associated with the shingle. Fine- to very fine-grained sands mantle seabed depressions.

The main accumulations of sand are:

- in the active sandbanks in the south and east of the sub-region: Inner Dowsing, Race Bank, Cromer Knoll

- as discontinuous deposits in several nearshore areas such as at the mouth of the Humber, off Mablethorpe and in the marginal areas of the Wash

- as sandy sea floor in the area north of Well Hole

- as sandy sea floor south and east of the Indefatigable Banks.

Within areas densely sampled by the marine aggregate industry the database indicates a sand resource of 674.3Mm^3 in the Wash sub-region, 434.0Mm^3 of which are potentially workable (Figure 5.3).

5.3.4 Yorkshire-Humber

The relatively narrow nearshore zone is the primary area for locating potential marine aggregate resources although most of this zone is not currently prospected. This sub-region also includes the large shallow water area of the Dogger Bank.

There are generally only reconnaissance geological survey data available in this sub-region and only parts of the sub-region have been prospected by the marine aggregate industry. No parts of the sea floor within this sub-region are considered to have been densely sampled by the marine aggregate industry. There are currently no areas licensed for aggregates dredging in the Dogger Bank area, although the central part of the bank has been prospected (though not to modern standards) with no resources located.

The seabed sediments rest largely upon Pleistocene deposits, mainly Weichselian till, although Triassic, Jurassic and Cretaceous rocks crop out widely beneath the sediment cover off the Yorkshire coast. Over much of this sub-region the cover of superficial sediment is thin (<0.3m) and bedrock is extensively exposed at seabed. Locally within bays and in the lee of headlands thicker accumulations are found. Muddy sediments are mainly restricted to seabed depressions such as the Outer Silver Pit.

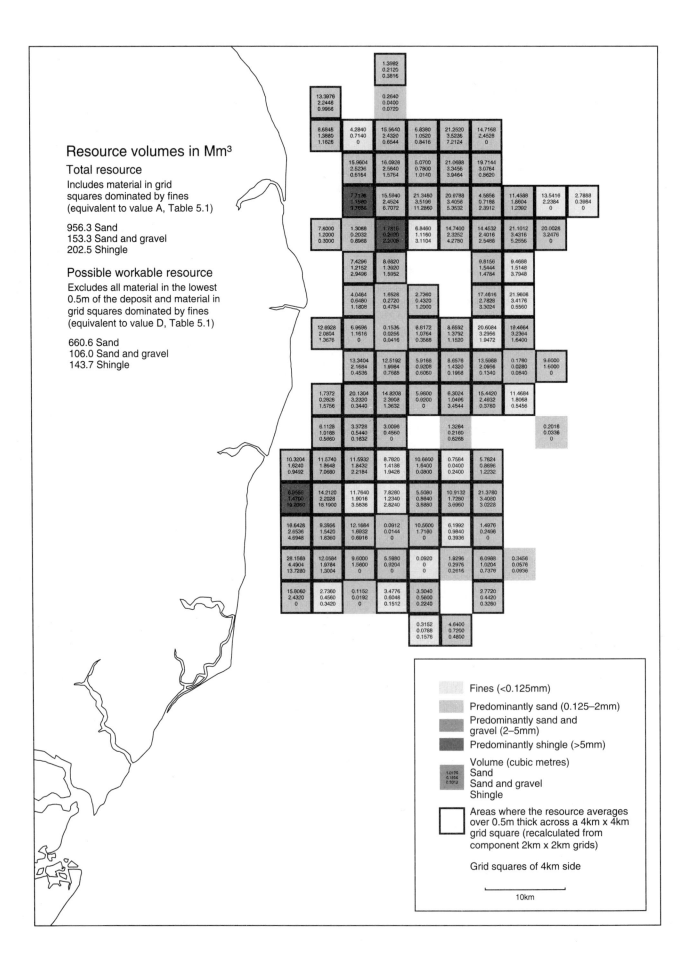

Figure 5.2 *Resources in areas densely sampled by the marine aggregate industry: East Anglia*

CIRIA Report 154

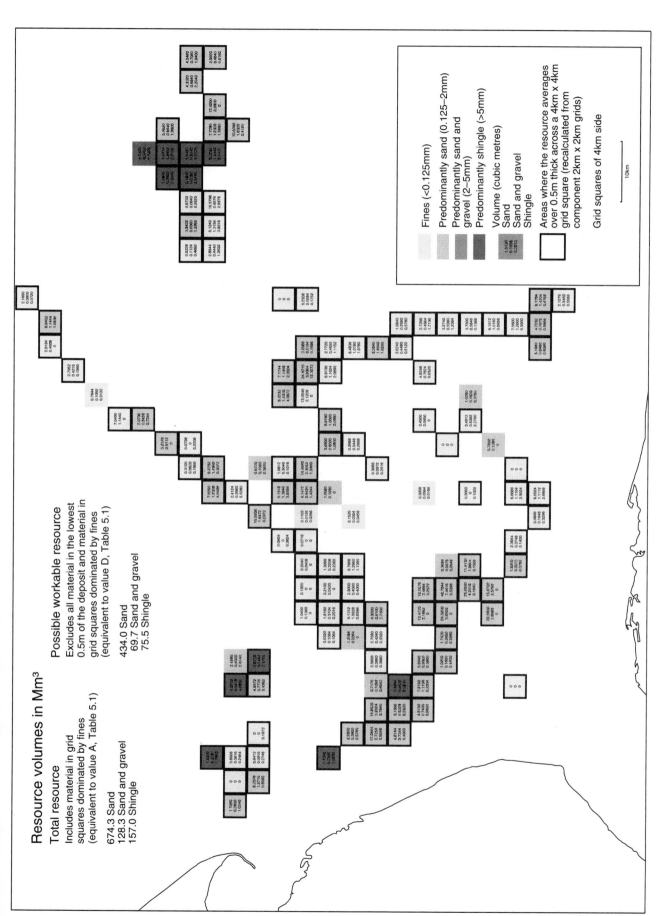

Figure 5.3 *Resources in areas densely sampled by the marine aggregate industry: Wash*

The Dogger Bank is an extensive area of relatively shallow water (25—40m depth) above a broad, flat-topped seabed feature of positive relief formed during the last glaciation. It is composed of a core of glacimarine clays, locally pebbly, which are covered, in part, by superficial sediments. A number of small open channels or closed depressions less than 15m, and some major channels to 50m deep, break up the otherwise smooth seabed of the Dogger Bank. Details of sediment distribution are generally known only from BGS reconnaissance surveys. Holocene laminated muds and sands and present-day bedforms rest upon the eroded glacial deposits of the Dogger Bank.

Shingle and coarse shingle

There is a general paucity of shingle grade material occurring on the seabed in this area. Where it is present the shingle often includes a large shell component. The distribution of coarse sediments is also irregular, with bedrock locally widely exposed in areas scoured by strong tidal currents, such as around headlands, and in areas of high topographic relief.

Shingle deposits occur off Flamborough Head and Whitby. The shingle deposits occurring offshore from Whitby lie mostly in water over 50m in depth. The shingle is shelly with pebbles of dolerite, red sandstone and quartzite. Evidence from 14 shallow cores suggests the deposits are typically 0.1m in thickness and overlie Jurassic bedrock or till. Shingle occurs widely off Flamborough Head, between Filey Bay and Bridlington Bay. Almost all the shingle is in water depths less than 55m and over half is shallower than 50m. The shingle is of veneer thickness (probably less than 0.1m) and directly overlies bedrock. It has a variable sand and shell content. In small areas east of Flamborough Head and Bridlington Bay, around 54°07′ and 0°04′E, and 54°04′ and 0°05′E, the thickness may be up to 3m or more. Areas of the Dogger Bank containing potential shingle resources are in less than 40m water depth.

Available reconnaissance data indicate significant concentrations of shingle in the region of Dogger North Shoal (54°53′N, 1°35′E), North West Riff (54°35′N, 1°20′E), South Dogger Ground (54°12′N, 1°57′E to 2°13′E) and Eastermost Shoal (54°40′N, 2°38′E). The shingle deposits generally range in thickness from 0.1m to 2.0m. Data points are few in number and widely spaced, but shingle thicknesses of 0.5 to 0.8m are indicated around North West Riff and several vibrocores in the Dogger North Shoal deposits proved c.0.5m of sandy shingle overlying till. Over 1.0m of shingle-bearing sediment was proved in one core from the Eastermost Shoal. The shingle is often very sandy, and the component clasts show considerable compositional variation, containing large amounts of igneous and metamorphic rock types as well as large proportions of sandstone and limestone. Locally (e.g. Eastermost Shoal) the shingle is shell-rich, resulting from the accumulation of modern mollusc shells in an area of low sedimentation.

Mixed sand and gravel

Sediments in this category are likely to be found in at least small quantities in association with some of the shingle deposits mentioned above.

Sand

The sandbanks of Sand Hills lie southwest of the Dogger Bank at around 50m water depth. The banks are 12m to 21m high. In the west the banks are mantled by large sandwaves whose presence is thought to indicate the banks are still active, although in the east the banks have smooth surface profiles and no sandwaves and are therefore considered to be moribund. To the north-west of the Dogger Bank, the East Bank Ridges are sandbanks in water depths of 50—60m, and are considered to be moribund. Sand covering large parts of the Dogger Bank is fine-grained, with coarser grades associated with the localised shingle deposits.

5.3.5 Tyne-Tees

Over the greater part of the sub-region water depths exceed 50m, shallower waters being restricted to an approximately 10km wide nearshore zone. Over much of this sub-region the cover of superficial sediment is thin (<1.0m) overlying till or bedrock. Locally within bays and in the lee of headlands thicker accumulations are found. The sediment cover is very thin around Holy Island and the Farne Islands.

There are generally only reconnaissance geological survey data available in this sub-region and only parts of the sub-region have been prospected by the marine aggregate industry. No parts of the sea floor within this sub-region are considered to have been densely sampled by the marine aggregate industry.

Much colliery waste has been dumped on the Durham coast and has been widely redistributed by marine processes.

Shingle and coarse shingle

There is a general paucity of shingle grade material occurring on the seabed in this area. Shingle deposits in the nearshore zone are particularly thin, generally less than 0.3 m. Thicker accumulations of sandy sediment occur in deep water troughs or valley features and also in extensive sandbanks, such as the Hills, or in the isolated banks inshore of the Farne Islands.

Shingle deposits occur off Tynemouth and the Farne Islands, although they are likely to be thin (probably less than 0.5m) and of patchy distribution. The shingle deposits off Tynemouth are thin (often c. 0.1m thickness) and directly overlie till or Coal Measures bedrock. One sediment core has recorded 0.7m of sandy shingle, but this core may have penetrated into weathered Coal Measures bedrock. Coal is a common component of shingle in this area and in many cases it is the major lithology. The shingle commonly includes mud contaminants. South of the Farne Islands, offshore Beadnell Bay, thin, patchy shingle deposits overlie till, but large areas of exposed bedrock also occur locally. Some localised shingle deposits are associated with hummocky mounds of till east of the Farne Deeps, but in water depths of 70m to 80m.

The shingle comprises clasts of hard Carboniferous sandstones, together with igneous and metamorphic rock types and some dolomite, limestone and chert. The shell content of the shingle is highly variable. Coal and carbonaceous material are locally major shingle components, particularly off Tynemouth and the Durham coast.

Mixed sand and gravel

This sediment category occurs in areas of weaker tidal currents where the sand has not been winnowed. Small deposits may occur in close association with patches of shingle.

Sand

Sands, gravelly sands and shingle predominate although a large area of silts and muddy sands occur in a linear north-south trending deep water trough off Blyth/Hartlepool. Between Amble and Teeside the seabed sediments are usually muddy. In part this is due to spoil but it is also due to the reworking of older muddy sediments which are present in the area.

5.4 ADDITIONAL SELECTED AREAS STUDIED

5.4.1 Location

Details on the location and material required for planned beach recharge schemes and maintenance of existing recharge sites were provided in Section 3. Five additional areas for detailed study were chosen which had sufficient detailed data available and were accessible to likely recharge sites. These study areas lie outside the areas intensely sampled by the aggregate industry, although along the Suffolk coast (Figure 5.6) grid squares are considered which fill gaps in the Crown Estate database.

5.4.2 Thames Estuary

Goodwin Sands

The Goodwin Sands are a large resource of sand. Despite removal of 2.5Mm³ of sand for use in the landfill for the Folkestone Terminal of the Channel Tunnel (Jones, 1989), a large resource remains. The report data indicate that up to 833.1Mm³ of sand and 21.4Mm³ of mixed sand and gravel occur in this area (Figure 5.4). These estimates are based on Hydrographic Office surveys across the Goodwin Sands undertaken after the extraction of sand for the Channel Tunnel project. Numerous shipwrecks on and around the Goodwin Sands could hinder exploitation of this resource.

Inner Thames Estuary

Data were available from construction companies who had undertaken surveys in the inner Thames Estuary for a variety of construction projects, including the now abandoned project to build the third London airport at Foulness. These sediments support an important flora and fauna and environmental considerations will affect plans for exploiting this resource. The report data indicate that up to 639.8Mm³ of sand and 27.7Mm³ of mixed sand and gravel occur in this area (Figure 5.5).

5.4.3 East Anglia

Offshore Yarmouth-Southwold

Due to the complex arrangement of sandbanks and sandwaves on the sea floor off the Suffolk-Norfolk coast, Hydrographic Office data have helped locate a number of sand bodies not recorded on the Crown Estate database. These deposits may lie contiguous to identified resources. The additional resource identified is quite large, up to 338.0Mm³ (Figure 5.6)

Offshore Happisburgh, NE Norfolk

Large resources of sand exist in the Norfolk Banks. In the banks closest to Happisburgh, over 5241Mm³ of sand have been identified (Figure 5.7). Major pipelines extend offshore from the Norfolk coast and cross this study area. These include submarine cables and pipelines linking the offshore gasfields to the onshore terminal at Bacton.

5.4.4 Tyne-Tees

Approaches to Teesport

A series of sandwave fields occupy depressions on the sea floor, often between ridges of exposed bedrock in this area. The bedforms occur at between 35m and 55m depth. Rippled sands and thin gravel ridges occur in the vicinity of the larger bedforms which are locally up to 6.5m thick. Some shipwrecks occur in the area, but the scattered nature of the bedforms detracts most from the potential of the deposits. Nevertheless, the report data indicate that up to 79.8Mm³ of sand occur in this area which could supply local recharge schemes (Figure 5.8).

Table 5.2 *Summary of resources in areas selected for detailed study*

	Sand		Sand and gravel		Shingle	
	Volume Mm³	Tonnage Mt	Volume Mm³	Tonnage Mt	Volume Mm³	Tonnage Mt
Thames Estuary:						
Goodwin Sands A	833.1	1333.0	21.4	38.5	2.5	5.0
Goodwin Sands B	828.1	1325.0	21.4	38.5	2.5	5.0
Goodwin Sands C	823.4	1317.4	19.6	35.3	0.1	0.2
Goodwin Sands D	753.5	1205.6	15.0	27.0	0	0
Inner Thames Estuary A	639.8	1023.7	27.7	49.9	7.6	15.2
Inner Thames Estuary B	634.8	1015.7	27.7	49.9	7.6	15.2
Inner Thames Estuary C	634.8	1015.7	27.7	49.9	7.6	15.2
Inner Thames Estuary D	567.7	908.3	22.9	41.2	4.7	9.4
East Anglia:						
Offshore Yarmouth-Southwold A	338.0	540.8	0	0	0	0
Offshore Yarmouth-Southwold B	338.0	540.8	0	0	0	0
Offshore Yarmouth-Southwold C	336.5	538.4	0	0	0	0
Offshore Yarmouth-Southwold D	278.5	445.6	0	0	0	0
Offshore Happisburgh A	5241.2	8385.9	75.9	136.6	101.2	202.4
Offshore Happisburgh B	5238.5	8381.6	75.9	136.6	101.2	202.4
Offshore Happisburgh C	5194.6	8311.4	56.6	101.9	99.4	198.8
Offshore Happisburgh D	4613.8	7382.1	44.2	70.7	80.3	160.6
Tyne-Tees:						
Approaches to Teesport A	79.8	127.7	4.5	8.1	0.4	0.8
Approaches to Teesport B	77.7	124.3	4.0	7.2	0.36	0.72
Approaches to Teesport C	54.0	86.4	0.25	0.45	0.25	0.5
Approaches to Teesport D	30.3	48.5	0.13	0.23	0.07	0.14

A: estimated total material identified in the areas sampled
B: as A but excluding material in grid squares where fines are the dominant lithology
C: as B but also excluding material in deposits averaging less than 0.5m thick
D: as C but excluding all material in the lowest 0.5m of the deposit

All resource estimates were calculated in cubic metres and have been converted to tonnes using the following density values:

Shingle	2.0 tonnes/cubic metre
Sand and gravel	1.8 tonnes/cubic metre
Sand	1.6 tonnes/cubic metre

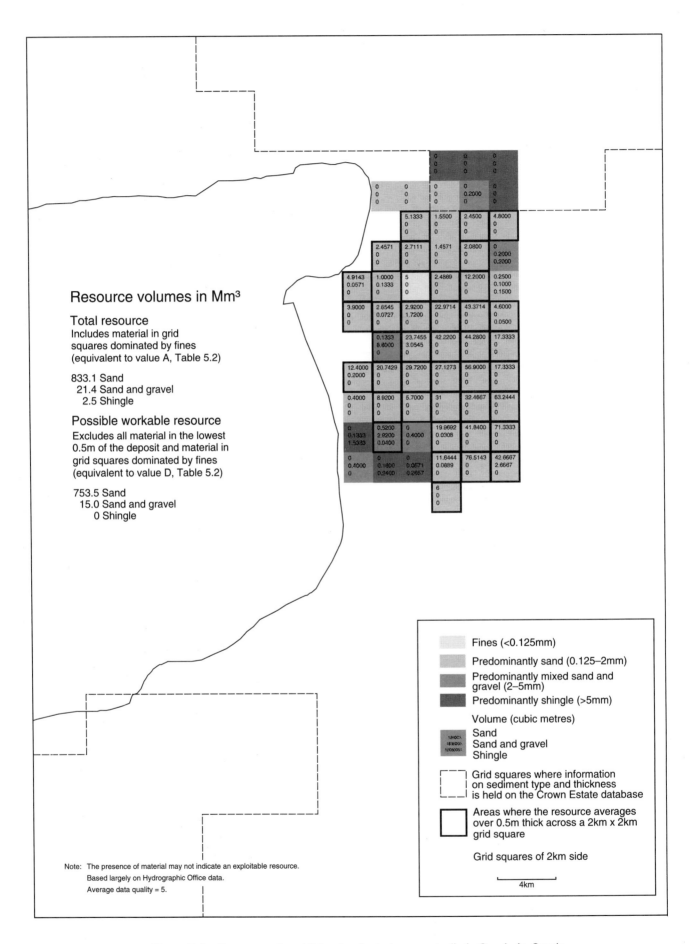

Figure 5.4 *Resources in additional selected areas studied: Goodwin Sands*

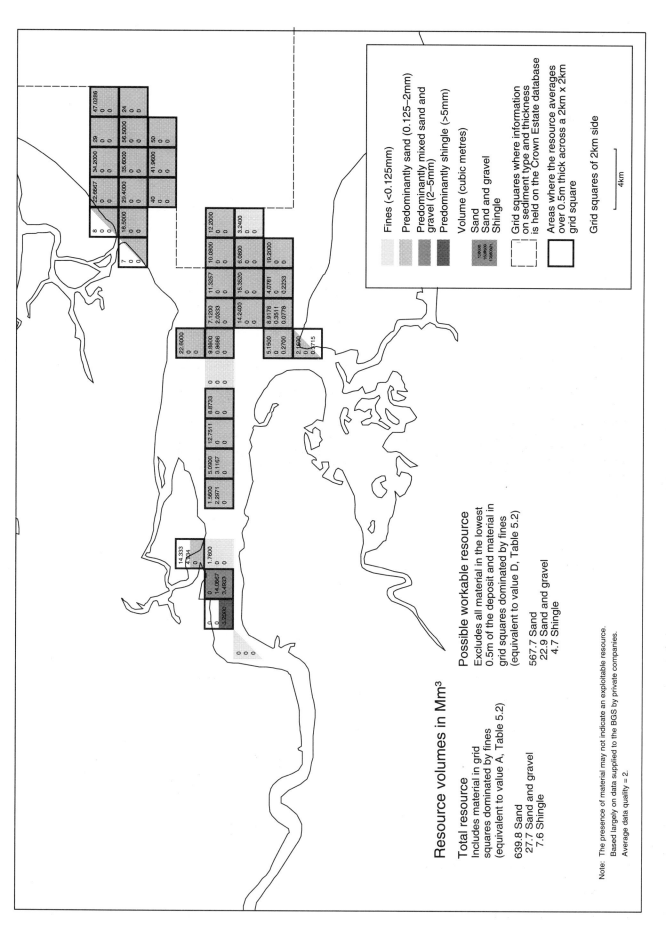

Figure 5.5 *Resources in additional selected areas studied: Inner Thames Estuary*

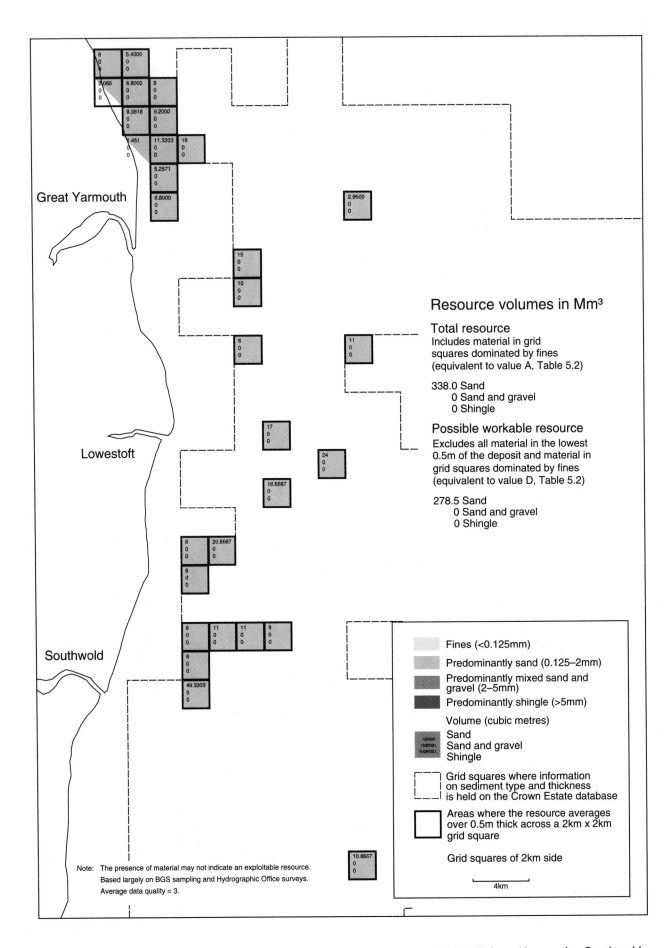

Figure 5.6 *Resources in additional selected areas studied: Offshore Yarmouth - Southwold*

CIRIA Report 154

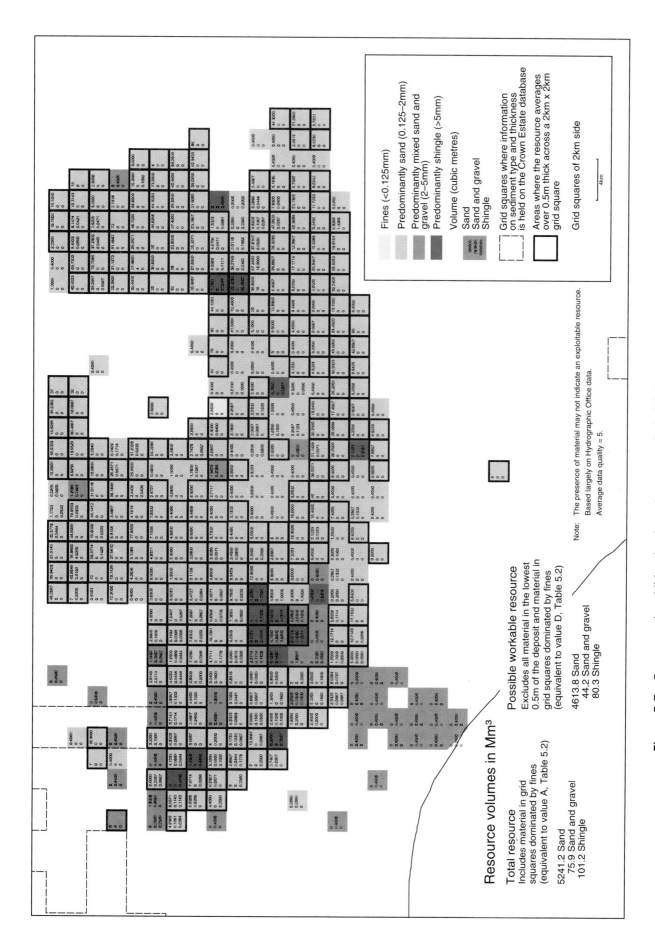

Figure 5.7 *Resources in additional selected areas studied: Offshore Happisburgh, NE Norfolk*

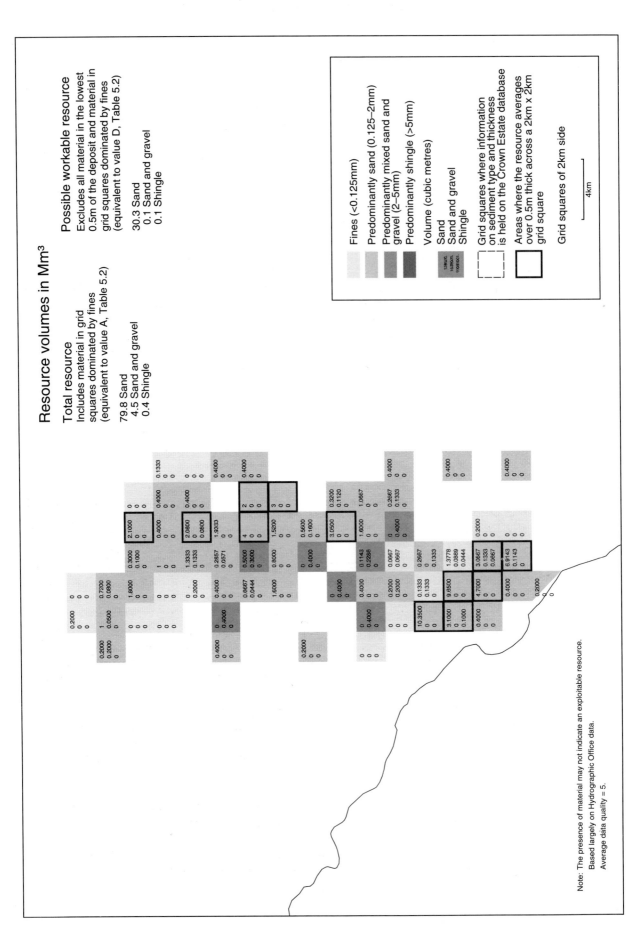

Figure 5.8 *Resources in additional selected areas studied: Approaches to Teesport*

6 General distribution and quality of marine materials suitable for beach recharge off the coasts of Wales and western England

6.1 BACKGROUND

This section assesses the distribution and quality of offshore material suitable for aggregate and non-aggregate purposes in the area offshore from Land's End in Cornwall to the Scottish Border at the Solway Firth. The area is divided into five sub-regions - Bristol Channel South, South Wales, North Wales, Lancs-Cheshire and Cumbria - to accord with the regional areas for material demand estimates in Section 3.

The section includes an outline of the geological history and hydrography of the Celtic Sea - Irish Sea area, information which pertains both to the distribution and to the origin of the seabed sediments. A regional description of material distribution and volumes provides an overview of the total offshore resource. For areas studied in detail resource volumes within grid squares are provided. The database created specifically for the project holds over 1400 points of data (excluding Crown Estate data) for areas off the coasts of Wales and western England which have been manipulated into 562 2km-a-side grid squares of averaged data. Some logistical factors affecting exploitation are discussed in Section 8.

6.2 REGIONAL REVIEW

6.2.1 Sea floor topography

The topography of the present-day seabed is largely the product of Quaternary glacial activity in the Irish Sea, and marine planation concomitant with periods of rising sea level both during Quaternary interglacials and since the last glaciation. The seabed takes the form of a gently inclined submarine erosion surface, locally modified by enclosed deeps and the superficial sediment cover. Tidal sand ridges, sandbanks, sand ribbons and trains of sandwaves locally modify the sea floor topography by up to 20m. The occurrence of bedforms is governed by the tidal current paths in the Celtic Sea—Irish Sea (Section 6.2.2). Relict bedforms also occur, considered to have formed in shallower water depths than now occur. "Sarnau" are low ridges that occur normal to the coastline in Cardigan Bay which may represent relict glacial moraines. Anastomising nets of channels in St George's Channel, individually up to 200m wide and up to a few kilometres long, may be a relict braided river system developed on a subaerial sandur (outwash) plain. Periglacial features and moribund tidal sand ridges have also been reported from the sea floor of this sub-region (Tappin *et al.*, 1994).

Water depths exceed 60m over most of the area of the Celtic Sea west of Lundy and of St George's Channel west of St David's Head and the Lleyn Peninsula (Figure 2.1) and therefore the sediments occurring in these westerly areas are not considered in this Report. The Irish Sea east of the Isle of Man is, in contrast, an area of relatively shallow water, commonly less than 40m water depth.

From Land's End to Barnstaple Bay the sea floor generally slopes steeply from the coast and the 50m bathymetric contour lies mostly less than 20km offshore.

The Bristol Channel is a wide estuary mostly shallower than 50m, the centre of which has developed from a palaeo-Severn Valley which was exhumed during the Holocene transgression. The broad expanse of Cardigan Bay and smaller bights including Caernarfon Bay are shallower than 50m.

A trough exceeding 100m in depth runs up the western side of the Irish Sea. East of the trough the Irish Sea is characterised by a shallow floor with water depths rarely exceeding 35m. A broad zone of shallow (<10m) water occurs in Liverpool Bay, Morecombe Bay and the Solway Firth; intertidal zones form over 50% of the areas of these great embayments. The major anomalous bathymetric feature in the east Irish Sea is the Lune Deep at the mouth of Morecambe Bay which attains a depth of over 80m.

6.2.2 Tidal streams

The strength of tidal and wave induced currents has an important influence on the distribution of sediment. Winnowing of sediments to leave shingle lags and the growth of sandbanks occur under a strong tidal current regime, whereas fine sediments tend to accumulate in sheltered bays and offshore deeps. The twice-daily reversing tidal streams produce bottom stresses which create bed-load partings in St George's Channel and the Bristol Channel, from which net transport paths converge, and an area of fine-grained sediment deposition occurs in the Celtic Deep. Mobile sediment is thin or lacking in areas of high bottom stresses, with sand winnowed by erosion leaving thin, patchy shingle lags.

There is a strong correlation between tidal current velocities, the particle size of sand and the distribution of bedforms. Coarse sand fractions are concentrated in areas of higher tidal velocities. Sand becomes finer down the tidal current gradient and mud belts are associated with tidal current nodes.

Over much of the area from Land's End to Anglesey tidal currents are of moderate strength at 0.75—1.25m/s, generally exceeding 1.0m/s around the Pembrokeshire coast, in St George's Channel and in most of Caernarfon Bay. Stonger currents occur locally around exposed headlands such as St David's Head, the tip of the Lleyn Peninsular, and Hartland Point. They are also strong in major tidal inlets, most notably in the Bristol Channel which has a large tidal range and strong currents. The maximum tidal currents generally exceed 1.5m/s, and exceed 3.0m/s in the eastern part of the Channel (east of Cardiff). In bays sheltered by headlands, currents are weaker especially in shallow water, commonly less than 0.5m/s. Relatively weak tidal currents of less than 0.5m/s are typical in the deeper waters north-west of Cape Cornwall. In Cardigan Bay tidal currents reach no more than 0.5m/s in the inner part of the bay. The Welsh coast receives a persistent south-westerly swell from the Atlantic Ocean.

Tides enter the Irish Sea from both the north and south with the two paths meeting near the Isle of Man. The strongest tidal currents with values greater than 1.0m/s are confined to St George's Channel around Anglesey and the area between Galloway and the Isle of Man. Tidal currents are weakest both east and west of the Isle of Man and in Liverpool Bay and Morecambe Bay tidal velocities generally range from 0.6m/s to 0.8m/s. The eastern part of the Irish sea is exposed to only moderate wave energy. There is a net sand transport direction eastwards into Liverpool Bay from the North Wales coast.

Bedrock is locally exposed in areas scoured by strong tidal currents (e.g. around headlands) and also in areas of high topographic relief (e.g. Isles of Scilly, Seven Stones, Cape Cornwall Bank).

6.2.3 Geological setting

In many areas the shingle components show a relation to the lithology of the underlying bedrock or the erratic content of underlying glacial deposits.

The southern coast of the Bristol Channel is composed of a sequence of rocks that become younger towards the east, with structurally complex Devonian and Carboniferous slates, grits with igneous intrusions south of Minehead, and younger, structurally simpler, Triassic and Jurassic rocks dominating to the east. Holocene estuarine flats flank the inner Bristol Channel. Triassic, Rhaetic, Liassic, and Carboniferous mudstones, limestones and sandstones crop out in cliffs on the north side of the Bristol Channel east of Swansea Bay. Southern Pembrokeshire and the nearshore sea floor is composed of a wide range of rocks ranging in age from

Precambrian to Carboniferous including Coal Measures sandstones, shales and coals. West of the Pembrokeshire coast the St George's Channel Basin contains Mesozoic sediments, over 5km thick. The coast of Cardigan Bay is underlain by Ordovician, Silurian and Cambrian slates with intercalated sandstones which extend offshore in NE-SW alignement into the Cardigan Bay Basin. The Tremadoc Bay Basin includes a thick sequence of early Tertiary sediments underlain by Jurassic strata. The Lleyn Peninsula is mainly composed of Ordovician sedimentary, volcanic and igneous intrusive rocks. Anglesey is composed of a mixture of metamorphic and igneous rocks of Precambrian and Palaeozoic age which extend onto the surrounding sea floor. Carboniferous Limestone crops out along the North Wales coast.

The East Irish Sea Basin and Solway Firth Basin are filled by thick sequences of Permo-Triassic sedimentary rocks, commonly overlying Carboniferous rocks including Westphalian Coal Measures. A narrow ridge of older sedimentary rocks stretching from Cumbria to the Isle of Man separates the two large basins.

6.2.4 Quaternary geological history of the Celtic Sea — Irish Sea

A rudimentary understanding of the glacial history of this region is important because winnowed, sorted and redistributed glacial sediments are the source of many of the present day seabed sediments. The sea floor off the west coast of England and Wales was shaped during the last glaciation, and over wide areas Pleistocene deposits (mostly till) underlie the thin veneer of seabed sediments. Glacial deposits were exposed above sea level in early postglacial times, and thereafter suffered coastal and marine reworking as sea level rose.

Although large parts of the Celtic Sea and St George's Channel fall outside the scope of this report on account of water depths, the Quaternary history of the area between Britain and Ireland has significance for understanding the distribution of sediments close to the coast of Wales and western England.

During the Quaternary geological period, the climate fluctuated between glacial and interglacial cycles. Major oscillations in sea level were associated with the growth and decline of the continental ice caps. Due to melting of the ice sheet and isostatic rebound, sea level fell to approximately 120m below present sea level in the north Celtic Sea after 11 000 years B.P., and to lesser levels in Cardigan Bay before 9000 years B.P. Previously deposited glaciomarine deposits were subsequently eroded. Thereafter sea level rose eustatically until attaining its present tidal level approximately 5000 years B.P.

The ice-sheet that originated from the Welsh landmass during the last glaciation reached its maximum southern extension along the south coast of Wales. The ice sheet terminated in an irregular margin and extended offshore into Swansea Bay and between the mouths of the Usk and Taff in the Severn Estuary. However, the contemporaneous ice-sheet which filled the Irish Sea extended as a broad tongue well to the south, into the Celtic Sea. Scattered glacial deposits are found as far south as the Scilly Isles. The interaction of the two ice-sheets along the northern and western coasts of Wales led to the deposition of especially complex glacial deposits. Evidence from offshore boreholes and isolated coastal sections suggest more extensive older ice-sheets once covered the area.

Where the coastal and offshore area of Wales was overrun by ice during the last (Devensian) glacial stage, a very extensive mantle of sub-glacial till is usually present. The till comprises a stiff to very hard clay with admixed sand, gravel and boulders which is commonly over 55m thick. The deglaciation sediments comprise a complex sequence of sandur (outwash), glacilacustrine and glacimarine deposits. They form a discontinuous sequence of sediments ranging from a few metres up to 200m thick within overdeepened channels cut through the till and older deposits in Tremadoc Bay. Scattered hollows and channels occur, the upper parts of which are filled, or part filled, by fine-grained sediments, and more extensive sheets of such sediment to less than 10m thick occur over the till in the extreme south-east of Cardigan Bay and in Tremadoc Bay. The latest glacial sediments may be boulder deposits which extend as shoals up to 20km long and 3km wide from the coast into inner Cardigan Bay. These shoal ridges ("sarnau" in Welsh) may represent moraines of late Devensian ice or the dissected remains of sandur (outwash plain) sediments from the last mountain glaciers of Snowdonia.

Buried palaeovalleys in the Bristol Channel were cut during glacial periods when the southern limit of the ice lay somewhere in South Wales. Streams flowing from the ice would probably have carved the valleys and laid down the sheets of shingle and local valley infills. These offshore shingle deposits are probably equivalent to the extensive fluvio-glacial spreads in the lower part of the Taff valley. The shape of the proto-Severn Channel was modified during the last glaciation, but probably formed during an older glaciation.

6.2.5 Renewability of resources

It is important to note that the source of the shingle offshore are the deposits laid down during the last glaciation. The present distribution of the shingle reflects the marine reworking of these Pleistocene fluvial and glacial deposits during the early stages of the Holocene transgression across the area. The shingle is therefore a "relict" deposit, redistributed by wave action during the major sea level rise that took place between 8000 and 5000 years ago. Many patches of shingle now lie too deep to be affected by wave or tidal currents. The shingle resource must be considered finite and thus if shingle is removed from the offshore region by dredging it will not be replaced.

At present rivers around the coast of Wales and western England are not considered to be significant contributors of sediment to the seabed offshore. The main input from rivers is mud at the present day. Many river mouths and estuaries in this region are also sinks for fine sediment driven by onshore directed sediment transport such as in the Severn Estuary.

Sand is being supplied by cliff erosion from some outcrops of glacial and post-glacial sediments. Deposits susceptible to coastal erosion are found along the North Wales coast east of Llandudno, on the Lancashire coast from the Mersey to Morecambe Bay, and along the coast of Cumbria. Eroded cliff material does not appear to be transported far offshore, generally remaining in the nearshore zone. Material eroded from the North Wales coast is transported eastwards to the estuaries of the Dee and Mersey. In the Bristol Channel bed-load parting occurs in the inner channel with an easterly movement of shingle along the southern coast of the estuary from Barnstaple Bay.

Replenishment of dredged sand may therefore occur in some instances where local sediment transport paths and wave currents would allow bedforms to reform. For example, there is some evidence for natural mobility of tidal sandbanks in the Bristol Channel. The shape of Culver Sands, for example, may change as part of a natural equilibrium process. Evidence from banks being dredged is that the tidal regime around the banks may be strong enough to repair any minor change in form due to dredging.

6.3 GENERAL DISTRIBUTION OF MARINE MATERIALS: RESOURCES AND VOLUME ESTIMATES

The offshore resource is considered in relation the regional divisions as specified in Section 3. The West Coast region is divided into Bristol Channel South, South Wales, North Wales, Lancs-Cheshire and Cumbria sub-regions.

Dredging for sand and gravel is restricted to the Bristol Channel, Liverpool Bay (north-west of the Dee Estuary), a small area half way between the Isle of Man and the coast of Cumbria, and a very small concession in the mouth of the River Mersey at Liverpool. In the Bristol Channel the main licensed areas are in the outer Severn estuary, around the Holm islands, and off Porthcawl south of Nash Sand. For all dredging licenses within Liverpool Bay only sand is extracted.

6.3.1 Bristol Channel South

This sub-region extends from Land's End in the west to the Severn Bridge. Over much of this sub-region the seabed sediments are a mix of sand and gravel which occurs in extensive sheets of less than 1m thickness overlying a smooth bedrock surface. Most of the area lies in water depths in excess of 50m. Muddy sediments occur in the deeper water areas off the south Celtic Sea. Sediment generally moves eastwards from Barnstaple Bay along the coastal zone of north Devon and Somerset.

A proto-Severn Valley extends along the centre of the inner Bristol Channel and Severn Estuary. The valley base falls to —50m OD, with local overdeepening, in the outer Bristol Channel. Minor tributaries to this palaeovalley system are filled with sediment, but the main channel is covered only by the present veneer of seabed sediments.

The amount of sediment presently transported into the area is small and most of the seabed sediments are derived from former fluvio-glacial deposits which were reworked during the Holocene transgression across the area. This transgression resulted in the formation of a thin, shingle lag deposit and a general movement of sand into the inner Channel.

Shingle and coarse shingle

Although areas of seabed in this sub-region are covered by shingle, the deposits are of veneer thickness (typically less than 1m, commonly less than 0.15m) and bedrock is widely exposed. The shingle consists of a mixture of chert, sandstone, siltstone and igneous and metamorphic rock types. Some shell material occurs in most sediments and shell beds are locally developed.

Within areas densely sampled by the marine aggregate industry the database indicates a resource of 45.9Mm^3 for the Bristol Channel South sub-region, 24.1Mm^3 of which are potentially workable (Figure 6.1). In addition, a further 126.0Mm^3 are located in the additional areas of detailed study (Table 6.2, Figures 6.4 and 6.5).

Mixed sand and gravel

Material with a modal size of 2—5mm tends to occur scattered across the study area. Many sediments with abundant comminuted shell debris fall within this category.

Within areas densely sampled by the marine aggregate industry the database indicates a resource of 15.4Mm^3 for the Bristol Channel South sub-region, 13.7Mm^3 of which are potentially workable (Figure 6.1). In addition, a further 55.8Mm^3 are located in the additional areas of detailed study (Table 6.2, Figure 6.4).

Sand

The sands in this sub-region are quartzose, mainly medium- to coarse-grained although fine-grained sands occur within bays and in the lee of headlands. Sand at seabed may pass down into a lag gravel resting upon the bedrock surface.

The main accumulations of sand are:

1. Sandbanks up to 15m thick some 25km west and north-west of Bude.

2. Small, nearshore, sand ridges between Cape Cornwall and St Ives.

3. Sandbanks at the mouth of the Bristol Channel immediately to the north-west of Lundy (Section 4). These deposits of sands, which probably contain some gravel, are of potential commercial interest. Some prospecting has been carried out in this area, but further detailed prospecting is recommended to fully evaluate their potential.

4. Inner Bristol Channel where important sand resources occur.

Sandbanks in the sub-region formed of finer-grained material may be partially replenished by modern sediment movement though the volume of this material is uncertain.

Within areas densely sampled by the marine aggregate industry the database indicates a resource of 96.1Mm^3 for the Bristol Channel South sub-region, 66.9Mm^3 of which are potentially workable (Figure 6.1, Table 6.1). In addition, a further 3863.2Mm^3 are located in the additional areas of detailed study (Table 6.2, Figures 6.4 and 6.5).

Palaeovalley deposits

Palaeovalleys are overdeepened river channels cut during glacial sea-level lowstands. Small but relatively thick deposits of seabed sediments are locally present off the north Cornish coast where they infill submarine channels.

6.3.2 South Wales

This sub-region is a major source of marine dredged aggregate, principally sand. The aggregates occur in a number of well defined areas and across much of the rest of the area bedrock is at or close to the seabed. The existing licensed areas fall into three categories; linear tidal sand banks such as Nash Sand, parts of the main channel in the lower Severn Estuary such as in the Bristol Deep, and areas of shingle sheets of uncertain thickness such as south of Culver Sand. Parts of Carmarthen Bay have been prospected for aggregate resources.

The sand tends to occur in clearly defined linear sand banks and extensive sand wave fields. The sandbanks are up to 10m thick with some rising up to 20m above the surrounding seabed. Some of the sand has been considered too fine for aggregate use and some deposits (e.g. Cardiff Grounds) are contaminated with coal particles. There are nevertheless extensive resources of medium-grained sand suitable for use as fine aggregate. Potential shingle resources are less extensive; despite much of the sea floor being covered by a veneer of shingle, these lag deposits are often thin and patchy, but seismic evidence indicates locally thicker sheet deposits, often located nearshore, but the composition of these is uncertain. Fines form extensive deposits in those parts of the estuary with least tidal energy such as Bridgwater Bay and Cardiff Bay.

On account of the strong tidal currents in the Bristol Channel, sediment up to sand grade is mobile over most of the tidal cycle and in the inner Channel the tidal currents entrain sand as bedload. This has led to the sand grade sediment being well sorted and formed into a variety of bedforms. Sand has almost filled the estuary east of Newport to leave only a narrow tidal channel, but further down the estuary the tidal regime has produced fields of sandwaves and a series of linear sandbanks aligned nearly parallel to the major tidal flow.

The tidal sandbanks contain a variable coal content derived from the coal loading industry that was centred on Barry and Cardiff during the earlier part of the century. The coal content may limit the use made of some sand from the banks, particularly Cardiff Grounds.

Shingle and coarse shingle

Areas between the sand bedforms in the Bristol Channel are characterised by a lag deposit of coarse shingle or exposed bedrock.

Across parts of the sub-region there are extensive spreads of shingle at seabed. East of Cardiff Grounds, in water depths of about 10m, is an extensive area of thin shingle. The precise thickness of the unit is not known but seismic profiles suggest that at least a metre covers bedrock though the seismic resolution is poor. A prospecting licence covers an area south of this shingle spread in the deeper water of the Bristol Deep.

Gravel waves, formed mainly of shingle-rich sediments, occur in several isolated, small areas particularly in St George's Channel and are between 1m and 3m in height. Gravel waves occur in a small area off Dinas Head (52° 03′ N, 4° 57′ W).

Table 6.1 *Summary of resources in areas densely sampled by the marine aggregate industry*

	Sand		Sand and gravel		Shingle	
	Volume Mm³	Tonnage Mt	Volume Mm³	Tonnage Mt	Volume Mm³	Tonnage Mt
Bristol Channel South A	96.1	153.8	15.4	27.7	45.9	91.8
Bristol Channel South B	88.4	141.4	14.2	25.6	41.3	82.6
Bristol Channel South C	85.5	136.8	13.7	24.7	38.6	77.2
Bristol Channel South D	66.9	107.0	10.8	19.4	24.1	48.2
South Wales A	183.5	293.6	30.0	54.0	16.6	33.2
South Wales B	175.8	281.3	28.8	51.8	15.5	31.0
South Wales C	168.6	269.8	27.7	49.9	13.2	26.4
South Wales D	134.4	215.0	22.1	39.8	6.1	12.2
North Wales A	406.2	649.9	65.8	118.4	24.5	49.0
North Wales B	389.6	623.4	63.3	113.9	13.5	27.0
North Wales C	387.4	619.8	63.0	113.4	12.4	24.8
North Wales D	295.6	473.0	48.0	86.4	9.2	18.4

A: estimated total material identified in the areas sampled
B: as A but excluding material in grid squares where fines are the dominant lithology
C: as B but also excluding material in deposits averaging less than 0.5m thick
D: as C but excluding all material in the lowest 0.5m of the deposit

All resource estimates were calculated in cubic metres and have been converted to tonnes using the following density values:

Shingle	2.0 tonnes/cubic metre
Sand and gravel	1.8 tonnes/cubic metre
Sand	1.6 tonnes/cubic metre

Within areas densely sampled by the marine aggregate industry the database indicates a resource of 16.6Mm³ for the South Wales sub-region, 6.1Mm³ of which are potentially workable (Figure 6.2).

Mixed sand and gravel

Material with a modal size of 2—5mm tends to occur scattered across the study area. Many sediments with abundant comminuted shell debris fall within this category.

Within areas densely sampled by the marine aggregate industry the database indicates a resource of 30.0 Mm³ for the South Wales sub-region, 22.1 Mm³ of which are potentially workable (Figure 6.2).

Sand

The main accumulations of sand are:

1.   Tidal sandbanks occurring along the northern flanks of the estuary from Helwick Sands in the west (off Gower) to Cardiff Grounds in the east. These form discrete sediment bodies resting on a largely flat, rocky seabed which may crop out around their flanks. These bodies have been targets for sand extraction for many years and have shown subtle changes in bathymetry during this time. Sand size varies in the major sand accumulations. In the upper estuary, around Middle Ground, most of the sand is fine-grained. Further west, in the vicinity of Cardiff Grounds and Culver Sand, the sands are medium-grained. In Swansea Bay, Nash Bank has the coarsest sand and Scarweather Sand the finest, whereas Helwick Bank off the Gower contains

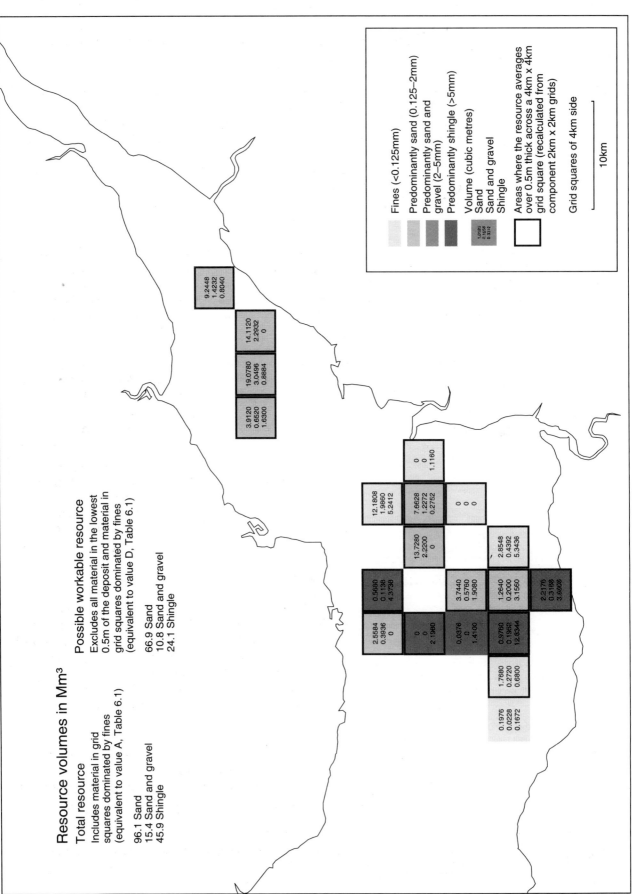

Resource volumes in Mm³

Total resource

Includes material in grid squares dominated by fines (equivalent to value A, Table 6.1)

96.1 Sand
15.4 Sand and gravel
45.9 Shingle

Possible workable resource

Excludes all material in the lowest 0.5m of the deposit and material in grid squares dominated by fines (equivalent to value D, Table 6.1)

66.9 Sand
10.8 Sand and gravel
24.1 Shingle

Fines (<0.125mm)

Predominantly sand (0.125–2mm)

Predominantly sand and gravel (2–5mm)

Predominantly shingle (>5mm)

Volume (cubic metres)
Sand
Sand and gravel
Shingle

Areas where the resource averages over 0.5m thick across a 4km x 4km grid square (recalculated from component 2km x 2km grids)

Grid squares of 4km side

10km

Figure 6.1 *Resources in areas densely sampled by the marine aggregate industry: Bristol Channel South*

sand typically ranging between fine-grained and medium-grained. Holm Sand comprises medium-grained sand at its centre, with coarse to very coarse sand on the flanks.

2. Tidal sand ridges of Bais Bank north-west of St David's Head. Most of the sand is medium-grained.

Coarse-grained sands are widespread in St George's Channel and in patches in Cardigan Bay. Fine-grained sands are typical of the inner parts of Cardigan Bay.

Within areas densely sampled by the marine aggregate industry the database indicates a resource of 183.5Mm^3 for the South Wales sub-region, 134.4Mm^3 of which are potentially workable (Figure 6.2). In addition, a further 151.6Mm^3 are located in the additional areas of detailed study (Table 6.2, Figure 6.6).

Palaeovalley deposits

Palaeovalleys are overdeepened river channels cut during glacial sea-level lowstands. Thick deposits infill restricted valleys on the flanks of the main buried Severn valley. A borehole put down by Wimpol in 1987 for the Severn Tidal Power Group (STPG) approximately 800m north of Steep Holm penetrated 23m of fine to coarse sand and shingle. Two other STPG boreholes in the Holms area penetrated about 13m of medium- to coarse-grained sand and shingle.

Shingle infills occur offshore in valleys that extend south of Barry and Aberthaw to join the main Severn valley. The material used to recharge Sand Bay north of Weston-super-Mare came from a small spread of shingle-rich sand around the Holms that formed a local infill.

6.3.3 North Wales

This sub-region includes the major licensed dredging areas within Liverpool Bay. There are currently three areas licensed for dredging marine aggregates (mainly sand) in the Liverpool Bay—Irish Sea area. Much of the Liverpool Bay—east of Isle of Man area has been prospected by the dredging industry, but prospecting has not been as intensive as in the southern North Sea and English Channel. Large areas of resistant bedrock are exposed on the rugged sea floor to the west and north-west of Anglesey.

Shingle and coarse shingle

A large area of shingle-rich sediment extends in a belt existing to the south and west of Anglesey and extending north of Anglesey towards the Isle of Man. The shingle deposits are discontinuous, and a part of the deposit lies on the till and glacial deposits from which many of the clasts were derived. The shingle clasts comprise a diverse range of lithologies, mainly Lower Palaezoic rock types including gneiss, schist, greywacke, andesite, rhyolite, agglomerate, slate, sandstone, limestone and conglomerate. In southern Liverpool Bay Carboniferous components are particularly common as clasts, principally sandstone and limestone.

Shingle and coarse shingle deposits occur as shoals up to 20km long and 3km wide which extend from the coast into Cardigan Bay. These shoal ridges ("sarnau") are probably erosional remnants of late glacial moraine deposits. From north to south they are known, respectively, as Sarn Badrig (NW of Barmouth), Sarn y Bwch (NW of Aberdyfi) and Sarn Cynfelin (NW of Aberystwyth).

Shingle derived from glacial deposits in this region generally has a low calcium carbonate content (<20%).

Within areas densely sampled by the marine aggregate industry the database indicates a resource of 24.5Mm^3 for the North Wales sub-region, 9.2Mm^3 of which are potentially workable (Figure 6.3).

Mixed sand and gravel

Material with a modal size of 2—5mm tends to occur scattered across the study area. Many sediments with abundant comminuted shell debris fall within this category. Within areas densely sampled by the marine aggregate industry the report database indicates a resource of 65.8Mm³ for the North Wales sub-region, 48.0Mm³ of which are potentially workable (Figure 6.3).

Sand

The main accumulations of sand are:

1. Tidal sand banks south-east of Bardsey Island off the Lleyn Peninsula.

2. A sandwave field in Caernarfon Bay (James and Wingfield, 1988).

3. Constable Bank north of Llandudno. This is the largest of a number of sandbanks that are generally aligned sub-parallel to the coast. Constable Bank lies 5km off Llandudno, it is over 8km long and has an amplitude of over 12m.

4. The floor of Liverpool Bay which is mostly covered in sand. A sandwave field occurs at the mouth of the River Dee.

On the eastern Irish Sea platform tidal currents are such that sandwaves are commonly associated with most of the major expanses of sand.

Within areas densely sampled by the marine aggregate industry the database indicates a resource of 406.2Mm³ for the North Wales sub-region, 295.6Mm³ of which are potentially workable (Figure 6.3). In addition, a further 57.3Mm³ are located in the additional areas of detailed study (Table 6.2, Figure 6.7).

6.3.4 Lancs-Cheshire

The seabed is covered mainly by sands and shingle-rich sediment in this sub-region. The eastern Irish Sea has a coastline characterised by well developed tidal flats reflecting in part the high tidal range in Liverpool Bay. A major area of mud deposition, corresponding to an area of low-tidal current velocity, occurs east of the Isle of Man.

Shingle and coarse shingle

The largest expanse of shingle-rich sediments covers an area between Anglesey and the Isle of Man. Another substantial spread occurs north of the Isle of Man towards the Galloway coast. Small, discontinuous patches of shingle occur in Liverpool Bay, Morecambe Bay (south of Barrow-in-Furness) and in the Solway Firth. The shingle-rich sediments are mostly thin (<0.5m) and directly overlie till and other glacial sediments from which the gravel is derived.

Mixed sand and gravel

This sediment category occurs in areas of weaker tidal currents where the sand has not been winnowed.

Sand

Glacial sediments are believed to be the primary source of sand in the Irish Sea. The main accumulations of sand are:

• tidal sandbanks in Morecambe Bay

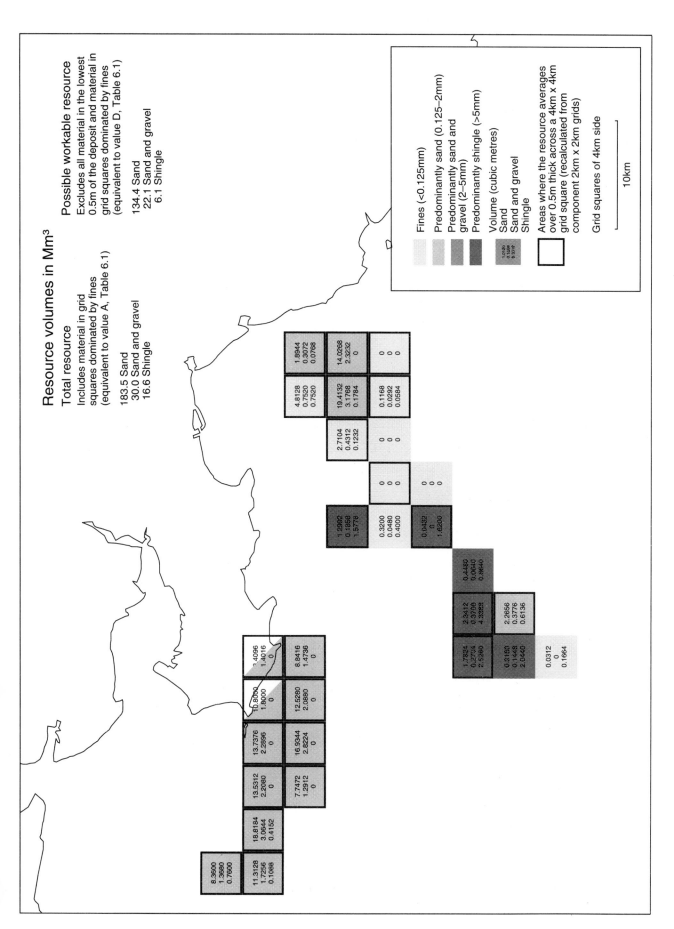

Figure 6.2 *Resources in areas densely sampled by the marine aggregate industry: South Wales*

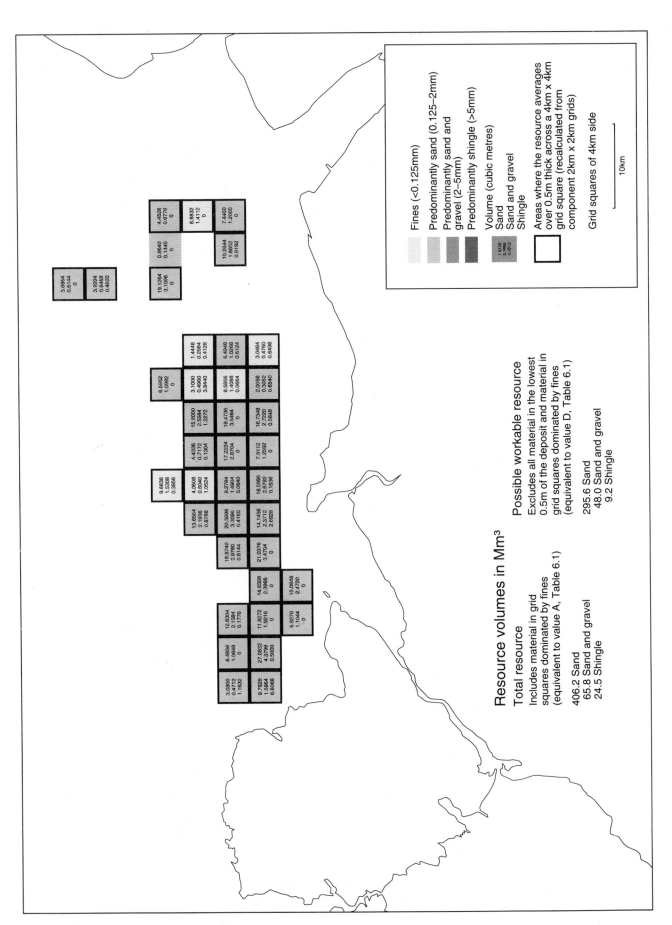

Figure 6.3 *Resources in areas densely sampled by the marine aggregate industry: North Wales*

- sandwave fields at the mouth of the River Ribble, south-east of Lytham St Anne's

- tidal sandbanks and fields of sandwaves occur in south-east Liverpool Bay near the mouth of the River Mersey.

A possible 150.7Mm³ of sand are located in the additional areas of detailed study (Table 6.2, Figure 6.8).

6.3.5 Cumbria

Much of this sub-region is blanketed by mud or mud-rich sediments. Sediments of sand or coarser grade are confined the the nearshore zone around Cumbria and in areas north and south of the Isle of Man.

Shingle and coarse shingle

A deposit of shingle occurs to the south-west of the Solway Firth, north of Whitehaven. Small areas of shingle also occur in the inner Solway Firth but these are probably of artificial origin. These sediments have a low carbonate content, less than 20%.

Mixed sand and gravel

This sediment category occurs in areas of weaker tidal currents where the sand has not been winnowed.

Sand

A sand-rich nearshore zone occurs between Barrow-in-Furness and Seascale, and in a small zone immediately offshore from Whitehaven. Sand is trapped within the Solway Firth and tidal sandbanks up to 20m thick occur. Tidal sandbanks occur off the north-east of the Isle of Man.

6.4 ADDITIONAL SELECTED AREAS STUDIED

6.4.1 Location

Details on the location and material required for planned beach recharge schemes and maintenance of existing recharge sites were provided in Section 3. Five additional areas for detailed study were chosen which had sufficient detailed data available and were accessible to likely recharge sites. These study areas lie outside the areas intensely sampled by the aggregate industry. Of the sites chosen the area chosen north of Lundy is furthest from potential recharge sites, but is considered because of the very large resource of sand which could supply many sites in southwest England and Wales.

6.4.2 Bristol Channel South

North of Lundy

At the mouth of the Bristol Channel, north of Lundy Island, sandbanks occur in water ranging from 27m to approximately 50m in depth. These banks have been surveyed in some detail by the Hydrographic Office and have been sampled by BGS. Sandwaves commonly occur on top of the banks. The sands here have a carbonate content typically of 10—20%, and live fauna and worm tubes are frequently recorded as contaminants in BGS samples. South of Lundy Island the sands have a high carbonate content, often greater than 40%.

The report database indicates that over 2855Mm³ of potentially workable sand occur in this area (Figure 6.4, Table 6.2). Although this volume estimate relies heavily upon side-scan sonar data, and upon the assumption that the bodies are composed wholly of sand, nevertheless there appears to be a very substantial resource north of Lundy. This has yet to be fully evaluated.

Inner Bristol Channel

Bridgwater Bay and the nearshore area between Cardiff and Newport are areas of mud deposition, but both sand and shingle deposits occur elsewhere in this inner channel region. Deposits in addition to, and often located contiguous to those recorded on the Crown Estate database are recorded on the database. These deposits occur in relatively shallow water, ranging in depth from 5m to 40m. Sediments are likely to include some live fauna and worm tubes, and may be contaminated by coal particles. Seismic evidence has been used to determine the thickness of some shingle-capped sheets in this sub-region, but it is uncertain whether these shingle sheets are wholly composed of coarse material. The large recorded shingle resource in this sub-region (Table 6.2) should therefore be treated with considerable caution. Further geological investigation is recommended, preferably to include drilling boreholes at key offshore sites.

The report database indicates that potentially workable deposits of $544.6Mm^3$ of sand and $126.0Mm^3$ of shingle occur in this region in addition to the volumes recorded on the Crown Estate database (Figure 6.5, Table 6.2).

6.4.3 South Wales

Outer Swansea Bay, off Porthcawl

The depth of water over Nash Sand ranges from 2m to 15m, and over Scarweather Sands from 2m to 20m. The report database indicates that up to $152.0Mm^3$ of sand occur in banks averaging over 0.5m thick in this area in addition to the volumes recorded from Scarweather Sands on the Crown Estate database (Figure 6.6, Table 6.2)

6.4.4 North Wales

Inner Cardigan Bay

Details on bedforms in outer Cardigan Bay are provided by James and Wingfield (1988). West of $4°20'W$ fields of sand ribbons oriented SW-NE, parallel to the direction of maximum tidal currents, occur in the outer part of the bay. They have a length:breadth ratio in the order of 40:1, and may be covered by sandwaves. They may coalesce, but are commonly isolated and pass laterally into sand streaks. The deposits studied in the inner part of Cardigan Bay are spread generally thinly across the sea floor, with thicker accumulations in Barmouth Bay. The sands may contain a live fauna and worm tubes, and occasionally seaweed. The report database indicates up to $42.7Mm^3$ of sand in accumulations averaging over 0.5m in thickness.

6.4.5 Lancs-Cheshire

Lancashire Coast

The Report database indicates that over $144Mm^3$ of sand occur in accumulations averaging over 0.5m in thickness.

Table 6.2 Summary of resources in areas selected for detailed study

	Sand		Sand and gravel		Shingle	
	Volume Mm³	Tonnage Mt	Volume Mm³	Tonnage Mt	Volume Mm³	Tonnage Mt
Bristol Channel South:						
North of Lundy A	3075.4	4920.6	55.8	100.4	2.8	
North of Lundy B	3049.2	4878.7	55.8	100.4	2.8	5.6
North of Lundy C	3039.3	4862.9	54.6	98.3	0.5	1.0
North of Lundy D	2855.1	4568.2	46.8	84.2	0	0
Inner Bristol Channel A	787.8	1260.5	0	0	246.6	493.2
Inner Bristol Channel B	667.0	1067.0	0	0	182.2	364.4
Inner Bristol Channel C	665.2	1064.3	0	0	181.6	363.2
Inner Bristol Channel D	544.6	871.4	0	0	126.0	252.0
South Wales:						
Outer Swansea Bay A	151.6	242.6	0	0	0	0
Outer Swansea Bay B	151.6	242.6	0	0	0	0
Outer Swansea Bay C	149.6	239.4	0	0	0	0
Outer Swansea Bay D	121.6	194.6	0	0	0	0
North Wales:						
Inner Cardigan Bay A	57.3	91.7	0.1	0.18	2.8	5.6
Inner Cardigan Bay B	57.3	91.7	0.1	1.18	2.8	5.6
Inner Cardigan Bay C	42.8	68.5	0	0	0	0
Inner Cardigan Bay D	28.8	46.1	0	0	0	0
Lancs and Cheshire:						
Lancashire Coast A	150.7	241.1	1.1	2.0	0.5	1.0
Lancashire Coast B	150.7	241.1	0.97	1.75	0.5	1.0
Lancashire Coast C	144.3	230.9	0	0	0	0
Lancashire Coast D	128.3	205.3	0	0	0	0

A: estimated total material identified in the areas sampled
B: as A but excluding material in grid squares where fines are the dominant lithology
C: as B but also excluding material in deposits averaging less than 0.5m thick
D: as C but excluding all material in the lowest 0.5m of the deposit

Conversion from cubic metres to tonnage used the following density values:

Shingle	2.0 tonnes/cubic metre
Sand and gravel	1.8 tonnes/cubic metre
Sand	1.6 tonnes/cubic metre

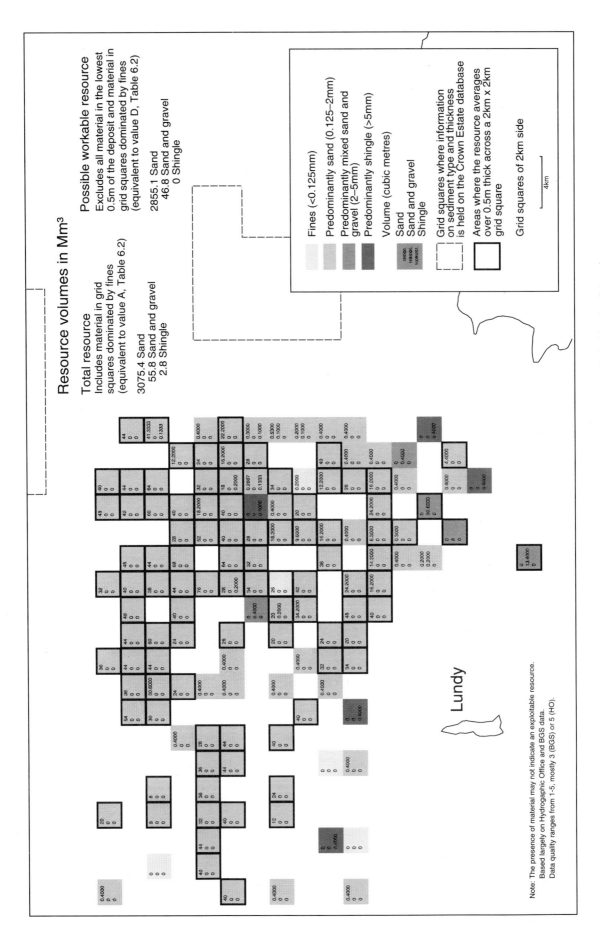

Figure 6.4 *Resources in additional selected areas studied: North of Lundy*

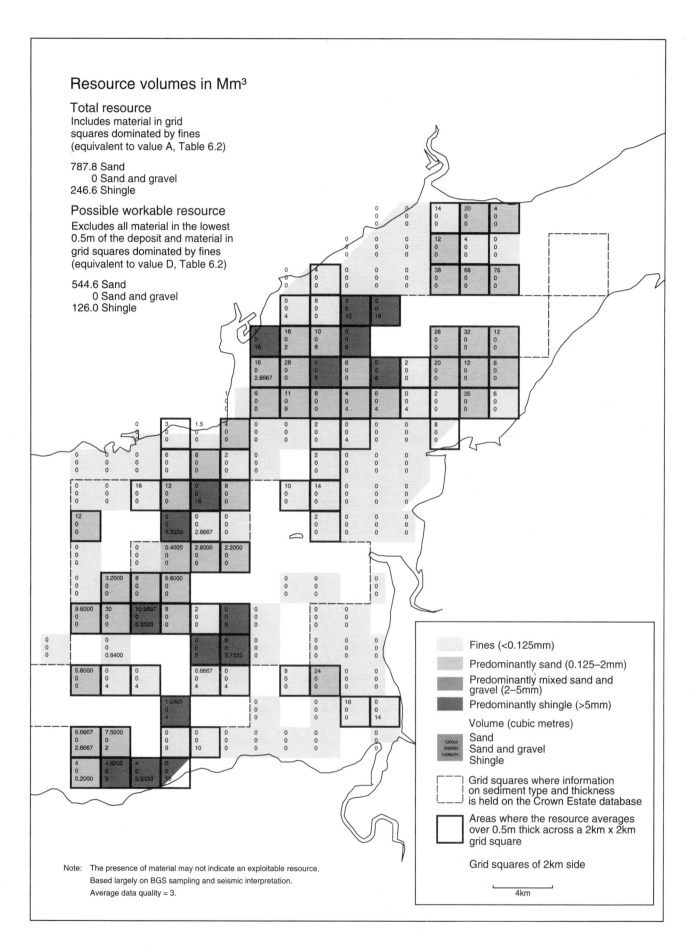

Figure 6.5 *Resources in additional selected areas studied: Inner Bristol Channel*

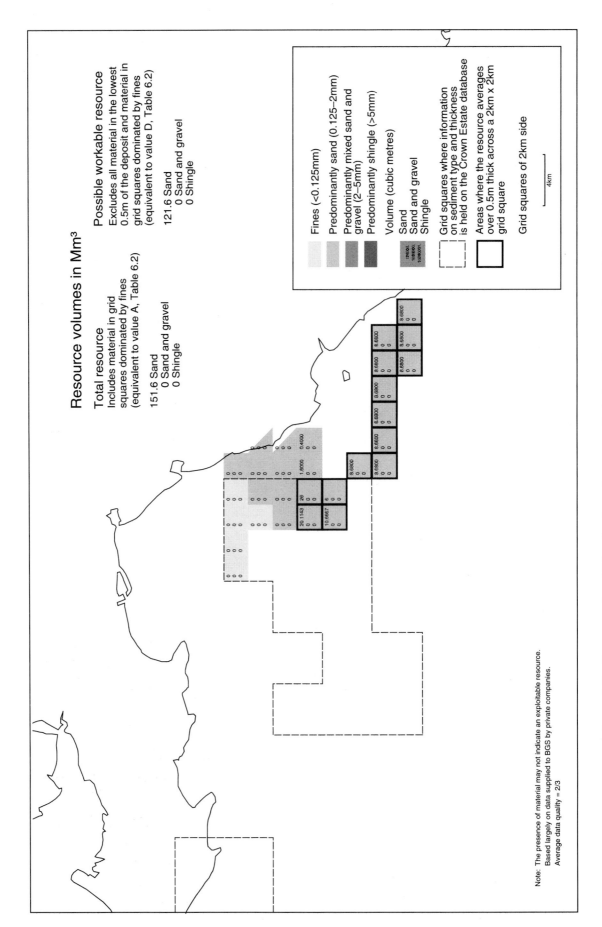

Figure 6.6 *Resources in additional selected areas studied: Outer Swansea Bay, off Porthcawl*

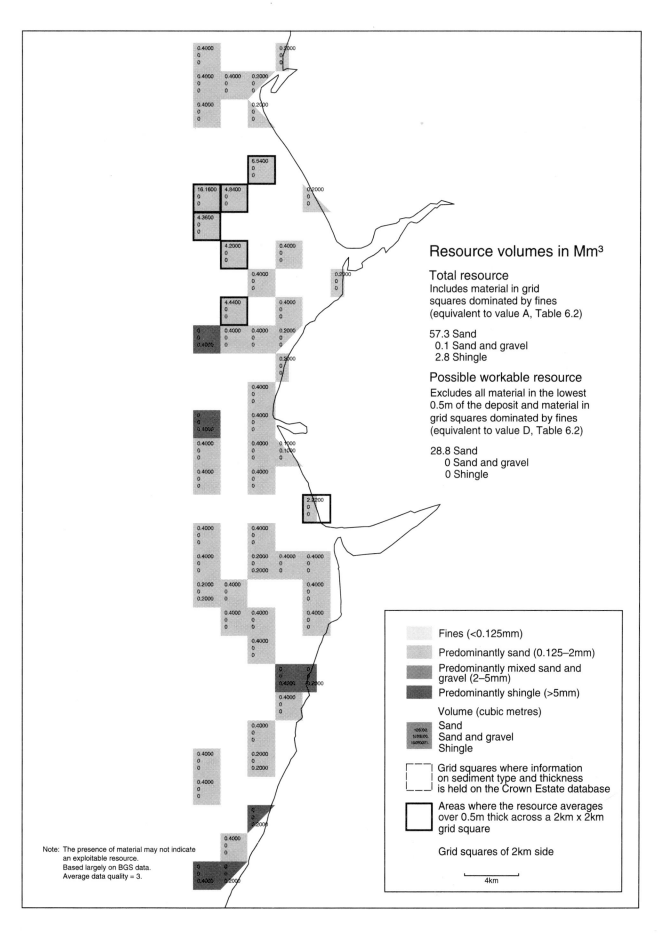

Figure 6.7 *Resources in additional selected areas studied: Inner Cardigan Bay*

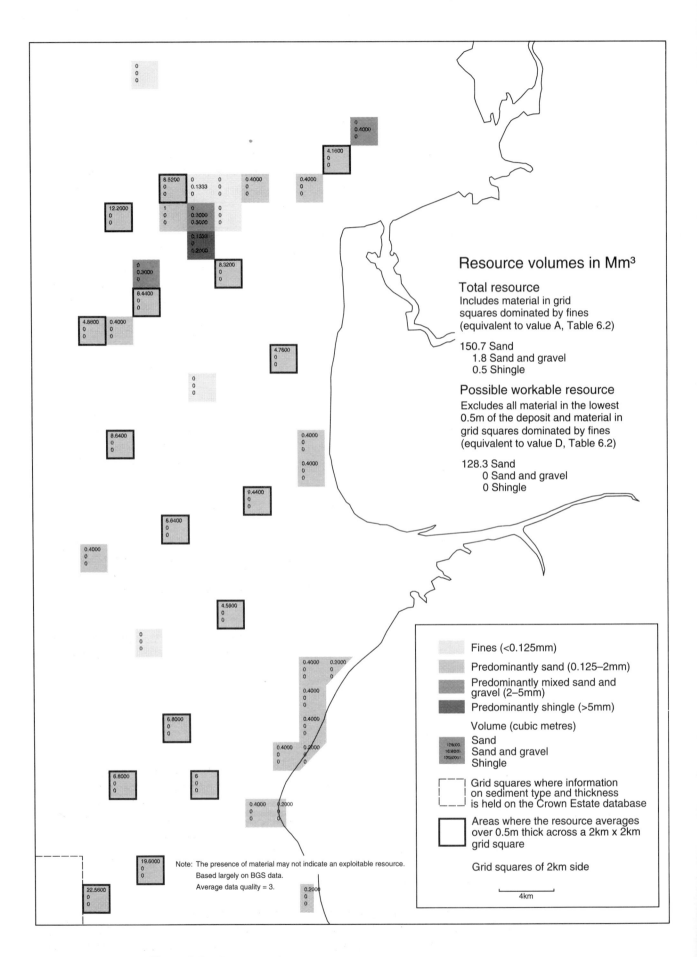

Figure 6.8 *Resources in additional selected areas studied: Lancashire coast*

CIRIA Report 154

7 Alternatives to marine sources for beach recharge

7.1 INTRODUCTION

7.1.1 Background

Most of the material used for beach recharge in the UK comes from marine-dredged sediments. Some schemes, however, have used material won from land sources such as sand and gravel pits. The presence of large stockpiles of waste materials from such industries as china clay production and slate quarrying has led to speculation about their suitability for use in beach recharge. Similarly, there is interest in the use of materials from navigation dredging, which are at present dumped as a waste material, but could be a potential source of material for beach recharge purposes. There is, therefore, a need to investigate the quality, quantity and potential in-service performance of these alternative sources of materials, to consider also the economic and environmental effects of their extraction and usage, and to balance these considerations with the similar constraints involved with the use of marine materials in beach recharge.

An aim of this report is to summarise existing information on alternative sources of materials which are potentially useful for recharge schemes. Such materials include land-won primary aggregates (natural sand, natural gravel and crushed rock), secondary aggregates (mineral wastes) and navigation dredgings.

Data on land-based sources have been collated by the British Geological Survey which has its own mineral databases and an extensive literature archive. Further information has also been obtained from mineral producers, coastal local authorities and other institutions. Data on navigation dredgings have been collated by HR Wallingford from its own information holdings and also from external data searches.

7.1.2 Section outline

This Section describes land-based sources of alternative materials for beach recharge and navigation dredgings. Each sub-section includes details of the location, available volumes, lithology and technical quality of each material. Consideration is also given to the likely mode of transportation of the materials to coastal sites. Where appropriate, indications are provided of relative costs.

The main conclusions are detailed in Section 9 which also includes recommendations for the appropriate use of alternative materials and for the requirement for further investigations.

7.2 LAND-BASED SOURCES

7.2.1 Constraints

The working of any mineral deposit is constrained by a range of factors including quality control, environmental impact, national and local planning controls, the capital costs of production and processing, the provision of suitable and economical transportation facilities, customer acceptance of the mineral product and the ability to displace existing products from the market. Some of the most important constraints relating to potential alternative beach recharge materials are outlined in the following text.

Technical specifications

The principal physical characteristic of a material which affects its performance in beach recharge is its grading. It is generally accepted for sand beaches that the recharge material should be at least as coarse as the existing beach material. Specific recharge schemes usually specify a sediment grading, although this may be to some extent modified to match the grading of the most suitable supply of material. The material should also be clean and non-toxic. In the case of shingle beaches, particle shape may also be specified (i.e. the material should be rounded). In addition, it is usual to specify that the materials should be of a similar nature to those occurring naturally on the local coastline.

Even when a material is technically suitable for a particular scheme, there may be resistance to its use due to a perception of inferior quality. In order for the customer to accept the material, it must be fully demonstrated that it is both reliable and consistent.

Geographical locations

As haulage costs are a significant element of the cost of any bulk fill material, local deposits are usually preferred for any civil engineering scheme. The geographical location of available materials is therefore a fundamental factor in the choice of materials for beach recharge schemes.

Transport considerations

The large volumes of material required for beach recharge schemes are usually most effectively moved by sea-going bulk transport, from where the sediment is pumped to the point of use. In some schemes, road haulage has been used, but this requires careful consideration of road access to many beach recharge sites. In some cases it may be economic to deliver land-sourced materials by sea.

Costs

The costs of producing aggregates derive principally from the capital and running costs of extraction and processing, together with the cost of transportation to the point of use. Other costs may include royalties or an environmental component, such as costs involved in site restoration or extraction monitoring procedures.

Production costs of land-based materials, both primary and secondary, and marine-dredged materials are variable, reflecting the variety of materials worked and the various types of extraction. It is therefore difficult to compare the production costs of the various materials and there is no clear advantage to any material.

The cost of transportation means that the extractive industry generally operates from quarries or pits which are comparatively close to their markets. In the South-East, however, substantial volumes of aggregates are imported (chiefly by rail or ship) from neighbouring regions and the trend here is towards longer-distance transportation.

Environmental considerations

All surface mineral working has some adverse effects on the environment. The main problems with land-based pits and quarries are visual intrusion on the landscape of both the extraction site and any associated waste tips, although noise, dust and transportation of the material all give rise to concern. Other aspects such as loss of land, hydrogeological impacts and the need for site restoration may be equally important environmental considerations. Such environmental impacts need to be considered on a case-by-case basis. There is generally, however, an environmental benefit in substituting secondary aggregates (mineral wastes) for primary aggregates.

7.2.2 Sand and gravel

Sand and gravel are naturally occurring particulate deposits. They are mostly relatively young, unconsolidated and superficial, deposits derived from the redistribution of rock weathering products by water, ice or wind. They are usually Quaternary alluvial (river channel, terrace or fan deposits) or glacial deposits (morainic, fluvioglacial outwash or periglacial materials).

Sand and gravel may also occur in older (Solid) consolidated or partially consolidated bedded deposits as conglomerates, pebbly sandstones or sands.

Superficial (Quaternary) deposits

River sand and gravel
Extensive spreads of sand and gravel occur along the bottom of many major river valleys and as terraces on valley sides. The deposits from the Thames, Trent and Severn are important sources of sand and gravel.

Glacial sand and gravel
Glacial deposits were formed in close association with ice sheets and include fluvioglacial deposits laid down by meltwaters from the decaying ice. They are much more variable than river gravels both in their lithology, particle size and in their geographical extent. Although geological maps show extensive spreads of glacial deposits in England and Wales, considerable variations occur within a given deposit and resources of glacial sand and gravel can be difficult to identify. Nevertheless, aggregate workings in glacial deposits are widespread, particularly in East Anglia.

Wind-blown sands
Deposits of wind blown sands occur in south Humberside, Lincolnshire and around Merseyside and Manchester, but they are not extracted for aggregates as their grain size is both too fine and too uniform for use in concrete.

Solid deposits

Sands
Loose or partially consolidated sands occur in geological formations of varying geological age. The oldest deposits occur at the base of the Permian in north-east England. Jurassic sands are worked for mortar sand near Oxford and in Wiltshire. The Cretaceous Greensand is an important source of sand in southern England and is quarried extensively at several sites. Such sands tend to be relatively fine and are mainly extracted for mortar, asphalt or industrial sands. Sandy formations are also extensive in the Tertiary rocks of southern England, but the deposits are mostly too fine-grained for use as aggregates, although some building sand is produced.

Sands and gravels
Substantial deposits of loosely bound sandy pebble beds of Triassic age occur in the Midlands and in the area around Exeter. They are an important local source of gravel and sand for concrete.

Production of sand and gravel in England and Wales

Table 7.1 shows the production of land-won sand and gravel in England and Wales in 1989. Since 1989 production of aggregates has fallen due to the depressed state of the construction industry. The greater downturn in housebuilding and commercial construction compared with road building and maintenance has resulted in sand and gravel production declining faster than crushed rock production. In 1991 production of land-won sand and gravel in England and Wales had fallen to 73 253 thousand tonnes (BGS, 1993) and may have declined further since, as there has been no improvement in economic conditions affecting the construction industry.

The bulk of the production is from the superficial deposits, the river and terrace gravels of southern England and the Midlands. Glacial and fluvioglacial material assumes a greater importance in northern England and East Anglia. Only relatively small amounts of sand and gravel are extracted from the solid formations; the main sources are the Triassic rocks of the Midlands and the Greensand of south-east England. Figures 7.1 and 7.2 show the current distribution of sand and gravel pits in England and Wales from both superficial (Quaternary) and solid deposits.

Table 7.1 Production of land-won sand and gravel in England and Wales (source: DoE, 1991)

Producing Region	Production (thousands of tonnes)	Production as a % of the England and Wales total
South East	37 653	36.9
East Anglia	9 359	9.2
East Midlands	16 032	15.7
West Midlands	14 458	14.2
South West	6 781	6.6
North West	6 120	6.0
Yorks & Humberside	5 968	5.8
Northern	3 585	3.5
South Wales	247	0.2
North Wales	1 819	1.8
TOTAL	102 022	100.0

Use of land-won sand and gravel in beach recharge

Land-won sand and gravel has been used in a small number of beach recharge schemes such as in the replenishment of Hurst Spit by the New Forest District Council. In this scheme, a coarse beach material was required with a D_{50} of 16mm, and oversized (i.e. reject) material from local gravel pits has been used for maintenance. In 1989, 30 000 tonnes of this material was used. The current plans for Hurst Spit involve the use of much larger volumes of material dredged from Shingles Bank in the Needles Channel. The scheme will, if approved, use around 600 000 tonnes of coarse, marine-dredged material.

Most land deposits of sand and gravel are capable of producing materials which are likely to be suitable for beach recharge. They are, however, generally not used for this purpose primarily because of the difficulties and the costs of transporting large volumes of material across land to the point-of-use on a beach.

7.2.3 Crushed rock aggregates

Most hard ("Solid") rocks are potentially suitable for crushed rock coarse aggregates. However, demanding specifications of aggregate materials used in road pavements and structural concrete require that high quality crushed rock aggregate materials are used. These are commonly derived from indurated and cemented sedimentary rocks and from the tougher, crystalline types of igneous or metamorphic rocks. In Britain, the geologically young South-East is almost devoid of local hard rock sources and crushed rock (chiefly limestone and igneous rocks) is transported into the region by rail, road and ship.

Sedimentary rocks

Limestones of Carboniferous age

Most limestones are hard and durable and useful for aggregate. They are common rock types and usually occur in thick beds which are structurally simple and easy to quarry. As a consequence, they are widely extracted for aggregate materials, as well as for cement manufacture and for industrial processes which utilise the chemical properties of the stone. Limestones of particularly good aggregate qualities occur in the Carboniferous, and the Carboniferous Limestone currently provides about 60% of national crushed rock aggregate production. It represents the largest resource of good-quality aggregate in British sedimentary rocks. The main occurrences are in the Mendips, in South and North Wales, in the central and southern Pennines and on the borders of the Lake District.

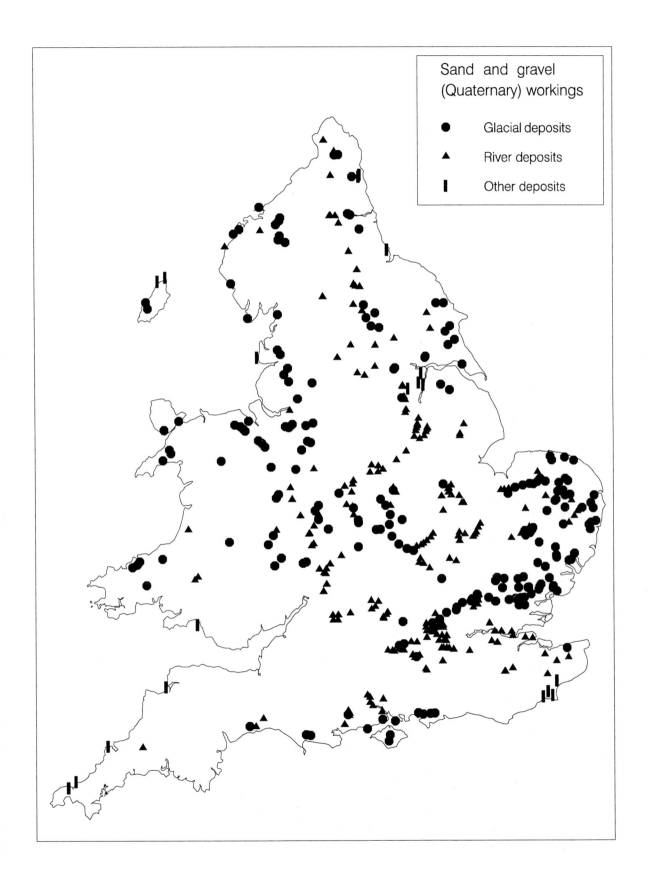

Figure 7.1 *Distribution of sand and gravel workings from superficial (Quaternary) deposits*

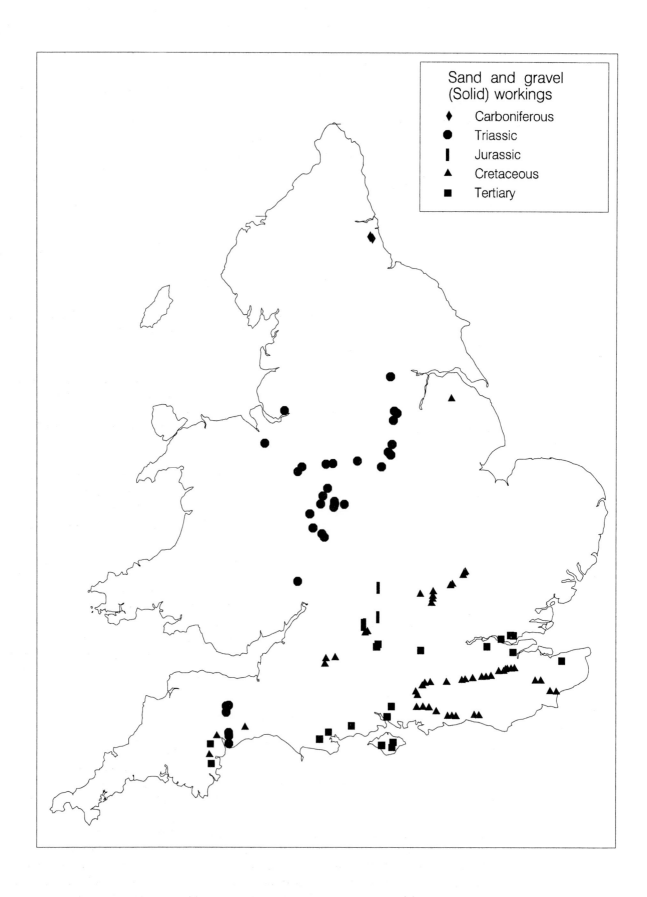

Figure 7.2 *Distribution of sand and gravel workings from Solid deposits*

CIRIA Report 154

Limestones of other ages

Other major limestones worked for aggregates include the Permian magnesian limestones which occur in a narrow outcrop between Durham and Nottingham, and the Devonian limestones between Torquay and Plymouth. The younger Jurassic and Cretaceous limestones (notably Cretaceous chalks) of eastern and southern England are generally too weak and porous to be used as aggregates.

Silicate clastic rocks

Sandstones, gritstones, arkoses (feldspathic sandstones) and greywackes (impure sandstones) are all used as aggregate materials, although their strength, porosity and durability directly depends on the degree of cementation. The sandstones and greywackes of the South Wales Coalfield and in North Devon are capable of producing strong, durable aggregate materials. Weaker and more porous aggregates are produced from the Carboniferous sandstones of the central and northern Pennines. Particularly strong aggregates are produced from quartzitic sandstones near Nuneaton and in Anglesey. A minor source of calcareous sandstone aggregates in southeastern England is represented by the Kentish Ragstone of the Cretaceous Lower Greensand.

Igneous rocks

Igneous rocks are widely quarried for crushed rock aggregates. The finer-grained varieties (such as dolerite, basalt or porphyry) are often preferred due to their high strength, although large amounts of aggregates are also produced from coarse-grained rocks (such as granites and diorites). The suitability of these rocks for aggregate depends on mineralogy, texture and degree of weathering and alteration.

Dolerites and basalts are quarried for aggregates in Devon, Wales and the Welsh Borders, in Derbyshire and in the Whin Sill of Northumberland. Granitic rocks and diorites are worked in large quarries in Leicestershire and supply large amounts of crushed rock aggregate to southern England. Granites are also extracted for aggregates in southwest England and in the Lake District.

The Strontian granite beside Loch Linnhe in south-west Scotland is being developed for crushed rock aggregates at Glensanda superquarry, with distribution exclusively by sea-going bulk carrier to southern England and other markets. Other planned coastal superquarry developments include proposals to extract anorthosite from South Harris, and similar rocks from south-west Norway.

Metamorphic rocks

The wide range of metamorphic rock types is reflected in their variable usefulness as aggregate. Coarse or medium grained, massive, granular rocks such as gneisses, quartzites, marbles and hornfels generally provide high-quality aggregates, whereas foliated and platy rocks such as schists and phyllites are usually weaker and may be less durable. In England and Wales there are few sources of metamorphic rock aggregate materials, apart from local deposits in Cornwall, Anglesey and Cumbria.

Production of crushed rock aggregates in England and Wales

Table 7.2 shows the production of crushed rock aggregates in England and Wales in 1989. The current economic recession has resulted in some reduction in output of crushed rock aggregates. In 1991 crushed rock production in England and Wales totalled 126 300 thousand tonnes (BGS, 1993), a reduction of 16% of peak output in 1989.

The bulk of the production is from the Carboniferous Limestone. Many very large quarries are situated in this limestone, particularly in the Mendip Hills, the Peak District, both North and South Wales and the southern and eastern fringes of the Lake District. Several large quarries in the Mendips have rail linked transportation to the south-east market. A further large and important source of crushed rock aggregate with rail links to the south-east region is the granite and associated igneous rocks of Leicestershire. Production of roadstone aggregate from the Leicestershire quarries amount to 25% of total igneous rock output in Great Britain. The large production figures for the South West region is largely the result of Carboniferous Limestone quarrying, and the similarly large figure for the East Midlands region reflects the importance of both Carboniferous limestone and igneous rock supplies. The Glensanda quarry in Scotland is the only operational coastal superquarry in the UK; it currently produces 5 million tonnes of crushed granite aggregates per annum and, when fully operational, its annual output is scheduled to be 7.5 million tonnes.

Table 7.2 Production of crushed rock aggregates in England and Wales (source: DoE, 1991).

Producing Region	Production in thousands of tonnes per annum	Production as a percentage of England and Wales total production
South East	3 146	2.1
East Anglia	674	0.4
East Midlands	33 651	22.4
West Midlands	12 900	8.6
South West	38 213	25.4
North West	7 535	5.0
Yorks and Humberside	16 936	11.3
Northern	13 810	9.2
South Wales	13 137	8.7
North Wales	10 497	6.9
TOTAL	150 500	100.0

Figures 7.3 to 7.7 show the current distribution of crushed rock quarrying in England and Wales. Sedimentary rock quarries for limestone, sandstone and chalk are separately distinguished; as are slate quarries. Quarries of metamorphic rocks other than of slates, and, igneous rocks are shown on one figure.

Use of crushed rock in beach recharge

Although some crushed rock has been used for beach recharge in North Wales, there is currently little demand for this material on beaches. The use of crushed rock in recharge would have a major impact on their appearance and amenity use. In addition, the demand for beach recharge material is in the south-east, which is devoid of "hard" rocks suitable for the production of crushed stone (see Figures 7.3 to 7.7).

Quarry wastes may provide potential sources of material as described in the following section.

7.2.4 Secondary aggregates

Many mineral wastes (secondary aggregates) are technically capable of substituting for primary aggregates obtained from sand and gravel pits, rock quarries and marine dredgers. Currently, about 10% of total aggregate demand is met by secondary aggregate material. Government guidelines recognise the significant potential for meeting long term aggregates demand from waste and recycled sources (DoE, 1994). The Government estimates that 40 million tonnes of secondary aggregates will be used annually in England by the year 2001 and this will rise to 55 million tonnes per annum by the year 2006, representing 12% of the total aggregate supply for the period 1992 to 2006.

There are many different types of mineral waste, but by far the most important are:

- colliery spoil
- china clay waste
- slate waste
- power station ashes

- metalliferous slags
- demolition wastes
- road planings.

There are particularly large stockpiles of waste materials from coal mining, china clay production and slate quarrying. If the use of waste materials in the construction and civil engineering industries could be increased it would have the dual environmental benefit of reducing a waste disposal problem and slowing the rate of demand for primary aggregates.

The major sources of secondary aggregates in Great Britain and their potential for utilisation in the construction industry has been reviewed in a recent report (Whitbread *et al.*, 1991) commissioned by the Department of the Environment. A summary of the occurrence of secondary aggregate material is given in Table 7.3 and Figure 7.8.

Colliery spoil

Colliery spoil is the waste material produced during coal mining. It consists of a mix of fine and coarse rock particles (mudstone, siltstone, shale and sandstone) and carbonaceous matter, and is generally of a greyish, shaley, appearance. Large colliery spoil tips occur in Yorkshire, Nottinghamshire and South Wales, and smaller volumes occur in other coalfield areas. In north-east England some colliery waste has been disposed of at sea.

The main use of colliery spoil is as constructional fill in road embankments and building sites. At the peak of motorway construction, in the 1970s, some 8 million tonnes/year were being used as bulk fill. Other commercial outlets for colliery spoil include brickmaking (mainly in Scotland), the manufacture of lightweight aggregate, and cement making. The main problem with the use of colliery spoil is its variability within a deposit. For this reason generally colliery spoil is suitable for use only in undemanding situations (e.g. for fill); although in some circumstances it can be upgraded by processing (washing, screening, blending) with a consequent increase in cost.

Table 7.3 Sources of secondary aggregates in Great Britain (adapted from Whitbread *et al.*, 1991)

Materials	Annual Production (Mt)	Stockpiles (Mt)	Location	Main end use
Colliery spoil	45	3600	Coal mining areas	Constructional fill
China clay waste	27	600	Cornwall Devon	Concrete, roadstone
Slate waste	6	500	North Wales Lake District SW England	Type 1 roadstone
Power station ash	13	(some)	Power stations	Constructional fill blockmaking, lightweight aggregate
Blast furnace slag	4	(some)	Steelworks	Aggregate, lightweight aggregate
Steel slag	2	12	Steelworks	Roadstone
Demolition waste	24	-----	Widespread	Constructional fill, recycled aggregate
Road planings	7	-----	Widespread	Constructional fill, minor roads

Despite the availability of large volumes of colliery waste in England and Wales, there is little scope for its use in beach recharge schemes due to its unsuitable lithology and variable quality. It may, however, be suitable in schemes involving reclamation of land from the sea.

China clay waste

China clay waste results from the extraction of china clay (kaolin) from kaolinised granites in Cornwall and Devon. The area around St Austell has the greatest production, with other quarries centred on Bodmin Moor and Lee Moor, Plymouth. The processing of the kaolinised granite results in the production of large quantities of granular waste material. Whilst it is primarily a sand, some 10% of it could be classified as coarse aggregate.

For each tonne of china clay produced, there are about nine tonnes of waste, of this about four tonnes are granular waste (china clay sand) material. Other fractions include rockwaste (known locally at Stent) 2.5 tonnes, overburden 1.5 tonnes, and mica wastes 1 tonne. The production of china clay sand is around 10 to 12 million tonnes per year, most of which is stockpiled. Sand is not usually separated from the other wastes, although English China Clay International (ECCI) do produce some mainly sand tips and estimate that some 100 million tonnes of china clay sand is accessible. The sand is typically a quartz sand (85%—88% quartz) with some tourmaline (9%—11%) and smaller amounts of feldspar (2%—3%) and mica (1%—1.5%). Details of the chemical properties and certain physical properties of the sand are given in Table 7.4.

Table 7.4 Typical chemical and physical properties of china clay sand (source: ECCI)

Chemical Analysis:	Silica	(% SiO_2)	87.20
	Alumina	(% Al_2O_3)	7.40
	Iron Oxide	(% Fe_2O_3)	1.59
	Titanium Oxide	(% TiO_2)	0.19
	Calcium Oxide	(% CaO)	0.10
	Magnesium Oxide	(% MgO)	0.29
	Potash	(% K_2O)	1.12
	Soda	(% Na_2O)	0.08
	% Loss on ignition		1.06
Physical Properties:	Specific Gravity	2.60 to 2.65	
	Water absorption (%)	0.5 to 1.9	
	Bulk Density (Concrete Sand)-loose (Kg/m3)	1540	
	Bulk Density (Concrete Sand)-compacted (Kg/m3)	1650	

China clay sand is available for use in the construction industry in three forms;

- dump sand - unprocessed material straight from the pit or tip
- screened sand - dump sand, dry screened to remove oversize material
- processed sand - sand from the pit or dump which is processed through a washing and grading plant.

Technically, the processed china clay sand is able to meet the required specifications for building and concreting sands and the unprocessed sand is an acceptable fill material.

In Cornwall and Devon china clay sand is used extensively in the construction industry as concrete aggregate, as a mortar sand and in road sub-bases and constructional fill. About 1.5 million tonnes per year are used in construction. 20 million cubic metres of dump sand was used as constructional fill at Colliford, Cornwall. Recent road-building schemes that used china clay sand in their construction include the Ivybridge, Lee Moor, Camborne, Bodmin and Liskeard by-passes. Small amounts have also been used in several building schemes in southeast England where it was preferred over local aggregates supplies due to the white finish of the concrete produced with china clay sand.

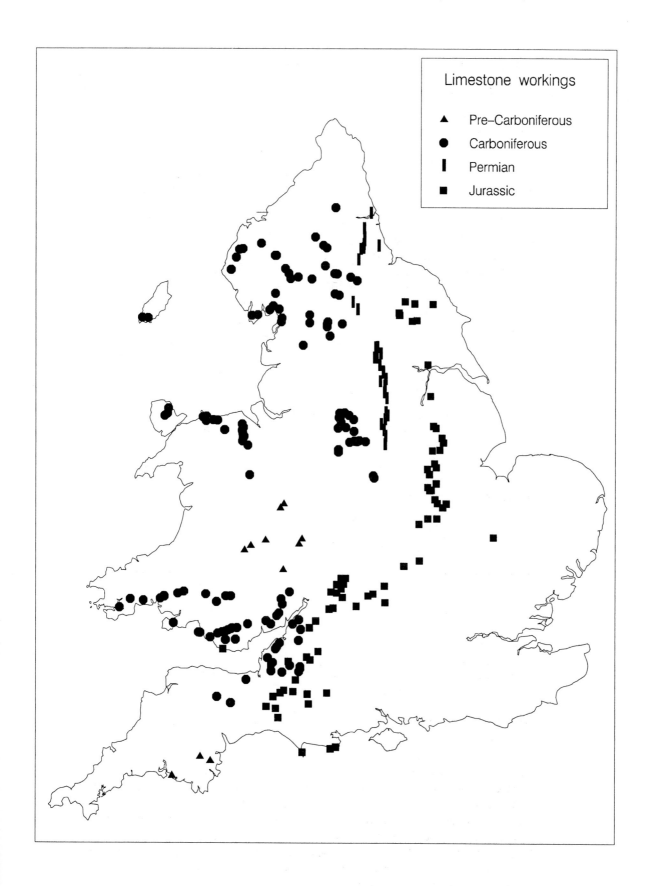

Figure 7.3 *Location of limestone quarries (excluding chalk)*

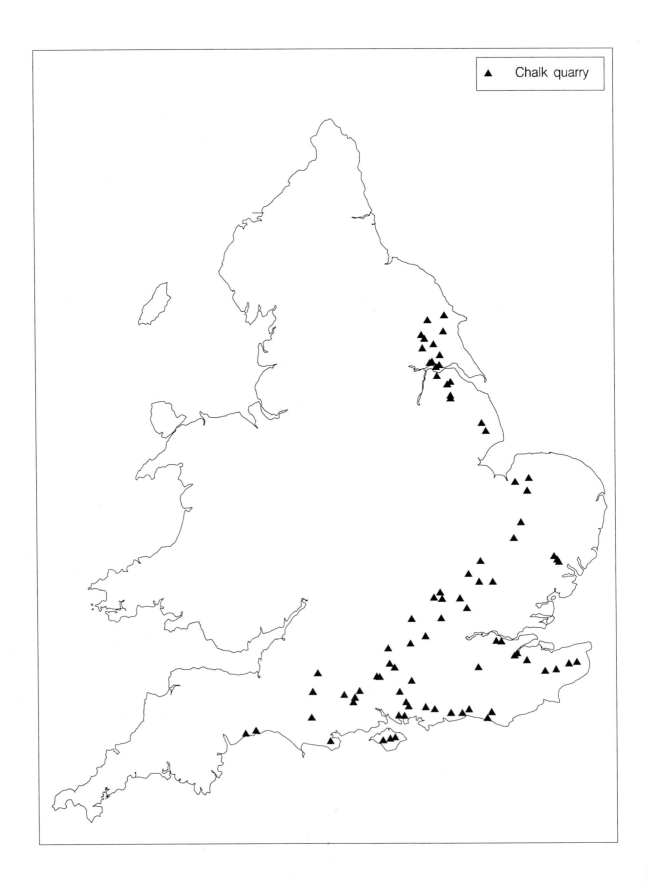

Figure 7.4 *Location of chalk quarries*

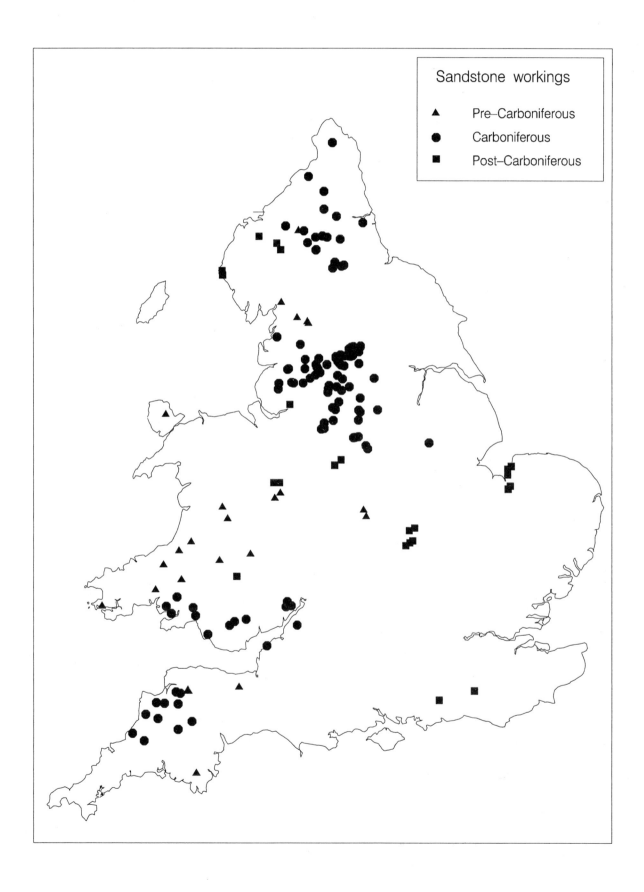

Figure 7.5 *Location of sandstone quarries*

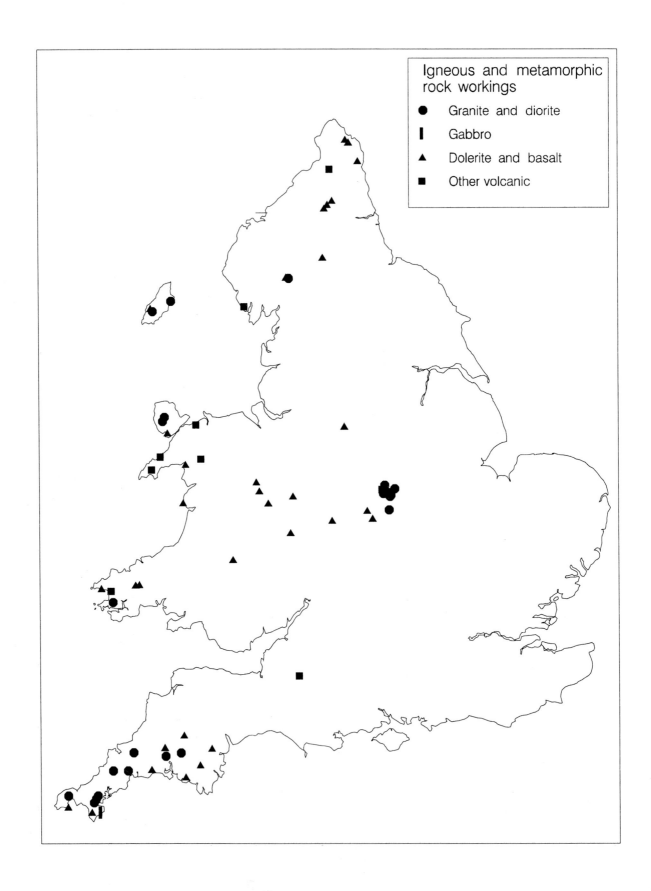

Figure 7.6 *Location of igneous and metamorphic rock quarries*

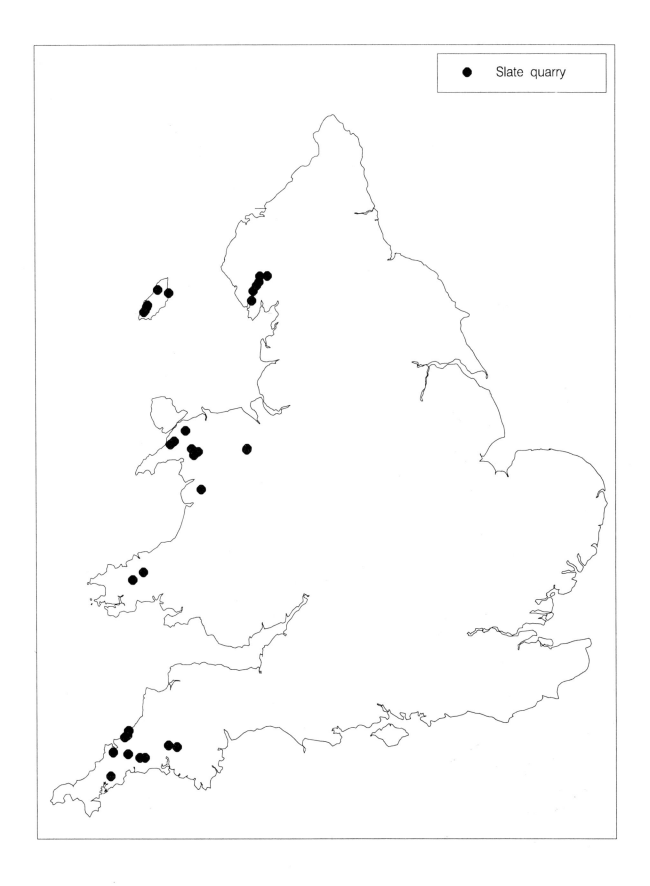

Figure 7.7   *Location of slate quarries*

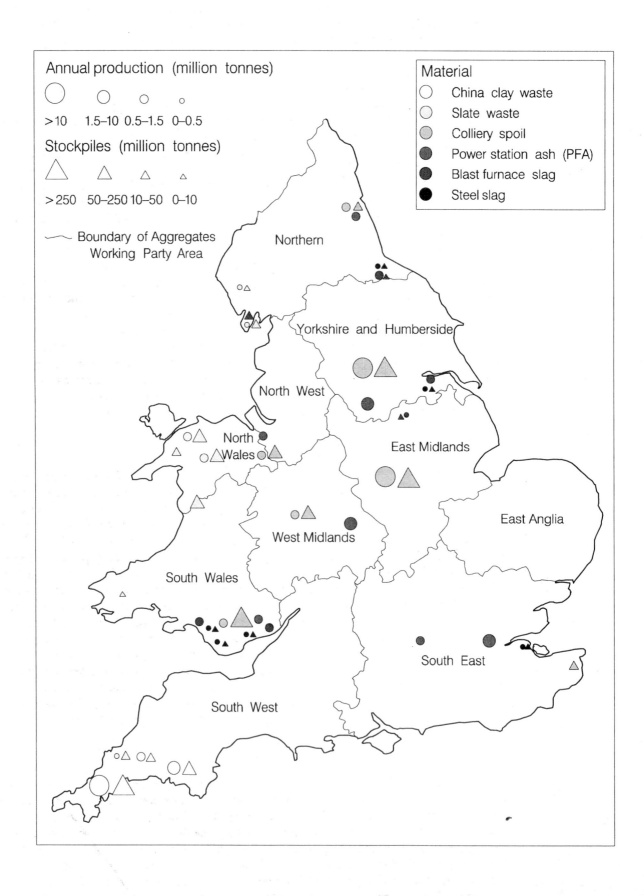

Figure 7.8 *Location of mineral wastes in Britain*

China clay sand is potentially an alternative resource of beach recharge material, and has been used for beach reclamation at Saltash (on the Tamar) and at Crinis Beach in St Austell Bay. The sand is similar to a Zone 1 (category C) concreting sand (BS 882) with a D_{50} between 1mm and 3mm. It also contains very small amounts of clay and other fines (material less than 75 microns). Grading curves of china clay sands are given in Figures 7.9 and 7.10. Beach slopes in china clay sand are expected to be about 1:7 which is similar to the profile of shingle beaches.

The most serious drawback for increased use of china clay sand is its high transport cost due to its relatively remote location. Road, rail and sea transportation are all options which can be considered, although sea-going bulk transport is likely to be most suitable for beach recharge schemes. A recent feasibility study (Whitbread et al., 1991) into bulk transportation of china clay sand to the South East, examined all three transport options and their costings. Road transport was thought to be not feasible, mainly on the grounds of cost, but also because of the limitations of the road system. Road transport, however, does have the advantage of being flexible and is able to deliver directly to site. Rail transportation would be preferable to road transportation, but the existing rail infrastructure in the South West would require costly major improvements to carry large freight trains regularly. Sea transportation of china clay sand from, for example, a port facility at Falmouth or Par would first require the materials to be transported from St Austell to the dock by such means as rail, conveyor, pipeline or aerial ropeway. The capital and running costs of such a loading facility would be considerable and, together with shipping and unloading costs, would result in a delivered price which would not work economically. Recent experience by ECCI in quoting for fill material for the Severn crossing and the Cardiff Bay Barrage, has shown that even though no charge was made for the material, the loading and transport costs resulted in a "delivered" price twice that of sand from local sources. Whitbread et al., (1991) in their study of the utilisation of mineral wastes, conclude that the wider and increased use of china clay sand could only be achieved by considerable financial support from Government measures, (by such changes as a tax on primary aggregates, or a subsidy on the uses of secondary aggregates).

Slate waste

The quarrying of slate for roofing has been an active industry in parts of western Britain for hundreds of years and has resulted in vast quantities of slate waste (Table 7.3), particularly in North Wales but also in the Lake District and Cornwall. Slate waste is, in effect, a crushed rock and is therefore potentially useful for all applications requiring coarse aggregates. Some slate waste has been used in local schemes for fill or road construction (Type 1 and Type 2 sub-base aggregate). The flaky shape of slate waste excludes it from some aggregate uses (e.g. concrete), and some processing is required to improve particle shape and hence its compaction properties, even when used as roadstone or fill. Slate waste is inert and, although the tips are usually relatively clean, the waste occurs in a wide range of particle sizes. Processed (crushed and screened) slate waste is a potential source of shingle-sized material for beach recharge, particularly in those areas of western Britain with similar natural beach material. There is, however, little local demand in these areas. The use of slate aggregate in areas of higher demand such as the south and east, will depend largely on the costs of transportation by rail or sea, although other factors such as appearance and durability may also affect the choice of material. Whitbread et al. (1991) conclude that only a small financial or administrative incentive may be required to initiate bulk shipping of slate waste to the South East.

Demolition and construction wastes

Approximately 24 million tonnes of demolition and construction wastes arise each year. Most of this material is dumped in landfill sites, but around 11 million tonnes are recycled for use in construction, mostly as fill, but also as graded aggregates. The waste materials are a mix of concrete, bricks and blocks as well as steel, timber and plastic. In order to produce acceptable fill, a certain amount of processing is required involving extraction of non-mineral material from the rubble, prior to rough crushing by mobile plant. Graded aggregates are mostly derived from concrete waste and are technically suitable for use as Type 1 and Type 2 roadstone. They require sophisticated crushing and screening plants and at the moment there are very few such fixed site plants in Great Britain. It is likely that production of aggregates from recycled construction and demolition wastes will increase in the future and will lead to the establishment of more fixed-site recycling plants. There will remain, however, the constraint of overcoming consumer resistance to the use of recycled materials. In the case of materials suitable for beach recharge, the technical performance of the material must meet certain physical specifications, and the material should not contain any contaminants. It is also an advantage if the material has an attractive appearance and is similar to the natural beach material.

Others

Other waste products which are used, or have the potential for use as aggregates, include furnace bottom ash (Fba) from coal-fired power stations and blast furnace and steel slags. Table 7.3 shows the annual outputs of these waste products.

Furnace bottom ash consists of fused conglomerates of ash particles which fall to the bottom of the furnace during the burning of pulverised coal. The main residue from this process is pulverised flue ash (Pfa) which is a fine powder and is collected from the flue gases by electrostatic precipitation. Pfa is used as fill or in the manufacture of concrete blocks. Fba particles are coarser and heavier than those of Pfa, with a particle size from coarse sand to over 300mm size. In 1990, about 2.5 million tonnes of Fba was produced in England and Wales (Whitbread *et al.*, 1991) and over 90% of this was sold to the construction industry for use as a road sub-base material and as a concreting aggregate.

Blast-furnace slag is produced as a by-product of pig-iron manufacture and results from the fusion of limestone with impurities in the iron ore. Steel slag is produced in the steel making process when pig iron is converted to steel. The slag is a mixture of various impurities and flux materials. Chemically and mineralogically both blast-furnace and steel slags are very complex mixtures of silica, alumina, calcium and magnesium oxides. Steel slag also contains some reactive lime and magnesia which can cause expansion on contact with water. Blast-furnace slag is either air-cooled or water-cooled and the type of cooling process influences the physical character of the slag. Most slag is air-cooled and is a dense, crystalline rock-like material. Water-cooled slag yields a granular, glassy product. Air-cooled blast-furnace slag can be processed to produce most forms of concreting aggregate and roadstone. Granulated slag (water-cooled) is used as a cement, in glass manufacture and as a lightweight aggregate. Blast-furnace slag is produced at Teesside, Scunthorpe, Llanwern and Port Talbot and all output is fully utilised in the construction industry.

Steel slag is denser than blast-furnace slag. Steel slags produced by the basic oxygen process (BOS) contain high free-lime contents. Steel slags produced from electric arc furnaces (EAF) has a lower free-lime content. For this reason, about 50% of EAF slags (from the Sheffield area) are after processing, used for roadstone, whereas only very small amounts of BOS slag find a secondary use.

There are many other mineral wastes which have the potential to be used as secondary aggregates:

- metalliferous mine wastes (e.g. tin, lead, zinc ores)
- fluorspar mine wastes
- waste foundry sand
- waste railway ballast
- quarry wastes
- glass waste.

Most of these miscellaneous mineral wastes occur in relatively small volumes, although small stockpiles of mine waste occur at many old mining sites. Most of the wastes from modern mining and quarrying is disposed of on site in restoration and landscaping schemes. Some spent railway ballast is recycled for use as roadstone.

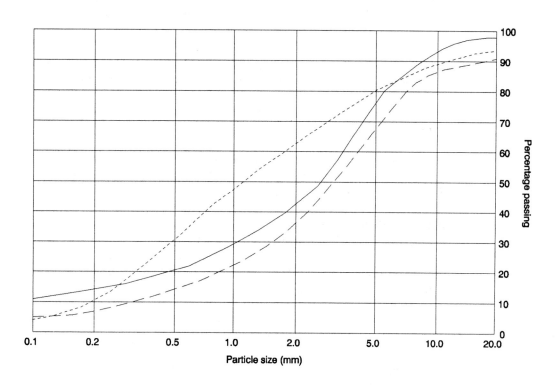

Figure 7.9 *Particle size distribution of three samples of china clay sand from Cornwall*

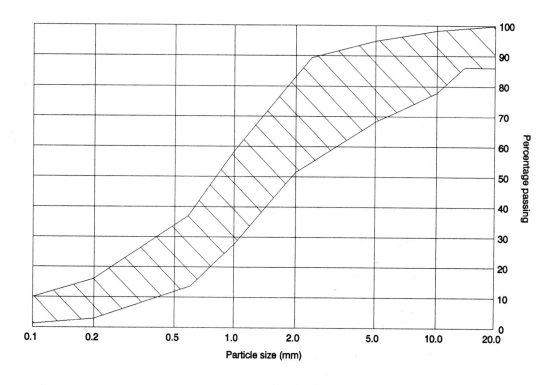

Figure 7.10 *Typical grading envelope of unprocessed china clay granular material*

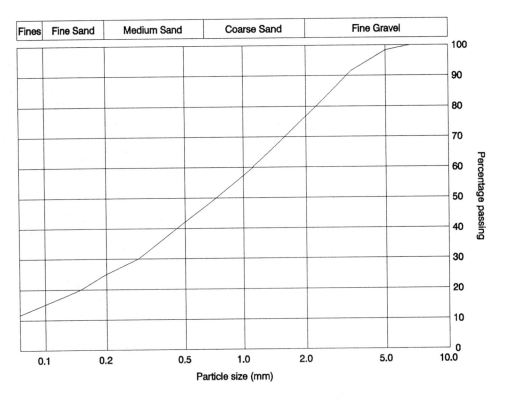

Figure 7.11 *Grading characteristics of Glensanda granite "dust"*

The large-scale quarrying of granite for crushed rock coarse aggregate at Glensanda in south-west Scotland (see Section 7.3.2) is resulting in the accumulation of large amounts of quarry fines ("dust"). Currently, there are estimated to be around 6 million tonnes of fines stockpiled at the Glensanda coastal superquarry, and annual production of this largely waste product is scheduled to increase in future years. The bulk density of the Glensanda fines is 1.55 tonnes/m³ and the material is strong, durable and clean. A grading curve is given in Figure 7.11. This shows that, though the granite "dust" is finer than china clay sand (see Figures 7.9 and 7.10), it is mostly of coarse and medium-sand size, with around 15% of fines (material less than 0.1mm). It is similar in size to material used for recharge of sand beaches. It is, however, composed of finely crushed granite, not quartz sand, and may, therefore, be unacceptable for beach recharge for reasons of amenity.

7.3 NAVIGATION DREDGINGS

7.3.1 Introduction

An assessment has been made of the volumes of material disposed offshore as a result of maintenance and capital dredging operations in the UK. This analysis has been undertaken using data available in the public records maintained by MAFF. These records indicate the volumes of material annually dumped at the licensed offshore sites around the UK. There are approximately 150 of these sites in use in any one year. The analysis has been carried out using data from 1985 to 1992. The public register does not contain information concerning the nature of the material dumped.

For this analysis the licensed sites have been grouped into 30 regions around the UK (Figure 7.12). For these regions the average annual disposal of maintenance and capital dredged material for the period 1985—1992 is given in Table 7.5.

An assessment has been made of the type of material (cohesive or sandy) dumped in the 8 regions that account for about 85% of the annual average disposal of maintenance material. This information is presented in Table 7.6.

7.3.2 Maintenance dredged material

Table 7.5 indicates the main areas of maintenance dredging in the UK. The majority of material dredged for maintenance is cohesive (Table 7.6). The estuaries of the Humber and the Severn account for about 60% of the entire UK dredging and marine disposal. The approximate breakdown of cohesive and non-cohesive material dumped in these regions has been determined through discussions with the Port Authorities. This breakdown indicates that about 20% of the material dumped offshore is sand.

Annual maintenance disposal on the south coast of England is about 2 million tonnes. This disposal is concentrated between the Isle of Wight and Dover. Between the Thames and the Humber about 1.5 million tonnes of material are disposed. Nearly all of this material is cohesive. Between Scarborough and Berwick-upon-Tweed 1.8 million tonnes of material are dumped offshore and the indications are that at least half of this material is sandy.

It is important to note that, at present, in only a few instances is maintenance-dredged material used in a beneficial manner. In the Liverpool Bay region about 1.5 million tonnes of dredged material is taken onshore and there the sand fraction is separated for use in the construction industry. Most of the time the material is unsuitable for beach nourishment purposes or the timescales for the letting of contracts associated with maintenance works are short: so that it is not practical to consider options, other than disposal, for the use of the material.

7.3.3 Capital dredged material

Capital dredging works around the UK may be a more suitable source of material for nourishment purposes. By their very nature capital schemes are more likely to result in the production of coarse material than maintenance works. However, coarse material dredged during a capital development is often used within the development for reclamation purposes. The timescales associated with developments are also more likely to allow options for nourishment to be taken advantage of. The plant that is to be used can be adapted so as to be able to pump material ashore. Unfortunately capital dredging projects are not evenly distributed about the coast or through time and cannot therefore normally be considered a reliable source of material for nourishment schemes. In the years 1985 to 1992 over 60% of the UK capital dredging was undertaken in the three regions of Tyne-Tees, Harwich and Morecambe Bay.

Tyne-Tees and Harwich were schemes associated with major port development works and in Morecambe Bay the capital dredging was associated with deepening the approach channels for the Admiralty at Barrow.

An example of the use of capital dredged material for beach nourishment is the port of Poole. Here capital works in the approach channel to Poole Harbour in 1988/89 resulted in 604 000m^3 out of 675 000m^3 dredged being pumped onto Bournemouth beaches. Further capital works the following winter resulted in 420 000m^3 out of 510 000m^3 dredged being pumped ashore. The second scheme was only realised following the success of the first development. In 1991/92 developments to the navigation channel inside Poole Harbour resulted in 40 000m^3 of fine sand being jetted onto the beach at Sandbanks for Poole Borough Council.

7.3.4 Summary

Between 1985 and 1992 about 40 million tonnes of dredged material is annually dumped at about 150 licensed marine disposal sites. Over 80% of this material arose from maintenance work. The majority is dumped in the Severn and Humber estuaries. Most of the maintenance dredged material from UK ports is cohesive and unsuitable for beach nourishment schemes. However, in many regions some amounts of sandy material are dredged. Capital dredging projects generally produce coarser material and often quantities of this material are used within the development project with the finer fractions being dumped at sea.

Figure 7.12 *Locations of regions for disposal sites*

Table 7.5 Average annual sea disposal tonnages 1985—1992

Disposal region	Maintenance tonnage	Capital tonnage
Thames	57 000	78 000
Harwich	1 224 000	1 074 000
Great Yarmouth	115 000	6 000
The Wash	130 000	133 000
Humber	11 201 000	535 000
Scarborough	83 000	16 000
Tyne and Tees	1 711 000	1 384 000
Berwick-upon-Tweed	7 000	none
Forth	1 499 000	137 000
Dundee	198 000	4 000
Moray Firth	522 000	36 000
North West Scotland	63 000	95 000
Clyde	465 000	52 000
Solway Firth	197 000	46 000
Morecambe Bay	1 186 000	1 255 000
Isle of Man	7 000	none
Liverpool Bay	2 374 000	11 000
Anglesey	6 000	101 000
Pembroke	71 000	52 000
Outer Bristol Channel	2 614 000	37 000
Inner Bristol Channel	6 739 000	7 000
Plymouth	219 000	196 000
Lyme Bay	61 000	3 000
Poole	150 000	220 000
Isle of Wight	692 000	301 000
Brighton	378 000	32 000
Dover	493 000	36 000
Irish Sea	0	18 000
Northern Ireland (East)	367 000	141 000
Northern Ireland (North)	82 000	104 000
TOTAL	32 906 000	6 110 000

The timescales associated with capital projects are, by their very nature, such that it should be possible to examine local options for the beneficial uses of the dredged material. However, the use of dredged material in such a manner nearly always results in an increased cost for the dredging.

Table 7.6 Breakdown of maintenance dredged material

Region	Percentage of total	Average annual tonnage (1985-1992)	Cohesive	Non-cohesive	Unknown
Humber	34.0	11 201 000	9 300 000	1 900 000	
Bristol Channel:					
Inner	20.5	6 739 000	≈ 6 700 000		
Outer	7.9	2 614 000			2 600 000[a]
Liverpool Bay	7.2	2 374 000	1 100 000[b]	1 300 000[c]	
Tyne and Tees	5.2	1 711 000	500 000[d]	900 000[d]	300 000[e]
Forth	4.6	1 499 000	1 400 000	100 000	
Harwich	3.7	1 224 000	1 200 000		
Morecambe Bay	3.6	1 186 000			1 200 000[f]

Notes:

[a] - A mixture of material is disposed, ratios unknown. All is dumped in the Swansea Bay site.

[b] - Material dredged seawards of New Brighton is sand.

[c] - Some of the remaining material dredged is sand.

[d] - Data from Tees and Hartlepool Port Authority.

[e] - Some of the remaining material is sand.

[f] - A mixture of material is dumped, the majority is considered to be sand.

8 Environmental considerations

The resource volumes identified in this report should not be regarded as exploitable reserves. Even allowing for the retention of a minimum sediment thickness of 0.5m, a number of other quality and environmental factors may hinder or prevent exploitation of a sediment resource or otherwise restrict the reserves that it contains. Some of these factors are reviewed in brief here. This is not intended to be a comprehensive review, merely a reminder of other factors involved. Further information and references can be found in the *Beach Management Manual*.

8.1 COMPATIBILITY OF DREDGED MATERIAL AND BEACH SEDIMENT

The available offshore resource has been considered in terms of sediment size and available volume in Sections 4, 5 and 6, but sediment composition, colour and contaminants are also important factors (see *Beach Management Manual* Section 6.2.2 and Table 6.1). Knowledge of the composition of shingle clasts is important in order that dredged material can be matched as closely as possible to beach material. Factors such as the colour of clasts and their shape are significant both for aesthetic reasons and to maintain a suitable environment for flora and fauna. Information on biogenic material (seaweed and marine organisms), mud content and chemical contaminants will be required. The occurrence of abundant glauconite has also been recorded on the database and should be investigated for any proposed scheme, because this mineral is prone to oxidation when exposed on a beach, giving the sediment a rusty coloration. Shell content is generally not crucial in determining whether material is suitable for beach recharge although it could be a factor in long term degradation of the beach grading. However, shingle composed largely of shell debris would be unsuitable in some sites. For this reason attention is drawn in this report to the location of carbonate-rich shingle resources.

8.2 ENVIRONMENTAL IMPACTS

Issues that need to be considered in an environmental assessment of beach recharge and that also apply to the planning stage for offshore dredging are reviewed in the *Beach Management Manual* Sections 6.2.2, 6.6 and 7.9.1. The issues are also addressed by Campbell (1993). A brief outline of the main considerations is provided here.

8.2.1 Physical impacts

The resources discussed in Sections 4 to 6 extend into the nearshore zone. Removal of sediment from nearshore zones for beach recharge could interfere with the local hydrodynamic and coastal sediment regimes with potential adverse impacts on coastal stability.

If sandbanks are to be considered as a potential source of material for extraction, it is important to consider the extent to which the bodies contribute to the local coastal defences by reducing wave energy. In such cases where the materials are a possible source of recharge material there may be a need to assess the net environmental benefit, balancing any possible deterioration in the naturally occurring coastal defence against the economic advantage of exploiting a convenient and compatible material source (Arthurton, 1993). This can be judged only with the benefit of a wide perspective of the materials inventory and regional sediment transport information, using results from hydrodynamic studies where appropriate.

8.2.2 Biological impacts

The environmental impact of offshore dredging on marine ecology is also an important consideration. Dredging may disturb, remove or alter the nature of the substrate on which certain marine species depend. These effects, and especially the rates of recolonisation after dredging, are the subjects of ongoing research. In some cases environmental considerations may sterilise resource areas, or otherwise restrict the exploitation of a resource.

The biological effects of marine mineral extraction have been investigated in a number of projects funded jointly by the Crown Estate and the Ministry of Agriculture Fisheries and Food. Research undertaken by Kenny and Rees (1994) at an experimental dredging site off North Norfolk recorded a significant immediate reduction in the variety, abundance and biomass of benthic organisms as a consequence of dredging. Subsequent recolonisation of the substrate by the dominant taxa proceeded relatively rapidly, but the community structure had not fully recovered seven months after dredging.

Restricted licences are sometimes issued by the Crown Estate to dredge only part of the resource. This has been implemented around Hastings Bank for example, on account of the fisheries considerations. The EC Habitats Directive stresses the importance of conservation of certain internationally important marine areas.

Of particular importance in the East Coast region are the strong fishing interests on the Dogger Bank and the disturbance of dredging on crab breeding grounds, offshore from north Norfolk and Lincolnshire. The major commercial species of fish potentially endangered by dredging is the herring which spawns over certain shingle areas, the eggs being attached to the clasts within the shingle deposit. Most of the known herring spawning areas are well away from current dredging areas. The environment of the sandbanks may support a fauna of burrowing organisms such as sand eels and echinoids.

8.3 OTHER POTENTIAL CONSTRAINTS ON DREDGING

The positions of sea floor obstacles, determined from study of HO sources, have been recorded on the database. Telephone cables, areas designated as dumping grounds, shipping lanes and extensive submarine exercise areas all constrain resource exploitation. Dredging of sea floor sediments is prohibited from a corridor extending 0.75km either side of telephone cables and pipe lines. In The Wash and East Anglia sub-regions development of resources is locally constrained by the many gas pipelines and cable routes which cross the area. Substantial areas offshore from the Norfolk coast are constrained by pipeline or cable routes. Substantial areas in Morecambe Bay may be constrained by pipeline routes serving the Morecambe Bay gas field. Sterile ground for dredgers also occurs around shipwrecks. Development of hitherto unexploited resources in the South Coast region may be constrained by the existence of busy shipping channels.

Another aspect is the potential conflict of dredging activities with other users of areas for which dredging is proposed. These include areas close to ports, where commercial shipping or naval activities are confined to certain shipping lanes. Offshore dredging might also interrupt water sports and leisure activities and may be opposed by local residents. Sailing and water sports are important recreational activities in the Solent, Poole Bay and Christchurch Bay areas, but also occur on a smaller scale at numerous localities along the coast.

9 Recommendations and conclusions

9.1 AIMS AND LIMITATIONS

This report sets out the results of a study that has examined the relationship between the demand for marine-dredged materials and their resources, and in particular the potential for meeting the specific demand for beach recharge material over the long-term - the next 20 years. It focuses on the use of recharge materials from marine sources, although also considers a variety of alternatives. The study has involved a systematic assessment of demand and resources, carried out on a regional basis for England and Wales.

The quantitative assessments set out in this report produce volume estimates for grid squares in order to protect the interests of the owners of confidential information. The results are presented as a general view that has been built up from the best available sources of detailed data. Nevertheless, there remain areas of the sea floor where no information was available. The report serves as an indication, but no more, of local recharge demand in the long-term. It does not identify specific reserves of suitable recharge materials. The report does not in any way obviate the need for carrying out detailed prospecting surveys.

The report provides, for the first time, quantitative estimates of national recharge demand (in terms of shingle and sand) presented for the three main regions and the resources of suitable material to meet that demand, in the context of the likely requirements of the aggregate industry within the region. These estimates are of particular relevance in the determination of policy concerning coastal defence and minerals planning. In addition the report provides more detailed information on the distribution and quality of the resources of potential recharge materials, including resources outside existing licenced production and prospecting areas. Some of these additional resource areas extend into the nearshore zone. It is emphasised that assessment of these additional areas has been based essentially upon reconnaissance data. The information on the distribution of marine materials within regions is intended to guide minerals planning at the more local level and to inform coastal authorities and engineers of the likely resource options for consideration.

9.2 DEMAND AND RESOURCE OVERVIEW

The distribution of marine sand and shingle resources on the seabed around the coasts of England and Wales is uneven. The deposits vary in their thickness, grading and depth, and in their proximity to the shore. Some of these resources occur in places that are currently inaccessible to the aggregate industry, for example sterilized ground in the vicinity of seabed cables and pipelines, and in the nearshore zone because of perceived concern over negative impacts of extraction on shoreline stability.

Away from the littoral zone and places subject to extreme tidal currents, the resources of shingle offshore are relict deposits, formed under conditions quite different from those of the present-day seabed. Some sand resources may also be relict deposits, for example, the sand ridges that occur in the deeper waters of the southern North Sea. Most of the sand resources, however, occur in deposits that are ephemeral, with sand transported across the seabed according to the local hydrodynamic regime and its variation over time. Such a regime is largely a consequence of tidally generated currents and disturbance at the seabed due to waves. Except within parts of the littoral zone, any shingle extracted is not naturally replenished under the present-day conditions and therefore shingle deposits must be considered as non-renewable. Sand resources may be renewable locally, but sand resources may also be a diminishing asset but on a much longer timescale.

The sand and gravel resources of the nearshore zone, and the process regimes of that zone, have generally not been assessed in the same detail as the densely sampled resource areas farther offshore. Whether suitable resources are sufficiently abundant where required and whether their usage for beach recharge would satisfy the environmental *net benefit* principle in particular cases is not clear from the available data. The sand and gravel inventory in this zone and the processes that affect it are seen as priority topics for investigation.

The demand for beach recharge shingle (gravel) over the next 20 years will range from 23.37 to 47.43Mm^3, mostly for south coast beaches, and that for shingle for construction over this period, about 200Mm^3. The demand for beach recharge sand over the next 20 years is estimated to be in the range 36.46 to 82.78Mm^3, mostly for east coast beaches, and that for sand for construction, about 180Mm^3. The resource and total demand data are briefly reviewed in Sections 9.4 to 9.5 and summarised in Figure 9.1 and Table 9.1. It should be noted that recharge demand estimates are not available for mixed sand and gravel because available numerical models cannot yet simulate complex mixtures of sediment types. Demand estimates have therefore been derived from models using material of either sand (0.125—2.0mm) or shingle (>5mm) size for specific sites, and then the results are extrapolated along sections of coastline. Resource estimates are based on assessment of the areas densely sampled by the aggregate industry, together with additional selected areas of significant resource potential. Volumes presented for shingle should be treated with some caution because shingle in low concentrations (uneven, patchy distribution) may not prove practical to extract even though the volumes appear workable.

9.3 SOUTH COAST REGION

The main demand for beach recharge schemes in the English Channel East sub-region is for shingle grade material. The maximum requirement is estimated to be 22.4Mm^3 over the next 20 years, although maintenance might increase this volume slightly. In the English Channel West sub-region the demand is for shingle and sand in equal quantities, but gradually decreasing in amount.

The total volume of identified resources in the South Coast region would appear easily to meet the identified demand for sand and mixed sand and gravel for aggregate and recharge material over the 20-year period (Table 9.1).

The potentially workable resources of shingle in the English Channel East sub-region (225.4Mm^3) would appear significantly to exceed anticipated total demand (64.4Mm^3). However, shingle in low concentrations may not prove practical to extract. Moreover, the South Coast region also supplies marine materials for export to NW Europe. Other factors such as fisheries, unsuitable specification and contaminants may also restrict availability for beach recharge purposes.

Shingle resources south of Beachy Head, and sand and gravel resources in the nearshore zone between Bexhill and Hastings could be considered for supplying recharge sites in East Sussex. Coarse material required for beach recharge in West Sussex, Hampshire or the Isle of Wight could be most easily supplied from the broad area of shingle-rich deposits densely prospected by the marine aggregate industry located east of the Isle of Wight. Shingle occurring on the margins of large shingle deposits might be available for recharge purposes but, as noted above, all economically viable shingle resources will be in demand from the aggregate industry over the next 20 years.

The sand resource within Poole-Christchurch bays could be suitable for supplying material to beaches in Poole Bay and Colwell Bay. The shingle required to recharge beaches flanking the western end of the Solent might be supplied from resources identified south-west of the Isle of Wight. Localised resources of sand in Lyme Bay could supply the recharge schemes on the adjacent Dorset coast.

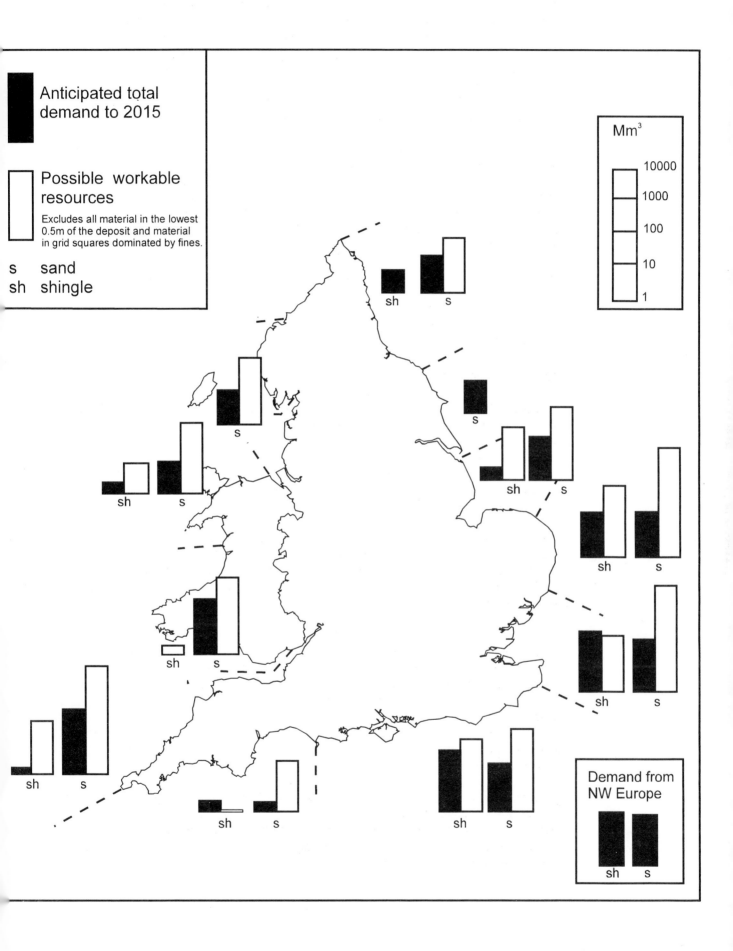

Figure 9.1 *Comparison of total regional demand and resource estimates*

Table 9.1 Comparison of regional demand and resource estimates

	Anticipated total demand by sub-region to 2015 Mm³			Possible workable resources Mm³			Difference between demand and possible resources Mm³		
	Shingle	Sand and gravel	Sand	Shingle	Sand and gravel	Sand	Shingle	Sand and gravel	Sand
Tyne-Tees	6.0	1.1	16.0	0.07	0.13	30.3	-5.93	-0.97	+14.3
Yorks-Humber	3.0	0.6	11.9	not investigated					
Wash	2.1	0	15.4	75.5	69.7	434.0	+73.4	+69.7	+418.6
East Anglia	8.6	0.6	9.5	224.0	150.2	5552.9	+215.4	+149.6	+5543.4
Thames Estuary	97.5	13.3	53.2	90.9	367.4	3373.9	-6.6	+345.1	+3320.7
English Channel E	64.4	6.7	25.6	225.4	92.1	761.6	+161.0	+85.4	+736.0
English Channel W	2.9	0	1.6	0.02	0.9	42.8	-2.9	+0.9	+41.2
Bristol Channel S	0.7	0	18.9	150.1	57.6	3466.6	+149.4	+57.6	3447.7
South Wales	0	0	44.8	6.1	22.1	256.0	+6.1	+22.1	+211.2
North Wales	1.5	0	9.9	9.2	48.0	324.4	+7.7	+48.0	+314.5
Lancs-Cheshire	0	0	10.3	0	0	128.3			+118.0
Cumbria	0.7	0	6.4	not investigated					
NW Europe	60.0	11.1	31.3						
Totals	247.4	33.4	254.8	781.3	808.1	14370.8			

Based on data presented in Tables 3.10 and 3.15
Sub-region demand volumes are based on the maximum estimated requirement for beach recharge plus the forecast aggregate demand for construction.
The possible workable resources exclude areas where fines predominate and exclude the lowest 0.5m of material.

Negative values: shortages anticipated in the sub-region
Positive values: surplus material should be available to work, assuming environmental and other constraints to not prevent extraction of the resource.

Demand estimates have been converted from tonnes using the following density values:

Shingle (>5mm)	2.0 tonnes/cubic metre
Sand and gravel (2—5mm)	1.8 tonnes/cubic metre
Sand (0.125—2mm)	1.6 tonnes/cubic metre

9.4 EAST COAST REGION

The main demand for planned beach recharge schemes is for sand grade material. The estimated maximum recharge demand over the next 20 years from this region is 51.5Mm³ including maintenance demand. The identified resources lying off the coast of eastern England would appear easily to meet the estimated demand for sand and mixed sand and gravel for aggregate and recharge material over the 20-year period (Table 9.1).

Offshore sand resources suitable in grain-size and quantity occur close to many of the proposed sites of beach recharge. Excluding environmental constraints it appears that local marine supplies of sand are readily available to meet demand from contiguous coastlines. Parts of these areas are currently inaccessible to the marine aggregate industry for a number of reasons, summarised briefly in Section 8.

Marine supplies are not likely to be sufficient to supply all of the total demand for shingle in the Thames Estuary sub-region. Anticipated total UK demand of 97.5Mm³ for the next 20 years, of which 11.5Mm³ could be required for recharge purposes, exceeds identified workable resources (90.0Mm³). Additional exports to NW Europe will exacerbate the supply situation in this sub-region. It is therefore significant that additional shingle deposits are identified in this report in the adjoining East Anglia sub-region, especially around sandbanks occurring offshore from north-east Norfolk. However, environmental factors such as fisheries and disturbance to fauna, the location of pipelines, and the uncertain effects on local sediment transport paths might inhibit removal of shingle close to major tidal sandbanks.

9.5 WALES AND WESTERN ENGLAND REGION

The identified resources off the coasts of Wales and western England would appear easily to meet the estimated demand for sand and gravel for aggregate and recharge material over the 20-year period (Table 9.1).

Offshore resources suitable in grain-size and quantity occur close to many of the proposed sites of beach recharge. Subject to investigation of environmental considerations it appears that local marine supplies of sand are readily available.

Potentially workable offshore shingle deposits are very limited in this region, apart from spreads of shingle located in very shallow water in the inner Bristol Channel. The extent of these deposits has been indicated by seismic survey, but their composition remains uncertain. Their location in environmentally sensitive areas may argue against further investigation. Although the anticipated demand for shingle is low in this region, there is nevertheless an estimated demand from the Irish Sea coasts of 5.5Mm³ which may have to be met from distant sources.

9.6 USE OF ALTERNATIVE MATERIALS

As discussed in Section 7, there are many potential sources of alternative materials for beach recharge in England and Wales. Such materials include land-won sand and gravel, crushed rock aggregates, mineral wastes and navigational dredgings. However, the technical and environmental quality of these materials and the costs of their development and transportation indicates that most of these potential alternative materials are unlikely to be used in beach recharge schemes.

The preferred materials for beach recharge are materials similar to those occurring naturally on the local coastline. In most cases these are sands and gravels. Land-won sand and gravel is in many cases technically suitable and small amounts have been used on recharge schemes. In general, however, these materials are not in favour because of the difficulties, and high costs, of placing large volumes on beaches.

Crushed rock aggregates are unlikely to be widely used in beach recharge because of the major adverse impact on beach appearance and its amenity value. Also, Government policy is to encourage less reliance on traditional land-won sources. Small amounts may, however, be the appropriate economic option for some schemes in Wales and western England.

Mineral waste materials (secondary aggregates) are available in large volumes in many parts of England and Wales and these may be technically capable of substituting for primary aggregates. There is currently little scope, however, for the use of most of these materials in beach recharge schemes due to unsuitable lithologies, their variable quality and their cost of processing, transportation and placement. Possible exceptions may be slate waste as a potential source of shingle-sized material particularly in parts of western Britain with similar natural beach materials; china clay sand, small amounts of which have been used for recharge schemes in Cornwall but because of high transportation costs is unlikely to be able to compete with local material supplies in eastern and south-eastern England; and quarry wastes if they are available close to the point of demand.

Most material resulting from maintenance dredging in the UK is fine or cohesive material, unsuitable for beach recharge schemes. Some sandy sediment is dredged but most is dumped as waste material. Capital dredging works tend to produce more coarser-grained materials, which are often separated from the finer materials and used for reclamation fill.

9.7 RECOMMENDATIONS FOR FURTHER STUDY

Marine shingle deposits are in great demand, particularly in the south and east regions. With very little natural replacement, the supply cannot last indefinitely. New shingle resources need to be identified and investigated as a matter of priority. The following sources merit further consideration:

1   The resources identified in the additional areas selected for detailed study in this report require more detailed investigation. Offshore from Happisburgh and the inner Bristol Channel are the two additional areas with significant potential resources of shingle.

2   Coarse deposits occur in some nearshore areas. Although exploitation of material from the nearshore zone could be environmentally sensitive, the resource potential of the nearshore zone merits further investigation. There is a need for greater understanding and analysis of coastal processes to ensure that net benefits are achieved if such deposits were to be exploited. Such exploitation may well have to be considered in the context of recycling or "short circuiting" of natural circulation processes.

3   Known shingle deposits occurring further offshore in water depths exceeding 50m such as south-west of the Isle of Wight require prospecting.

4   Shingle lags occur between and around tidal sandbanks offshore. Partial exploitation of these lags might be an option.

5   Palaeovalley fills such as the palaeo-Solent buried valley, the valley systems south of Beachy Head, and the Thames-Medway valley system represent possible sources of shingle to supply the demand for sand and gravel from southeast England, but little is known of the precise make up of the fill materials.

6   Further research is required to investigate the quality, the economic costs and the issues involved in developing the use of coarser material from capital dredging works for recharge schemes.

The work undertaken on beach recharge for this report has highlighted the need for the following further studies to improve the design of future schemes and the accuracy of the demand estimates:

1   Investigate the use of coarse land-based material as a potential supplement to marine materials.

2   Establishment of a database and analysis of post-construction surveys to assess the success of the design procedures.

3   Further research on control structures and littoral transport to improve the estimation of maintenance demand volumes.

References and published data

ARTHURTON, R.S. (1993)
Marine sand and gravel: resources and exploitation.
Proceedings of a Seminar "Towards a better coast - a strategic approach to coastal management". 4pp. Natural Environment Research Council.

BALSON, P.S. (1988)
East Anglia. Sheet 52°N-00° including the Wash (part of 53°N-00°). Sea Bed Sediments. 1:250,000 Series. British Geological Survey.

BALSON, P.S. (1990)
Spurn. Sheet 53°N-00° including part of Humber Trent Sheet 53°N-02°. Sea Bed Sediments. 1:250,000 Series. British Geological Survey.

BALSON, P.S. and D'OLIER, B. (1990)
Thames Estuary. Sheet 51°N-00°. Sea Bed Sediments and Quaternary geology.
1:250,000 Series. British Geological Survey.

BENBOW, J. (1990)
Marine aggregates: money in the banks.
Industrial Minerals, no. 275 (August 1990), 35—45.

BRITISH GEOLOGICAL SURVEY (1993)
United Kingdom Minerals Yearbook, 1992.
Keyworth, Nottingham: British Geological Survey.

BRITISH MARINE AGGREGATES PRODUCERS ASSOCIATION (1993)
Aggregates from the Sea: Why Dredge?
Information Publication

CAMPBELL, J.A. (1993)
Guidelines for assessing marine aggregate extraction.
Lab. Leaflet MAFF Dir. Fish. Res., Lowestoft, 73. 12pp.

CAMERON, T.D.J., LABAN, C. and SCHUTTENHELM, R.T.E. (1984)
Flemish Bight. Sheet 52°N-02°E. Sea Bed Sediments and Holocene geology.
1:250,000 Series. British Geological Survey.

CAMERON, T.D.J., CROSBY, A., BALSON, P.S., JEFFERY, D.H., LOTT, G.K., BULAT, J. and HARRISON, D.J. (1992)
United Kingdom offshore regional report: the geology of the southern North Sea.
HMSO for the British Geological Survey, 152pp.

CENTRAL DREDGING ASSOCIATION (1993)
Working Group Report: Marine Sand and Gravel in the EC Seas.
Report 93/01, (October 1993)

CLAYTON, K.M. (1989)
Sediment input from the Norfolk cliffs, eastern England - a century of coast protection and its effect.
Journal of Coastal Research, 5, 433—442.

CROSBY, A., GRAHAM, C.C., RUCKLEY, N.A. and PANTIN, H.M. (compilers) (1987) *Sea Bed Sediments around the United Kingdom (South and North sheets).*
British Geological Survey.

CROSBY, A. (compiler) (1983)
Portland Sheet 50°N-04°W. Sea Bed Sediments. 1:250,000 Map Series.
British Geological Survey.

DEPARTMENT OF THE ENVIRONMENT (1989)
Minerals Planning Guidance: Guidelines for Aggregate Provision in England and Wales
MPG 6, (1989)

DEPARTMENT OF THE ENVIRONMENT (1991)
National Collation of the results of the 1989 Aggregates Minerals Survey.
Department of the Environment.

DEPARTMENT OF THE ENVIRONMENT (1993)
Guidelines for Aggregates Provision in England and Wales: Revision of MPG 6
Draft Consultation Document/Policy Issues Paper, (January 1993)

DEPARTMENT OF THE ENVIRONMENT (1994)
Minerals Planning Guidance: Guidelines for Aggregates Provision in England
MPG 6, (April 1994).

DISERENS, A. P. and COATES, T. T. (1993)
UK South Coast shingle beach study - Storm response of shingle beaches.
HR Wallingford Report SR 323.

DYER, K. R. (1975)
The buried channels of the "Solent River", southern England.
Proceedings of the Geologists' Association, 86, 239-245.

EVANS, C.D.R. (1990)
The geology of the western English Channel and its western approaches.
United Kingdom offshore regional report: HMSO for the British Geological Survey, 93pp.

EVANS, C.D.R. (compiler) (1986)
Bristol Channel. Sheet 51°N-04°W. Sea Bed Sediments and Quaternary geology.
1:250,000 Series, British Geological Survey.

FOLK, R.L. (1954)
The distinction between grain size and mineral composition in sedimentary-rock nomenclature.
Journal of Geology, 62, 344-359.

HAMBLIN, R.J.O. (compiler) (1989)
Dungeness-Boulogne. Sheet 50°N-00°. Sea Bed Sediments and Quaternary geology.
1:250,000 Series. British Geological Survey.

HAMBLIN, R.J.O. and HARRISON, D.J. (1989)
The marine sand and gravel resources off the Isle of Wight and Beachy Head.
British Geological Survey Technical Report WB/89/41C.

HAMBLIN, R.J.O., CROSBY, A., BALSON, P.S., JONES, S.M., CHADWICK, R.A., PENN, I.E. and ARTHUR, M.J. (1992)
The geology of the English Channel.
United Kingdom offshore regional report: HMSO for the British Geological Survey). 106pp.

HARRIS, P.M. (1993)
Review of information on onshore sand and gravel resources in England.
British Geological Survey Technical Report WA/93/35.

HARRISON, D.J. (compiler) (1987)
Land's End. Sheet 50°N-06°W. Sea Bed Sediments and Quaternary geology.
1:250,000 Series, British Geological Survey.

HARRISON, D.J. (1988)
The marine sand and gravel resources off Great Yarmouth and Southwold, East Anglia.
British Geological Survey Technical Report WB/88/9C.

HARRISON, D.J. (1989)
Farne. Sheet 55°N-02°ᵂ. Sea Bed Sediments.
1:250,000 Series. British Geological Survey.

HARRISON, D.J. (1992)
The marine sand and gravel resources of the Humber.
British Geological Survey Technical Report WB/92/1.

HR WALLINGFORD (1993)
Coastal management: mapping of littoral cells.
Report SR328.

JAMES, J.W.C. and WINGFIELD, R.T.R. (compilers) (1988)
Cardigan Bay. Sheet 52°N-06°W. Sea Bed Sediments.
1:250,000 Series, British Geological Survey.

JELLIMAN, C., HAWKES, P.J. and BRAMPTON, A.H. (1991)
Wave climate change and its impact on UK Coastal Management.
HR Wallingford Report SR 260.

JONES, H. (1989)
Sand to land.
New Civil Engineer, 11th May issue, 26—29.

KENNY, A.J. and REES, H.L. (1994)
The effects of marine gravel extraction on the macrobenthos: early post-dredging recolonisation.
Marine Pollution Bulletin, Vol 28, No. 7, 442-447.

KELLAND, N.C. and HAILS, J.R. (1972)
Bedrock morphology and structures within overlying sediments, Start Bay, Southwest England, determined by continuous seismic profiling, side-scan sonar, and core sampling.
Marine Geology, 13, M19—26.

LAWSON, M.J. and HAMBLIN, R.J.O. (compilers) (1989)
Wight. Sheet 50°N-02°W. Sea Bed Sediments and Quaternary Geology.
1:250,000 Series. British Geological Survey.

LOTT, G.K. (1987)
California. Sheet 54°N-00°. Sea Bed Sediments.
1:250,000 Series. British Geological Survey.

MAFF (1993)
Project appraisal guidance notes - Flood and Coastal Defence.
Ministry of Agriculture, Fisheries and Food, PB1214.

McCAVE, I.N. (1987)
Fine sediment sources and sinks around the East Anglian coast (UK).
Journal of the Geological Society of London, 144, 149—152.

NICHOLLS, R.J. (1991)
Holocene evolution of the gravel coastline of East Sussex: discussion.
Proceedings of Geologists' Association, 102, 301—306.

O'CONNOR, B.A. (1987)
Short and long term changes in estuary capacity.
Journal of the Geological Society of London, 144, 187—195.

PANTIN, H.M. (1986)
Tyne-Tees. Sheet 54°N-02°W. Sea Bed Sediments and Quaternary geology.
1:250,000 Series. British Geological Survey.

PANTIN, H.M. and contributors (1990)
The Sea Bed Sediments around the United Kingdom.
British Geological Survey Research Report SB/90/1.

PRINGLE, A.W. (1985)
Holderness coast erosion and the significance of ords.
Earth Surface Processes and Landforms, 10, 107—124.

RIDDLER, G.P. (1994)
What is a mineral resource? In: Mineral Resource Evaluation II: Methods and Case Histories. Whateley, M.K.G. and Harvey, P.K. (eds.). Geological Society Special Publication, 79, 1—10.

TAPPIN, D.R. (compiler) (1983)
Lundy. Sheet 50°N-06°W. Sea Bed Sediments and Quaternary geology.
1:250,000 Series, British Geological Survey.

TAPPIN, D.R., CHADWICK, R.A., JACKSON, A.A., WINGFIELD, R.T.R and SMITH, N.J.P. (1994)
The geology of Cardigan Bay and the Bristol Channel.
United Kingdom offshore regional report: HMSO for the British Geological Survey, 107pp.

THE CROWN ESTATE (1989/1990/1991/1992/1993)
Marine Aggregates: Crown Estate Licences: Summary of Statistics 1989/1990/1991/1992/1993.

TUBEY, L.W. (1978)
China clay sand. The Use of Waste and Low-grade Materials in Road Construction.
LR817. Transport and Road Research Laboratory.

WATKISS, M. J. (1992)
The Development of a Marine Aggregate Industry - the British Experience
Proceedings of XIII World Dredging Congress (April 1992)

WENTWORTH, C.K. (1922)
A scale of grade and class terms for clastic sediments.
Journal of Geology, 30, 377-392.

WHITBREAD, M., MARSAY, A. and TUNNELL, C. (1991)
Occurrence and utilisation of mineral and construction wastes.
Arup Economics and Planning. Department of the Environment. HMSO.

WINGFIELD, R.T.R. (compiler) (1983a)
Lake District. Sheet 54°N-04°W. Sea Bed Sediments and Quaternary geology.
1:250,000 Series, British Geological Survey.

WINGFIELD, R.T.R. (compiler) (1983b)
Liverpool Bay. Sheet 53°N-04°W. Sea Bed Sediments and Quaternary geology.
1:250,000 Series, British Geological Survey.

Appendix A A review of procedures for obtaining beach recharge material

A.1 INTRODUCTION

This Appendix describes work to investigate the existing procedures for obtaining material for beach recharge schemes in the United Kingdom. It also examines existing procedural constraints and other difficulties, and makes recommendations which could lead to improvements. This work is closely related to CIRIA Report 153: *Beach Management Manual*.

The text is a consolidation of the views expressed to the author through a series of consultations undertaken in the latter part of 1994. The opinions expressed and the conclusions drawn are primarily those of individual consultees and their inclusion should not be taken as implying endorsement by any particular government department, public body or other organisation represented on the steering group.

A.1.1 Objectives

The objectives of the work were originally defined as follows:

- to examine existing administrative procedures for obtaining material for UK beach recharge schemes, using recent projects as examples

- to identify the constraints of existing procedures and the practical difficulties experienced by coastal authorities seeking beach recharge material

- to propose and document procedures for obtaining beach recharge material which could operate within current constraints

    - for marine materials
    - for alternative material sources

- to make recommendations for improvements to the documented procedures which could lead to the development of a nationally accepted framework within which materials suitable for beach recharge can be obtained.

The output from the third objective - a procedural guide for obtaining beach recharge material - is integrated into the main body of the *Beach Management Manual*. This Appendix covers the work carried out under the other three objectives listed above.

A.1.2 Method of approach

The work was carried out by interviewing members of a number of organisations who have ongoing beach recharge schemes, or had implemented such schemes in the past, together with representatives of other organisations whose work relates to the obtaining, licensing or controlling of aggregate dredging, and the development of coastal defence schemes. A full list of the organisations consulted is given in the Foreword.

A.1.3 Beach recharge schemes reviewed

The beach recharge schemes reviewed are shown in tabular form below, together with their main characteristics and brief comments. The aim, in selecting these particular schemes, was to obtain as much variation as possible in terms of recharge material, location, size and source.

Brief descriptions of the schemes reviewed have also been prepared, together with salient points relating to the sourcing and behaviour of beach material. However, to preserve confidentiality these have not been included in the report.

A.2 EXISTING CONSTRAINTS TO OBTAINING MATERIAL

Analysis of the data collected during the study shows that there are a number of areas of concern which have a bearing on the ability of a promoter to source material for a recharge scheme. These are:

- an actual or perceived lack of suitable recharge material within reasonable distance of the site

- difficulties associated with obtaining material from licensed marine sources

- difficulties associated with licensing new marine sources, in particular, matters relating to the Government View procedure

- difficulties associated with obtaining data for environmental and morphological assessments

- inadequacies in environmental research and shortcomings in current scientific models in which environmental data are analysed.

In addition to the areas mentioned above, other concerns were raised relating to such matters as royalties for aggregate extraction, the requirement for onerous and repetitive procedural paperwork during scheme development and the like. As these issues are not directly relevant to the procedural framework under study, they are not discussed any further in this report. The five areas of concern identified above are discussed below.

A.2.1 Lack of suitable material

Whether or not suitable volumes of recharge material exist for a particular scheme is, currently, somewhat difficult to ascertain. Firstly, because reliable estimates of the availability of both licensed and unlicensed sources are not known or capable of being determined, and, secondly, because the size and timing of competing demands are indeterminate. This report will, to a large extent, give an overall picture of the potential for over or under supply, but cannot be expected to predict the year-by-year fluctuations in the size, number and location of schemes, the rate of release of newly licensed areas or the vagaries of the competing construction market.

Various parties have referred to the lack of coarse material in the South East region and the lack of licensed sources to the West of the Needles, but these may be perceived inadequacies which may not be borne out under more detailed scrutiny. A current problem in carrying out a regional resource/demand study is the difficulty of obtaining reliable information (see Section A.2.4). A compounding problem is that designers are not being given sufficient funds to carry out comprehensive sourcing studies in the conceptual stages of scheme development. This latter difficulty may be partly due to the fact that a regional study of this nature is too costly to be justifiable for a single scheme, particularly when viewed in the light of the cost and chances of obtaining a licence to extract material if a new source is selected.

Bearing in mind that a designer should be responsible for ensuring that suitable material exists (otherwise the client's funds may be squandered in wasted design and scheme development), and given that a lack of knowledge of available materials inhibits design, it is clearly desirable for there to be more detailed information available on a regional basis. The carrying out of regional resource studies by coastal groups is, therefore, to be encouraged, particularly if it can be combined with the collection of other data, as described in Section A.2.4, below.

Name of Recharge Scheme	Marine Sources						Other Sources	Comments
	Sand		Mixed		Shingle			
	New Source	Existing Source	New Source	Existing Source	New Source	Existing Source		
Aldeburgh						C	C	Navigation dredgings plus land source.
Bournemouth	C						C	1974 scheme obtained new licence, 1989 scheme used navigation dredgings.
Clacton/Jaywick				C				Tried to get new licence but eventually failed.
Dinas Dnlle							C	Mixed shingle and quarried rock from land source.
Eastbourne				P				Shingle with 30% sand.
Felixstowe (The Dip)							C	Navigation dredging
Glyne Gap (Hastings/Bexhill)						P		
Hunstanton/Heacham				C				Source and cliffing problems.
Hurst Spit					P			Awaiting Government View
Hythe/Sandgate						P		Explored for new source - nothing found.

Table (Appendix A): Procedures for obtaining materials for recharge schemes

| Name of Recharge Scheme | Marine Sources | | | | | | Other Sources | Comments |
| | Sand | | Mixed | | Shingle | | | |
	New Source	Existing Source	New Source	Existing Source	New Source	Existing Source		
Llandudno North							P	Probably to be land-based.
Llandudno West							C	Mixed sand, rock and shingle from land-based sources.
Llanelli		C						From licensed marine sources, but came overland to site.
Mablethorpe/Skegness	P	C						Current project from licensed source, but still awaiting Government View for future work.
Minehead			P	P				Mixed shingle and sand, sources not yet identified.
Penrhyn		C					C	Sand from marine source, shingle and cobble from quarried source.
Pevensey Bay					P			
Portobello		C						Onshore/offshore recycling. Source licensed to authority.
Prestatyn		C						Substitution by land-based source not permitted due to colour problem.

Table (Appendix A): Procedures for obtaining materials for recharge schemes

Name of Recharge Scheme	Marine Sources						Other Sources	Comments
	Sand		Mixed		Shingle			
	New Source	Existing Source	New Source	Existing Source	New Source	Existing Source		
Sandbay	C							1983/84 project. New licence obtained.
Seaford						C		Existing source, but positive Government view for uplift in annual quantities.
Sidmouth							P	Land-based source of rounded material identified.
Weymouth						P		

Legend: P = Planned
              C = Completed

In addition, after publication of the current CIRIA projects relating to recharge, clients should be more aware of the need to investigate sources of recharge material early and for making adequate provision in their budgets for the necessary investigatory work to be carried out.

A.2.2 Obtaining material from licensed sources

At the present time all the licensees of marine aggregate extraction licences issued by the Crown Estate are aggregate producers working in the fiercely competitive market to supply the construction industry, both in the United Kingdom and continental Europe. To compete in this market each company attempts to maintain a high degree of confidentiality with respect to the quantity and quality of its reserves and the proportion of its licensed annual tonnage available for extraction from each licensed block at any specific time.

The confidentiality attached by the marine aggregate producers to their resources is claimed by promoters and designers of beach recharge schemes to inhibit their implementation, or, at least, to increase the risk of the scheme being aborted at a late stage, thereby wasting both time and client's/public funds. For a beach recharge design to be made reliable and feasible it is necessary for the designer to ensure that the quality of his material source is known and will be available in sufficient volume within a certain price range at the time the tender is let.

The current view of many designers, whose schemes may be competing with one another in some areas and who believe that they are unable to obtain sufficient information on available material, is that their only course of action is to go to tender and let the market forces determine cost and availability. The results of this action will lead to either satisfactory tenders, qualified tenders or no suitable tenders being received. This method of scheme implementation, although practical in the circumstances, can hardly be described as optimum in view of the possibility of failure in the final stages and the lack of opportunity for fine tuning the design.

The situation described above has led scheme promoters to the view that it would be preferable for dedicated sources, whose quality and available reserves are known, to be identified and licensed for recharge schemes. This proposal is discussed further in Section A.2.3, below.

An alternative view to that expressed above is that the possibilities of using existing licensed sources have not been fully explored. There appear to be two areas where further progress could be made; in communication between scheme promoter and licensee, and in the licence conditions themselves.

Much of the information relating to potential material sources is obtained by consulting engineers on behalf of their clients. In their desire to be fair and unbiased consultants tend to send out rather general and open enquiries to a number of potential suppliers in the hope that they will receive sufficiently encouraging and detailed responses for them to complete their designs and go out to tender. In practice, for the reasons given above, licensees are generally unwilling to respond in much detail.

There appears to be no overriding reason why clients, or their consultants, should not develop a more detailed confidential dialogue with licensees, particularly when one specific licensed source appears to be suitable for the project envisaged. In such circumstances the benefits accruing from securing a source of known quality and quantity would, quite possibly, more than compensate for any premium arising from dealing with a sole supplier.

It is also apparent that most, if not all, licences issued by the Crown Estate contain a clause which prevents the licensee assigning or sub-licensing any part of the licence to any other party. This effectively prevents a marine aggregate producer from negotiating with a coastal authority with a view to giving the authority a sub-licence to remove material from an area of suitable quantity and quality for their coastal works over a defined period. The removal of this clause, with suitable safeguards added, might enable a number of suitable arrangements to be made, thereby reducing the uncertainty and removing some of the current pressure from authorities wishing to obtain new licences.

A.2.3 Obtaining a licence for a new source

The problems associated with attempting to obtain a licence for a new source may be categorised into:

- the "Government View Procedure"

- obtaining data for an application

- analyzing data for an application.

An additional aspect of developing a new source is, naturally, the selection of a suitable location. However, this has already been covered in Section 3.1 of this report and it is not proposed to expand the subject here. The problems of obtaining and analysing data are discussed in Sections A.2.4 and A.2.5 respectively. This section is confined to a discussion of the Government View (GV) procedure and its effect on licensing.

The perceived major shortcomings of the GV were summarised in the DoE/WO consultation paper *Review of Licensing Arrangements for Minerals Dredging in England and Wales* published in April, 1994, as:

- the possible conflict between the role of The Crown Estate Commissioners acting both as landowner and the quasi planning authority in respect of minerals dredging

- the insufficient attention being paid to the environmental effects of dredging

- the procedure not being sufficiently public

- the lack of a right of appeal/challenge against the decision whether to grant a licence or not

- the unreasonable length of time taken by GV to determine.

In addition to those concerns summarised above, the following points emerged from the consultations undertaken during the present study:

- the GV does not result in an evaluation of the "best environmental option", as it tends only to examine the extraction process and does not give full consideration to the end use

- the same weight seemed to be attached to unsubstantiated objections to applications as was accorded to scientifically derived advantages.

At the present time the responses to the above mentioned consultation paper are still being evaluated and any proposed revised future version of the GV is, as yet, unpublished. In spite of this, the idea of the GV being a statutory process appears to appeal to most organisations as it overcomes most of the perceived shortcomings identified in the consultation paper. However, what is not made clear in the consultation paper is how the statutory process would be carried out in terms of scope and evaluation, and this leads on to the secondary concerns described above.

The evaluation of licence applications under the GV has to be made in the light of a number of conflicting pressures

- the increasing demand for aggregates for both beach recharge and general construction use

- the desire to limit the disruption of the seabed to the minimum in terms of area of licensed blocks

- the desire to maintain a free market in the granting of licences

- the demands of the coastal defence lobby for special consideration and the licensing of dedicated sources for beach recharge

- the constraints placed on the overall process by EC Directives in terms of conservation and environmental assessment.

Clearly, a case could be made for granting licences for the extraction of aggregates in specific areas of the seabed solely for the purposes of beach recharge, no matter who the licensee is to be. However, it would only be possible to evaluate the benefits and disbenefits of an application of this nature if sufficient data were available and were capable of being analysed. In view of the precautionary approach adopted by the GV and the current lack of data (see Section A.2.4), the immediate effect of the GV becoming statutory would be a number of negative views. This is not a reason for rejecting the case for a statutory process, but rather an emphasis on the need for improvements in data collection and methods of data analysis.

As far as the GV is concerned, whether it is statutory or not, it would appear that any future version should set out clearly:

- the scope of the evaluation process in terms of the source and end use of the material extracted

- the philosophy behind the evaluation, i.e. nil effect, net benefit etc. and how this will be applied to the evaluation process

- the requirements for data, both from applicants and from objectors

- the way in which decisions will be published and any appeal procedure carried out.

A.2.4 Obtaining data for licence applications

For licence applications to be considered under the GV, a number of aspects of the proposed extraction have to be examined. These are:

- the characteristics and quantities of material to be removed from the seabed

- the effect of the proposed dredging on the physical environment

- the effects of the proposed dredging on the biological environment

- the effects of the proposed dredging on other users of the sea

- (in the case of beach recharge) the effects of the recharge on the biological and physical environment.

The first of the considerations mentioned above has been investigated by CIRIA (this report) in the broad sense and considerable amounts of data in specific locations are obtained by organisations wishing to obtain licences. This aspect of data collection does not appear to present great problems at this time, although the cost of prospecting for a dedicated source for a limited amount of material for beach recharge is somewhat prohibitive. The last consideration, that of the effect of the recharge scheme, would only be taken into account in a "net benefit" scenario, and the data required for an evaluation of this type is essentially land-based and, thus, relatively easy to collect. It is the other three considerations that present the greatest problem.

The specific areas of knowledge which would appear to be currently lacking in the marine environment are as follows (see Appendix 3, DoE/WO Consultation Paper):

- the wave climate and its effect on the coastline, both in terms of direct effects and effects on sediment transport

- the current regime in terms of effects on sediment transport and fines dispersal

- sediment transport in terms of supply of sediment, patterns of movement and sediment budgets

- geochemistry of sediments and water column in terms of potential effects of disturbance by dredging operations

- the distribution of commercial fish stocks, their spawning grounds and the conditions they require for optimum growth

- the distribution and relative importance (in terms of areal extent and numbers) of marine species and habitats

- the extent and nature of commercial inshore fisheries.

To some extent moves have already been made by local coastal groups to obtain this data. The work carried out by HR Wallingford and Southampton University for SCOPAC, relating to the mobility of sediments in the south coast dredging areas, being a good example. However, there is little doubt that further studies of this nature will be required in other areas.

It would appear to be acknowledged that data on fish and habitats is scattered and difficult to collate, although no doubt the work being carried out by English Nature and The Countryside Council for Wales to satisfy the EC Habitats and Species Directive will help in due course as far as the rarer examples are concerned. However, there would still seem to be considerable additional detail required generally around the coast.

Information on fisheries in general has become more accessible due to the formation of the Aggregate/Fisheries Liaison Committees, but it is clear that problems are still being experienced with respect to inshore fisheries. Some form of registration of legitimate inshore fisheries activities might be appropriate here.

The general consensus obtained from the investigations carried out under this study is that in future all applications for production licences will need to be supported by environmental assessments. In view of this, and the difficulty and expense of collecting the relevant data, there seems to be a clear case for co-funding arrangements being set up to obtain coastal environmental data, and also for a comprehensive database being developed to store the information obtained.

The rationale for co-funding is that, apart from the members of any coastal group, there will several organisations interested in environmental data in any specific coastal area, such as MAFF, English Nature/The Countryside Council for Wales, the NRA etc., and the cost of collecting the types of data at the same time may well be lower than collecting the same data individually. Having the information stored on a common database would make it accessible.

A.2.5 ANALYSIS OF DATA

There would appear to be two main areas of analysis involved in evaluating the effects of dredging for marine aggregates:

- the short and long-term effects of the dredging on marine ecology

- the long-term effects of the change in seabed character and level on the coastline, together with the cumulative effects of a number of dredging operations.

The study of the effects of dredging on marine ecology has been hampered in the past by a lack of knowledge of the actual disturbance caused by the dredging, the effect of this disturbance on marine organisms and any comparison of the disturbance from dredging with natural disturbances. Much of the problem of studying these matters relates to the difficulty of measuring these effects, particularly in storm conditions. Some advances have been made by the carrying out of full-scale dredging trials and subsequent monitoring of the benthos (such as that relating to recolonisation undertaken by the Crown Estate and MAFF on the East Coast), but there is still much to be studied regarding the short-term effects of dredging.

Recent advances in measuring techniques, relating to suspended sediment, are likely to make the collection of relevant data both faster and far more cost-effective in the future, although it is probable that the ability to collect this data over a wide area during storm conditions will still prove to be difficult. It is understood that the second stage of the Crown Estate/MAFF research will study the suspended sediment levels generated by working dredgers and the effects of this turbidity on fish.

Although the effects of individual marine aggregate dredging proposals on wave and current patterns and sediment transport are assessed as a prerequisite to every GV application, it has been suggested that, particularly for inshore zones, the hydrodynamic effects are too complex to be modelled by the current generation of numerical models. Further development of numerical models is, therefore, a prerequisite for improved analysis of complex nearshore areas.

In addition to this the macro cumulative effects of dredging on large areas of the seabed adjacent to coastal cells is still difficult to predict and may only be deduced from sediment transport patterns. Again, the collection of data on a regional or coastal cell basis would seem to be indicated.

A.3   CONCLUSIONS AND RECOMMENDATIONS

The following conclusions and recommendations are drawn from the above discussion on existing constraints:

1. Availability of suitable material from either licensed or unlicensed sources is currently difficult to ascertain due to lack of source data and uncertainties relating to the construction market. In addition, funding for investigatory work in the early stages of scheme development is lacking. Current CIRIA projects will give general guidance in this field but cannot be expected to predict market fluctuations.

    It is recommended that steps are taken by coastal groups to develop regional resource studies. All clients should be encouraged to make provision for sufficient funding for adequate resource studies at an early stage in project development (see Section A.2.1).

2. Difficulties in obtaining guaranteed supplies of material from licensed sources has encouraged clients to promote the idea of licensing certain new sources for beach recharge only. Alternative views are held that the client/supplier relationship has not been fully explored and, in addition, that simple changes to licence conditions would alleviate the material supply situation. It is concluded that each of these views is valid for particular cases.

    It is recommended that the following should be investigated (see Section A.2.2):

    •   *the feasibility of licensing, for beach recharge only, certain sources in the nearshore zone and others which would, under current procedures, not be licensed;*

    •   *the possibilities of making special contractual arrangements directly with licencees, including the sub-licensing of licensed blocks or portions thereof.*

3. The Government View procedure is currently being re-evaluated in the light of comments on the DoE/WO April, 1994, consultation paper. It is concluded that a statutory rather than a voluntary process would be of greater benefit to the coastal engineering community. However, the benefits of a statutory process will only be felt when sufficient data is collected to enable comprehensive evaluation of applications possible (see 4 below).

It is recommended that any statutory process should reflect (see Section A.2.3):

- *the scope of the evaluation process in terms of the source and end-use of the material extracted,*

- *the philosophy behind the evaluation, i.e. nil effect, net benefit, etc. and how this will be applied to the evaluation process,*

- *the requirements for data, both from applicants and from objectors, and*

- *the way in which decisions will be published and any appeal procedure carried out.*

4. Government Views on a number of licence applications have been held up recently due to a lack of data on which to determine a view. Environmental impact assessments are virtually obligatory for a view to be made. Extant environmental and fisheries data is often scattered and difficult to collate, whilst the collection of marine environmental field data is a lengthy and costly process, at times inhibiting scheme promoters from investigating new sources of material.

It is recommended that coastal groups should work to promote co-funded arrangements to obtain environmental data and that this data should be stored on a common database (see Section A.2.4). Existing databases should be examined to identify that which is most appropriate for this purpose.

5. Engineering and environmental data requires scientific analysis to enable licence applications to be evaluated. Currently there are a few inadequacies in the analytical techniques available. In particular, the short-term effects of dredging activities on marine organisms are not fully understood, nor have the effects of dredging and processing on water quality been fully investigated. In addition, numerical modelling of complex nearshore wave and current regimes is still problematic.

It is recommended that further research be put into quantifying the effects of dredging on water quality, and hence marine biology, and that studies be carried out to further refine numeric models with respect to predicting the effects of offshore dredging on the coastal zone (see Section A.2.5).

Appendix B   Recharge demand spreadsheet

This appendix presents the spreadsheet used to calculate beach recharge demand for England and Wales (see Section 3.3). The following information and assumptions have been used in the extrapolation of the demand estimates derived for the 19 representative sites:

1. Calculations include all lengths of the coast of England and Wales that are currently protected by seawalls and/or groynes, or that include property at risk from flooding or erosion that is of sufficient value to justify protection. All sites are assumed to be recharged within 20 years (see note 10).

2. A representative site has been selected to provide a recharge volume per metre length for each length of coastline. The selection considers wave climate and beach type.

3. Storm return period risk acceptance levels of 20, 100 or 50 years have been applied depending on whether the predominant land use is urban, mixed or high value rural. These levels are accounted for by altering the water level associated with the design storms used to determine the recharge volumes for the representative sites. This alteration influences the recharged beach crest elevation and therefore the required volume.

4. The difference in tide range at each site relative to its representative site is accounted for by adjusting the design storm water level, in increments of 0.25m. This adjustment influences the beach crest elevation and volume.

5. The "area factor" combines the risk and tide level adjustments.

6. Sites which are exposed to significantly greater or lesser wave conditions relative to their representative sites are accounted for by applying an exposure factor. This factor is applied to only a few cases where the representative site conditions are clearly not applicable, and where no other site is more suitable.

7. The drift rate calculated for each site is based on potential drift for an open beach. The impact of well designed beach control structures or beach management programmes on future recharge schemes is included by reducing the maintenance requirement relative to the potential drift. The need for beach control depends on whether losses form the frontage would substantially benefit an adjacent frontage or whether the frontage is an independent unit. The value of control depends on whether the beach is sand or shingle:

Situation	Drift factor
No control	1
Existing groynes	0.75
Controlled sand	0.5
Controlled shingle	0.2

8. Estimated sand beach recharge volumes are increased by 20% to account for differences between estimates from this project and design volumes for planned schemes.

9. A volume adjustment to account for future sea level rise (SLR) is included.

10. A likely year (rounded to 0, 5, 10, or 15 years from 1995) of scheme implementation is included in the calculation of maintenance demand. Predictions are based on local knowledge and discussions with coastal authorities.

11. The final demand volumes in the text combine capital and maintenance recharges up to the year 2015.

12. The future requirements are based on the climatic change estimates. The values are extremely speculative.

CIRIA

CIRIA is the Construction Industry Research and Information Association. It is a non-profit-distributing, private sector organisation carrying out research and providing information for its members, who include all types of organisations concerned with construction, including clients, professional practices, contractors, suppliers, educational and research establishments, professional institutions, trade associations and central and local government.

CIRIA focuses on providing best practice guidance to professionals that is authoritative, convenient to use and relevant. Areas covered include construction practice, building design and materials, management and productivity, ground engineering, water engineering and environmental issues.

Through active participation, CIRIA members choose research and information projects of most value to them. Funding contributions are sought from member subscriptions and from government and other sources on a project by project basis. Detailed work is contracted to the best qualified organisation selected in competition, and each project is guided by a project steering group, which contains both individual specialists and representatives of different groups with experience or interest in the topic.

Core Programme Sponsorship. Core Programme members, who include many of the most significant construction firms, choose the programme of research projects and obtain privileged early access to results.

Construction Industry Environmental Forum. The Environmental Forum (run in partnership with BRE and BSRIA) is a focus for construction and related industries on environmental issues. Members have free access to a substantial programme of workshops and seminars, monthly information bulletins, and publications arising from research undertaken.

Construction Productivity Network (CPN). CPN (a joint venture between CIRIA and BRE), exists to promote the sharing and application of knowledge on construction productivity issues. Members have free access to a substantial programme of workshops and seminars, a newsletter, and an annual conference.

Associates/Affiliates. Subscribers obtain copies of CIRIA open publications on favourable terms and get discounts on CIRIA seminars.

Purchase of Publications. CIRIA publications, together with selected publications from other sources, are available by mail order or on personal application.

Seminars/Conferences. CIRIA runs a number of events, often related to research projects or publications.

CIRIA News (quarterly detailed reports on CIRIA's research and information activities) and **CIRIA Spectrum** (occasional information on issues of wide interest) are available free on request.

For further details, please apply to the Business Development Manager, CIRIA, 6 Storey's Gate, Westminster, London SW1P 3AU
E-mail switchboard@ciria.org.uk
Tel: 0171-222 8891   Fax: 0171-222 1708

Core Programme Members (May 1996)

Acer Consultants Ltd
Alfred McAlpine Construction Ltd
AMEC Plc
Aspinwall & Co Limited
Babtie Group Ltd
Bachy (UK) Limited
Balfour Beatty Ltd
Binnie Black & Veatch
Building Design Partnership
Cementitious Slag Makers Association
Charles Haswell and Partners Ltd
Christiani & Neilsen Ltd
City Analytical Services Limited
Curtins Consulting Engineers plc
Davis Langdon & Everest
Department of the Environment
Dudley Engineering Consultancy
Edmund Nuttall Limited
Galliford plc
Golder Associates (UK) Ltd
Graham Consulting Group
Health & Safety Executive
Henry Boot & Sons PLC

Higgs & Hill Construction Holdings Ltd
Highways Agency, DoT
HR Wallingford Ltd
Hutter Jennings and Titchmarsh
Institution of Civil Engineers
Keller Foundations
L G Mouchel & Partners Ltd
Laing Technology Group Ltd
London Borough of Croydon
London Underground Limited
Mark Dyer Associates
Miller Civil Engineering Ltd
Montgomery Watson Ltd
Mott MacDonald Group Ltd
National Power PLC
North West Water Limited
Northumbrian Water Limited
Ove Arup Partnership
Posford Duvivier
Reid Crowther Consulting Limited
Rendel Palmer & Tritton
Rofe, Kennard & Lapworth
Scott Wilson Kirkpatrick & Co Ltd

Scottish Hydro-Electric plc
Sir Alexander Gibb & Partners Limited
Sir Owen Williams & Partners
Geotechnical Ltd
Sir William Halcrow & Partners Ltd.
South Bank University
South West Water Services Ltd
Southern Water Services Ltd
Tarmac Construction Ltd
Taylor Woodrow Construction Holdings Ltd
Thames Water Utilities Ltd
The Environment Agency
The Maunsell Group
Thorburn Colquhoun
Trafalgar House Technology
Union Railways Limited
Wardell Armstrong
Wessex Water plc
Wimpey Environmental Limited
WS Atkins Consultants Limited
Yorkshire Water Services Limited